ROADRUNNER

Also by Trisha R. Thomas

Nappily Ever After

ROADRUNNER

A Novel

Trisha R. Thomas

FACE PRESS
CALIFORNIA

This book is a work of fiction. Names, characters, and incidents are products of the author's imagination. Any resemblance to actual events or persons, living or dead, is purely coincidental.

Published by Face Press, United States of America

Originally published in hardcover by Crown, a division of Random House, Inc., in 2002

Printed in the United States of America

Design by Leonard Henderson

Library of Congress Cataloging-in-Publication Data
Thomas, Trisha R., 1964–
Roadrunner : a novel / Trisha R. Thomas
1. African American baseball players—Fiction. 2. Police—California—Los Angeles—Fiction. 3. Triangles (Interpersonal relations)—Fiction. 4. African American families—Fiction. 5. Los Angeles (Calif.)—Fiction. 6. Missing persons—Fiction. 7. Family violence—Fiction. I. Title.
PS3570.H5917 R63 2002
813'.6—dc21 2002003633

ISBN 978-0-578-01045-8

10 9 8 7 6 5 4 3 2 1

First Paperback Edition

Cameron,
all roads lead to you

I know I should forget about you
and go on with my life.
But I can't,
because you are
everything I've ever wanted.
You are the manifestation
of the culmination
of every fantasy
hope
dream
wish
vision
and Prayer
I have ever made

Firyali

chapter 1

WHEN THE HOUSE cleared and the kids were off to school, his wife off to work, he moved swiftly to his black Nike bag hidden in the garage, unzipping it with the excitement of a child left home alone. So many choices: Percocet, Demoral, and Vicodin for the pain, Xanex and Prozac for the mood swings, Diazapram or Valium to simply sedate. All his. The prescription stickers neatly typed in small black letters, *Dellonzo Fletcher* with instructions: two times a day, four times a day, two at bedtime, one before bedtime.

He decided on a small sample of each, swallowing seven tiny pills from six separate yellow prescription bottles. He grimaced at the bitter taste as the pills disintegrated before he could completely swallow them. Within minutes the numbness had set in, making his limbs feel like flat rubber inner tubes, his mind a hazy fog of irrelevance.

It didn't matter. He'd already arranged himself on top of Josh's skinny twin-sized bed, staring up, counting the baseballs on the tan papered walls. He had nowhere to go. Nowhere to be by a certain time. Off into the peaceful bliss he went floating above the storm cloud his life had become. No paparazzi, no reporters, no questions he couldn't answer. His long lashes comfortably closed over his dark brown eyes. Smooth sailing, riding the waves of oblivion where he was unknown, even to himself. He didn't recognize himself as the man that women used to throw themselves at. Nor the man who commanded more attention than the King of Pop himself when he walked into a packed stadium. Here, he was safe, worry free, until midday, when the smorgasbord began to wear off.

Always right on time. He didn't want to die, but by chance if he did, he wouldn't be too upset about it.

The hazy Los Angeles sun filtered through the miniblinds. He could sense the hour of the day by the alertness of his mind. Two o'clock, maybe three in the afternoon. Somehow the drugs had made an agreement with his internal clock, knowing precisely when to wear off, knowing exactly when to free his brain. His eyes involuntarily fluttered open. His elbows wobbled as he pulled himself up to focus on his surroundings. Again, the dancing baseballs, gloves, and bats, coordinated with the burnt red color on the upper portion of the wall. A large framed print of Dell himself, sliding into home plate. This was Josh's room. His safe place. Leah, his bride of fifteen years, rarely came down the hall past the point where organization and structure became disheveled, where mess and clutter lurked behind every closed door. Leah had given up making sense out of the household chaos when Josh started kindergarten. She simply asked that the children's doors be kept closed so what she didn't know wouldn't hurt her.

Dell took that for its full meaning. He could hide here as well, blending in with the chaos of dirty clothes, books, and decapitated still figures, Power Rangers, X-men, cars, and dinosaurs with lost seniority. If she ever came home unexpectedly, she'd never think to look for him here.

The mess strewn all over the floor faded in and out of foggy waves. He felt wobbly when he stood. His foot twisted on an empty plastic Knott's Berry Farm water bottle. Underneath, Snoopy smirking, *Had a wild ride at Knott's.* The door, only a few steps away, seemed an infinite distance. He inhaled deeply the mixture of dry musty air, knowing his own breath was partly responsible. Standing with his head sandwiched between the open door, he peered down the long wide hallway before taking his first step out. His feet sunk into the plush thick carpet, making him aware he was back in the real world. The one where elegant wood-framed art lined the wall. On the other side, pictures of the life and family he'd created. His fingers trailed the textured walls as if seeing them for the first time. Dell and Leah fifteen years ago in a wedding portrait. She wearing a white satin dress, smiling broad, and unabashed. Her short dark wavy hair wrapped with a thin white chiffon scarf that draped across her shoulders. He in a modest shirt and tie with black slacks, looking younger than his twenty-one years, still in college, barely able to afford the gold band he'd placed on her finger.

He'd come a long way since then. The $200 million dollar man. His team, the California Angels, had gone as far as insuring his limbs, making sure he was worth the same whether he was crawling or walking. But there was no price for what he did, rejuvenating the entire game of baseball for the city of Los Angeles, bringing back the same excitement that Mickey Mantle and Willie Mays once brought to the sport. He'd been the golden boy, clean and pure. His dark coffee skin, smooth. His teeth white rays of light, smiling with the confidence only a completely pedigreed athlete could know. This picture was the same one used for his baseball cards, he in the midst of a full swing, his arms still flexed, hands tight around the bat, his legs in a conqueror's stance.

In the next photo, he was dressed in a sleek tuxedo holding the ESPY award, Most Valuable Player. 1997, the year he'd signed the contract making him one of the highest-paid baseball players in the majors. He'd been the most seen face on television. Exposed. Cameras in the living room, cameras in the kitchen. Interviewers from ESPN, ABC, FOX sports, asking who'd influenced his life. Who'd made the difference in him becoming an all-star versus another Black man with his face framed between bars? He always had the same answer. "God, my mother, my teachers who believed in me. It's a collaborative effort. A kid needs to be honored, told that he can accomplish something great."

After a while his answer had begun to change, taken on a cockier tone. "I believed in myself when nobody else would. You've got to be able to get past all the negativity out there. I can only depend on three people, me, myself, and I." He'd been the leader, the big man, standing six feet four inches, and all heart. A passion for the game so deep and so strong that his team looked up to him, the fans adored him, the media had put a gold star next to his name. Anything about Dellonzo Fletcher could sell a million copies off the stand.

As he moved down the expansive hall, it became a chronological family tour. His daughter, Kayla, grinning with missing front teeth, not yet aware of life's disappointments. His son, Josh, in his baseball uniform, posed with a bat held too high, angled all wrong. He focused to see better the year etched in gold at the bottom of the photo. 1994 Blue Jays, Hollywood Hills Little League. Dell remembered the coaching sessions with his little guy, only in T-ball, but skills had to be learned early.

"Okay, Daddy. I'm ready."

"No, son. Like this. Squeeze your arms tight to your side. Now raise them up slowly until they're comfortable. Now you feel that. Now you're ready. You can hit any ball that comes your way when you're positioned right."

Dell smiled, graced with the thought of simpler times, when the children listened, hung on his every word. He'd had a sense of balance. All-American baseball hero, father, and husband, the roles fit neatly, intertwined with each other. No one liked the image of a pure star. A mogul needed the edges softened by a loving wife, healthy smiling kids. He was the full package.

The dull throbbing returned, but he accepted the pain. Pain as familiar to him as breathing. He moved unsteadily down the hall, using the wall for balance. He found himself staring at a family photo taken just six months ago. Leah believed in taking pictures, the documentation of time. This one she insisted on because it had been five years since all four of them had been captured together. They sat underneath the mid-April clouds that threatened to unleash a torrent of rain. Leah picked an evergreen-covered spot in their backyard. They sat on the picnic table pushed against the trees as backdrop. The children sat on the bench while Dell and Leah sat above them on the table, stiff like Ma and Pa Kettle, looking straight into the camera. They all held their puppet smiles in place while the photographer appraised his subjects.

"Okay, everybody. This way. Say pepperoni cheeezz." The photographer stopped to peer over the camera. He strummed his fingers through the oily pompadour on top of his head as if it had been a long day and it was only going to get worse. "I'm sorry I'm no stand-up comedian, but that's the best I can do, guys. Can you just smile, please? Quick and painless, one more time. Cheeeeze."

The flash went off.

Dell blinked hard, as if the brightness jarred him once again. He straightened the frame by touching it slightly. It fell back into a crooked slant.

Voices from downstairs sailed up, shaking him from his time travel. He swiftly moved to his bedroom, closing the door quietly behind him. The large white walls of his own bedroom seemed to be on an angle. A familiar but altered state. He tried to slow his panic. His flat footsteps echoed as he plodded onto the icy bathroom floor. He rushed the shower, reaching in to flip the brass knob for full pressure. The clothing he was wearing quickly fell to a heap near his feet. He stepped in and winced from the hot water scalding his face and naked body. He didn't adjust the temperature. Hot was necessary. The hotter the better. Maybe it could rinse away his shame.

On the rare occasions that he and Leah made love, he worried that she would smell the Vicodin mixed with Scotch, or the Prozac broken down by gin. Her face pressed into his naked chest, he pictured her gasping and choking while he lay on top of her, struggling to breathe through the toxins secreting from his body.

He swore, promised, he would never do it again, mixing one lethal dose with another, especially after the accident forced him to admit that the drinking had gotten out of control. A sickness spreading uncontrollably. The painkillers were okay, even understandable. An injury like his took time to heal. But the alcohol he used to numb his shame, his failure. It was a vicious cycle. Trying to stay sane and sober to prove his remorse only made him go deeper underground for relief of the humiliation.

He washed harder, squeezed more soap out of the dispenser, rubbing it into his, face, chest, and arms, determined to mask himself with the softly scented suds. He let the soap slide around his head and neck like a cloak, down his back, curving around his thighs and muscular calves. There wasn't enough soap in the world to lather away what he needed to hide.

Dell heard his name being called through the bathroom door along with a gentle tapping of small knuckles. "Dad, I'm home."

He could pretend he didn't hear his son over the powerful jet stream of water cascading over his gleaming bald head. Continue washing and scrubbing. Instead, he flipped the knob, shutting off the water. The steam encapsulated the glass walls and the surrounding air. He stepped out of the shower and wrapped himself with a towel.

"Dad?"

Dripping wet, he pulled the door open, grateful for the spurt of cold air and the sweet round face that greeted him. "Hey, big man. How was school?"

"It was okay. Elliot and Skeet got in a fight so we couldn't go out for recess." Josh backed his way to the edge of the king-sized bed. The bathroom steam floated out, thickening the air.

"Again? Boy, you may want to consider a new set of friends. Every time you mention those two, they've been in a brawl." Dell reached past his son and grabbed a clean but thoroughly broken-in T-shirt out of his drawer. He was momentarily shocked at how loosely it fell over his torso. In the past months his size had withered, leaving him only a shell of his former self. He'd always stayed in top physical condition when he played for the California Angels. Baseball was a slow sport compared with most, but the speed and agility he maintained during his twelve years on the field gave him the nickname "Roadrunner." Stealing bases at the blink of an eye was his MO. The announcers would sometimes be the opposing team's only hint he'd taken off. "And there he goes, ladies and gentlemen. Dellonzo Roadrunner Fletcher, stealing home." He looked at himself in the dresser mirror for confirmation. His eyes seemed too close together while his cheekbones and chin were now defined lines in his chiseled face. His rich chocolate skin had been replaced with a pale cookie dough...lack of sunshine. It seemed, now, he had no reason to go out, unless it was during the night.

"I keep telling those guys to stop fighting over dumb girls. It's the same one too, Jessica. She doesn't like either one of them." Josh dropped his head, knowing the secret of who the little red-head girl truly did like. He circled and traced the shapes of flowers on the silk duvet.

"I'm shocked they're fighting over girls in the first place. I didn't know fourth graders were interested in girls." Dell had forgotten his own childhood. Playing baseball was all he remembered. But to him it was no game. Never had been. It was his life, what he believed in, the only thing, he thought, that could never fail him.

"Dad, they've been fighting over girls since first grade." The way his son's face lit up eased any lingering strain Dell may have felt. He touched his son's downy head and pulled him in close. Josh's gangly height was more appropriate for a basketball career rather than the sport they both knew and loved. He had his mother's coloring, like fresh baked bread, but his eyes were courtesy of his father. Sensitive dark eyes that reflected light in the center of his irises, reminding Dell that he'd done something right in this world. It hadn't all been a waste.

Dell hugged him for a moment too long, turning away abruptly, fearful his earlier transgressions would surface. More than tea tree and peppermint soap could find its way into his son's nostrils. "Is Kayla home?"

"Yeah, downstairs on the phone."

"She doesn't waste a minute, huh? All right, big man. Let me finish getting dressed. I'll be down in five."

He dressed, ignoring the urge to crawl into his bed, pull the covers over his head, and sleep until Leah came home. His wife would know if he'd spent the day in bed, even if he popped up the minute she arrived. Leah had a special talent for knowing what went on without having seen it, and it made him constantly second-guess himself. Feeling analyzed all the time, he made choices that were sane and acceptable, at least he tried.

He stepped over Kayla sprawled on the bottom tier of the steps. Her conversation was loud and animated.

"Don't stay on the phone all day."

Kayla batted her long lashes and pouted slightly, swinging her long braids from one side of her slight shoulders to the other. He wondered if there was some secret class that taught teenaged girls how to get what they wanted in this world, if a meeting was called at some magical age informing them how to be witty and smile on cue. How to master womanhood, how to master man.

"I'm serious." He couldn't muster the sternness to go along with his statement.

She flagged him a talk to the hand, not missing a beat in her conversation. "Oh, no, he didn't. *Dang.*"

Eight bedrooms, six bathrooms, a sprawling hillside mansion with plenty of room to hide, and there was only one phone line. Their Northern Hollywood home was built in the early 1970s, a Spanish-style villa with adobe exterior and interior immaculately maintained by the original owner, a white movie producer who'd amassed a fortune producing Blaxploitation films. When word got out that Dellonzo Fletcher had purchased the million-dollar home, the media had a field day. Making him out as an accomplice to the exploitation as if he'd bought slaves with the plantation. What kind of message was he sending? Dell never had a chance to respond. If he had, he would've told them, every boy needs a hero; *Shaft* was mine. If it wasn't for those films, he would've never learned how to stand up for himself, *Jive suckas.*

"That's just scandalous." Kayla's laughter and conversation could still be heard when Dell reached the kitchen. He logged a mental note to call the phone company. Phone lines for everyone in their very own rooms.

He walked through the high arched entryway of the kitchen. It reminded him of a cathedral the way the light came through the colorful stained-glass window at the peak of the vaulted ceiling. They'd had the large butcher table that Leah had fallen in love with on a vacation in Provence dismantled and shipped back along with the matching chairs that looked like mini wooden pews.

Josh was sitting at the long butcher's table considering the homework before him. Dell cradled his son's chin and kissed him on the forehead.

"Let's go out, toss the ball around?"

In a blink Dell saw the empty chair and math book sitting open. Josh was outside and waiting with his mitt on his left hand and his fist balled in the middle before the door closed behind him. "Guess that's a yes." Dell followed him out the kitchen door to the backyard.

The backyard was as big and wide as a public park, with a swimming pool and full-sized tennis court. The fall season hadn't changed anything. The leaves still hung on the trees, the wild grasses stood strong. Southern California didn't have seasons. Life was one constant stretch of time. For Dell it ebbed even slower. Days didn't have definition. A Monday could easily be a Friday, a Saturday could be a Wednesday. Christmas could be Easter and vice versa.

Dell lobbed the ball back and forth with Josh, filled with pride when his son used techniques he'd shown him. How to flick his wrist and follow the ball, how to extend his body first, and move his feet second, for a catch. Days, moments like these, put things into perspective. Made him wish even harder that he could shut down the drive, the need for the cheering crowd, the high unmatched by any other, fans, superiority, and recognition. All-star status. It was like a tumor that had grown and attached to his psyche. The cells had multiplied rapidly out of control, taking over every part of his functioning mind. It seemed like such a small wish to be granted. All he wanted was to feel his heart steady in preparation for the pitch headed his way... to stand in front of home plate... to trace the shape of the batter's box with the tip of his foot before his swing. Crouched in stance, anticipating the speed and shape of the ball... the crack of the bat... the run!

"Dad! You let the ball roll right past you."

Dell looked behind him where the ball sat in a mound of uncut grass. His heart was still racing. His lips and mouth dry from anticipation. He kept his eyes on the ball, but he'd missed it.

It was moments like these when he understood that it was hopeless. No matter how hard he prayed for the release, to be free of the need, it wouldn't go away. The sorrow. He picked up the ball and squeezed it before throwing it high over the hedge of trees. He could feel his son's eyes follow it over and disappear. What number was that? He pictured the other side of the grounds scattered with embittered baseballs. He'd buy him another. Keep trying to replace what he'd lost.

"Let's go inside," he'd said before realizing Josh was already gone.

chapter 2

THE EVENING CREPT over the northern foothills. The smoggy haze had blown to the east, leaving a clear black sky. Leah was exhausted from the duck and dodge of the Los Angles traffic. Although the Hollywood studio where she worked was only five miles away, it felt more like fifty. Her eyes were weary from staring at a computer screen all day and reading text on white pages all evening. Then sitting around with five other people trying to figure out how to close the season with enough thrill to ignite the fans into a writing protest to keep the show from being canceled. Essentially for the last few weeks, they'd all been sitting around a dead body watching it stiffen, knowing the execs had already pulled the plug on the weekly teen drama, but there was always a chance of reprieve. Regardless of the outcome, Leah always had a job, writing for whatever would fill that time slot, and the next and the next. Squire made sure of that.

The garage door rolled up slowly. Dell's pearl-colored Porsche was parked neatly off to the right. Brand-new and shiny, special ordered to replace the one he'd destroyed in a car accident. Seeing this one in its place brought an immediate sense of relief. He was home. He was safe.

She entered the house through the garage door and kicked off her shoes in the spacious foyer and flung her purse over the banister rail. This house was her solitude and only source of peace. But a house is not a home, as Luther Vandross would say. She was grateful for her family, Josh and Kayla, and her husband who wasted no time greeting her with a firm kiss and hug before she could completely get out of her coat. Her arms were caught in the sleeves but her lips were working fine. She inhaled the freshly showered scent of his neck. He cupped her oval face and kissed her closed eyelids.

"How was your day?" He helped her out of the coat. "I have a surprise for you."

She had a wide, but tired grin on her face as he led her by the hand through the house into the kitchen. "It's not a surprise if I can already smell it." She sat down on the stool that he pulled out for her.

He stood over his masterpiece, lifting the pot top. "Your favorite, steak and onions." He moved about the kitchen like an old pro on a cooking show, easily maneuvering the large steel pan in his hand. It had been a while since Leah had seen her husband proud of anything. He turned his back to her and reached into the cabinet. She noticed he was wearing his favorite baseball shirt with their college alma mater printed on the back, UCLA Bruins. His walnut skin peeked through various jagged slits in the shirt. His equally worn jeans sagged around his slim waist. The ensemble was now his daily uniform. Even after she'd bought a replacement from the UCLA bookstore, he never gave up this one. It was a part of him, the strong part.

"Met with Squire today." Leah unbuttoned the cuffs of her blouse, rolling them up and exposing her slender wrists.

"Yes, I know. How'd it go?" He had a quickness to his movement. How long had it been since he'd been interested in her, what she was doing in her career? This new mood was appealing. She took notice of the glowing candlelight coming from the dining room.

"Squire seemed real excited about the project. But you know him, he says yes to everything but promises nothing."

She leaned in on her elbows, "Where're the kids?" The possibility that this evening could parlay into something more than dinner swept through her.

"Kayla's cheering at the basketball game. Josh is asleep, at least close to it." Dell handed her a glass, then uncorked a bottle of champagne that seemed to appear out of nowhere.

Her mood dropped like an elevator with no cables. "Why would you have champagne here?"

"It's just for you. I'm not touching the stuff. I wanted to celebrate your debut producing deal."

"But I don't have anything yet, just a lot of maybes." She eyed the glass as he filled it with bubbly. For himself sparkling apple cider.

"To my baby, the producer. This is going to happen if I have to back it myself."

He sipped, pinky extended.

Leah stood up, walked around to the sink, and poured her glass of champagne down the drain. She rinsed the glass out before turning it upside down on the counter. "You know there shouldn't be any alcohol in the house, honey. It's dangerous."

She turned back to him to wrap her arms around his shoulders; she felt his body stiffen underneath her touch.

"Thank you for that. I needed to be brought down to earth. I don't know what I'd do without you to remind me of my limitations." He nudged her out of his way and stormed out of the kitchen.

What just happened? She stood with her hands still searching for someone to hold.

She heard the garage door slam. The Porsche engine revved. She asked her feet to move in the direction of the garage. Her heart skipped when the engine shifted into gear. As badly as she wanted to stop him, she was unable to move, leaning against the counter, still trying to figure out how she'd come to this point.

The garage door rolled slowly back down, sealing out the drum of his engine. Her heart sank, settling in a dizzy whirl of time. A constant merry-go-round that she couldn't get off. Only moments ago they were about to sit down to a home-cooked meal, have a quiet romantic evening. Now she was standing alone, as she did on countless nights, listening to the buzz of the kitchen lighting overhead. The hum of the refrigerator, then the dropping ice. The steady click of the small hand moving in seconds on the kitchen clock. Alone.

She threw the spoon against the wall. Dumped the contents of the pan into the sink, jumping back when the hot drops of juice attacked her silk blouse. It was always her fault, wasn't it? Always something she'd said or didn't say. Always the button pusher. Then why was it she who was the one left in a rage? Her heart palpitating, her mind filled with words she wouldn't say out loud, her fingers wanting to claw at something, at him. She wanted to tell him it wasn't her fault. It wasn't she who'd driven to the store, or in Dell's case, ordered the champagne and had it delivered. He'd probably had the fresh flowers and the Brie cheese and grapes centerpiece sent over from Epicure's. He'd even set the table. White china traced in gold, and silverware perfectly placed. She blew out the candles and found herself sitting in darkness. Maybe it was her fault. All the trouble he'd gone through and she'd come along and snuffed it out as easily as the candles. He'd put forth a gallant effort and she'd crowned him a failure. She closed her eyes and momentarily replayed the evening. He greeted her with a kiss, led her to the kitchen, she watched him with a flutter of anticipation. Possibly they'd make love. She remembered thinking that she didn't want to ruin anything, how great it was to see him happy even for a moment. Then there was the champagne. A harmless bottle of Moët. She could have come down later in the evening and dumped it out. She didn't have to call him on it right then and there. Stupid girl. It *was* your fault. Wasn't it always?

Leah made her way up the stairs. She stuck her face into the bedroom where she knew Josh lay with open ears. The bar of light from the hall hit his face. His eyes squeezed tight in a fabricated sleep.

"Can I come in and kiss you goodnight?"

His eyes opened in a squint. "Yeah." The smile he was trying to suppress crept up slowly.

"You can't fool me, I know when you're sleeping or awake, if you're good or bad, you can't fake." She'd been singing those words to Josh since he was a baby. She stepped strategically, trying to avoid large objects on the floor. She flicked on the small lamp in the shape of a baseball bat. She sat on the edge of his bed. "How was your day?"

"Good." He wrapped his arms tightly around her neck. She squeezed him back and kissed the top of his head.

"Just good . . . no details?"

"I got an A on my spelling test." He let go and leaned back on his pillow, throwing his arms behind his head, proof of a proud scholar.

"All right, now that's what I want to hear. You got a big breakfast coming up for that one. Now sleep tight, okay." She kissed him again on his forehead and then on the lips.

Leah sometimes thought if it weren't for Kayla and Josh, she and Dell would have separated long ago. They needed both of them, two parents firm in their lives. Leah wanted that, too. She'd grown up with a single working mother. To to make it worse, she was an only child as well. There was something ominous about coming home after school with no one there to care for you. Constantly locked into her own thoughts, no one to hear her, to listen, to test or train. Eating makeshift meals with a book in front of her face, reading about the romantic lives of Yorkshire princesses and peasant boys who were forbidden to love. That was where she hid, in those books, in those stories. As an adult, she'd promised herself that she wouldn't hide anymore. She'd live in the real world and have a real live family, with children and a husband who loved her and wouldn't run off at the first sign of trouble.

Her family wouldn't fall apart. She'd worked hard at keeping it together. Making it last as long as it had. She pulled the cover up and tucked Josh in. For her son alone, her marriage was worth fighting for. It was her constant assignment, fighting to keep Dell near, from running off, or floating away.

• • •

The nightmare started a year ago when Dell tore his ACL, the ligament that held the knee joint together. A common injury, part of the territory that came with being a baseball player. No one thought it would end his career. He'd heal and be back on the playing field like the rest of the sewn-together athletes on his team. Having surgery was like applying a Band-Aid. All of the guys spent time under the knife, if not multiple times. So this being Dell's first, it would be a breeze.

The first surgery went well. Dell recuperated and spent six weeks in physical therapy and was back on the playing field, but not without assistance. The Vicodin was too mild, he'd said. He needed something stronger. Then came the Oxycontin, the legal equivalent to heroin. That scared Leah. She didn't understand how he could still be in pain with that much medication. She supported his doctor's decision for another surgery; maybe it hadn't healed properly.

The surgeons confirmed all was well, but Dell swore that he was in more pain than ever. Leah reasoned he wouldn't know what was going on with his own body, with such an obscene amount of painkillers. He was too numb to feel anything. But he knew pain, "so deep and real I dream about cutting off my own leg," he exclaimed. So she backed off. She didn't want him to suffer. But things got worse. The mood swings, the anxiety, it was more than she could handle.

His temper was the first thing she noticed. Dell had always been loving, sweet, and sometimes too nice, letting friends and family take advantage of him... cars, college tuition, and at last count, a cousin in need of $100,000 to fund a Church's Chicken franchise. She thought she'd have to put her foot down on that one, but Dell took care of it. The quiet warrior had become a raging bull, letting his feelings out at the drop of a dime, screaming at the top of his lungs in telephone conversations, accusing people of cheating him, conspiring against him.

His rage scared her. She went through the intervention, throwing away what she could find of his medications, calling his doctor with threats if one more prescription was written, asking Gervis, his manager and agent, for help. Couldn't they force him into rehab? He finally agreed to drug rehabilitation, first as an outpatient, then a three-week stay that seemed to work, until he returned to training camp. He needed the meds to get him through. He couldn't play in pain, he'd tell her before swallowing five or six pills before a game.

Gervis was the one who delivered the news. The team's management wanted to buy out the rest of Dell's contract. He set the papers down in front of them both with a list of infractions, the most obvious being the drug abuse; with that came the erratic behavior, attacking one of his teammates with a bat, punching out the windows in Kurt Brewer's office with his bare hands. They didn't know what else he was capable of and they didn't want to find out. He'd have to fight his own battle on someone else's turf because the California Angels were washing their hands of him. After all he'd given them. "Where's the fucking loyalty?" he'd asked as he scribbled his name to the dissolution of his life. She rubbed his shoulders while he signed page after page. She could offer nothing that could comfort him, only her love and support.

"It wasn't enough," Leah thought out loud while dialing Dell's cell phone. She knew he wouldn't answer, but when the phone lit up on his dash, he would know that she cared. Her words would whisper, *"Baby, come home where it's safe, where you're loved."*

chapter 3

JOSH STAYED UP all night waiting for his father to return. At some point he'd wished for sleep, but it never came. He watched the shadows in his room change shape from dinosaurs to mountains. Blurry movement in his peripheral vision would cause him to shut his eyes tight and start again. When he closed his eyes, he was harassed by moving pictures, scenes and images of things that happened earlier in the day, sometimes that hadn't happened at all. So many pictures, he couldn't keep track of which were real and which were only in his imagination. Had his father really left the house, or was he somewhere downstairs? By the time the sun had knocked on his window letting him know that the night had passed and he could relax again, it was too late. His eyes were burning from being open all night, and now it was time to get ready for school. Add another bad day to his list of many. His teacher would call on him to do the homework assignment on the board, and he'd look like an idiot in front of Jessica and Allie, too, dazed from lack of sleep, his brain functioning like a snail in sand.

He rubbed the dryness out of his eyes best he could and made his way to his parents' bedroom. That was the first stop. If his father wasn't in bed, then he'd follow his routine to check the kitchen, then outside to the backyard where he'd sometimes found him sitting on the patio reading the sports section of the paper as if all was right in the world.

Luckily, this morning he found his dad sitting in the sunny bright breakfast nook, leaning into a strong black cup of coffee. Josh kissed him on the cheek and inhaled the smell of fresh brew. He loved the smell of coffee in the morning. It reassured him everything was fine, back to normal. Josh rifled through the refrigerator for the ingredients of his famous toast and jelly. He had a second thought about the butter and slid it back in. It was sure to antagonize his dad's queasy stomach.

Josh slipped the plate of toast in front of Dell.

When Dell felt the touch on his shoulder, only then did he look up to see the wiry body and proud narrow shoulders standing in front of him. He reached out, pulling Josh toward him, his face to his chest. This boy, his link to possibilities, that somehow tomorrow was worth waiting for. He tried to contain the swell of tears. He didn't want to appear weak in front of his son. Crying over failures. That was no kind of example to set for a man-child, especially one of color where inner strength was depended on for survival, mere existence.

Leah walked in, speaking abruptly. "Josh, please finish getting dressed for school."

Josh backed away from his father slowly. He cupped his hands over the wet spot that had formed on his T-shirt. Tears. It would only cause more problems if she knew.

"What's wrong with your stomach?" Leah's hand covered his forehead. "You sick?"

"No, I guess just hungry."

"Remember the big breakfast I promised you? After you're dressed and ready for school, I'll have a cheese omelette waiting." She kissed him on the side of his head and patted him off.

She pulled up a chair and sat across from Dell. Her yellow cotton robe pulled tight around her hips. The sheen of her terra-cotta skin caught his eye when she crossed her legs, letting the robe fall slightly open. She crossed her arms under her breasts and let the fullness rest on her forearms.

Dell wasn't surprised that she was fed up. At times, he wondered how she put up with him at all. He was nothing near the man she'd fallen in love with so long ago. A college athlete with a future so bright he wore shades every day. He first gathered the nerve to approach her in one of his classes. Both stuck in a religion philosophy class to fulfill their humanities prerequisite, he didn't waste time asking anyone to introduce him to the pretty young lady with the thin shoulders, broad hips, and long legs. He did all the dirty work himself—picked up his one sheet of paper for notes and slid his pen behind his ear and moved seats to be beside her. She smiled throughout the entire boring lecture, and he knew he was in.

"Dellonzo Fletcher." He'd stuck out his hand, then quickly retrieved it, remembering his callused palms brought on by constant batting practice. She'd whispered her name in his direction but kept her eyes on the professor, the sweetest sound, shy and honest, "Leah Willow."

"You need help, real professional help, not advice from a nine-year-old boy," her voice sharp and now on edge. "You can't lean on him like this."

He met her gaze head-on. She didn't understand; how could she? The surgery was supposed to end all the madness. How could she know how it felt, to learn that all that you believed yourself to be no longer existed? What if she'd lost her hands, her sight, unable to write the drivel she wrote every day? She'd know then.

They stared each other down, Leah watching his face, the face she'd fallen in love with so long ago, when they were both so young. Dell watched hers. What had this imposter done with his sweet princess, the one who had said for better or worse, in sickness and in health? He wanted to ask, but then again, she'd accuse him of turning this thing on her like he always did. She'd say, the bed he made was his doing. But what had he done, besides love her, take care of his family... what had he done?

"It's not like I was sitting here asking his philosophy on life; what difference does it make? Can't a father talk to his son?"

"Dell, you're not the only one suffering. When you're like this, it affects us all. You're not in this alone, but you continually shut me out. How many times do I have to tell you that you're all that matters, not baseball, not money, nothing else but you? But you don't seem to hear me. I want you to make a choice, right here, right now, your family or your misery. You're going to have to choose which you want to live with because I can't do this anymore. I can't take it." She'd made this threat before, so many times it felt like she was crying wolf.

"You need to leave... for a while." Her words turned into one stream of purple ribbon, letters typed backward like a used typewriter cartridge, "... until you can get yourself together. I mean for God's sake, Dell, it's been a year."

The purple ribbon continued. Tick, tick, tick.

"I, we, can't live like this, always wondering when—if you're going to try and hurt yourself again, the pills, the drinking. What if one of the kids came home and found you comatose or worse? Josh is being destroyed by this, watching you unravel in front of his eyes."

Dell looked up. He was waiting for the usual sign of mercy, the stay of execution. But she continued.

Tick, tick, tick...

"It's time, Dell. I know we've tried other rehab centers, pain centers, there's got to be a place that can help. It won't hurt to try one more, and keep trying until we find something. I found a place in Arizona, the Sedona Mountains. Very discreet. You can go there. I'll go with you."

"No."

"What do you mean, no? You're not willing to try?"

"What part of no didn't you understand? I'm not ever going to suffer that humiliation again, sitting around in one of those pseudo groups, trying to figure out where my life went wrong. I already know, and it can't be fixed by hiding in the Sedona Mountains playing patty-cake with a bunch of sorry-ass losers who lost their way. I didn't lose my way... it was taken from me. Stolen. My whole damned life taken in the blink of an eye. Don't you understand that?"

"Of course I understand, baby. Nobody understands more than me."

"How the hell can you say you understand? How the hell can you know?"

"Calm down, Dell," she whispered, more to herself than to him.

"How in the world can you understand? You still wake up every morning and scurry off to your little studio, working with your ex-lover. Your life hasn't stopped, hasn't changed. You didn't wake up one day unable to dream up dialog for your buffoon cast of characters. You weren't suddenly stopped at the studio gate and told your services were no longer needed. If you were, I don't remember hearing about it. You have everything. You've always had everything. You've got your damned cake and eatin' it, too."

"What's that supposed to mean, Dell? Are you trying to accuse me—"

Dell leaned over the table. "What? Thought I was so immersed in my own shit that I wouldn't notice yours? I'm not stupid. I'm not blind. All these years I've put up with you and Squire behind my back."

"You've gone way too far this time, Dell. I will not sit there and listen to you accuse me—"

He cut her off. "... of fucking another man. Why not... it's true. You think I don't know?"

"Get out!" Tick, tick, tick... "I've put up with your insanity long enough. You want to kill yourself, waste away, well do it somewhere else. I want you out of this house! Until you get some help and snap out of—"

The hand whipped across her face connecting skin to skin, a hollow pop. The chair kicked over, the plate of toast shattered on the floor. Someone had quieted her nonsense.

"If you want out, then you get the hell out. This is my home! These are my children. I will not be sent away like some wayward delinquent." His words came out between gritted teeth. It took him a moment to realize her face was in a state of shock. The sting, the hurt, the look of horror, he understood quickly, was caused by him. His hand, her face. In Dell's lifetime he'd never put his hands on a woman, and he knew he'd regret the day he did. But the look on her face, the finality of her words, left him spiraling, falling into a dismal point of no return. He looked at the offending hand as if it had a mind of its own. As if to question its intention, as if asking why. She was still on the kitchen floor where the chair had turned over with her fall. She rose up, holding her jaw, stumbling back away from him until she was cornered by the stone fireplace.

"Get out!" she screamed. "Go, Dell!"

chapter 4

TO JOSH, IT SOUNDED like a crack. A broom handle falling to the floor perhaps, but nothing as intimate as flesh. But still he knew. His life would forever be changed from that moment on. He slid into his room and closed the door before his father rounded the corner. He grabbed his backpack and headed down the stairs.

His mother was still in her yellow robe, standing at the stove. If it hadn't been for the red splotch on her cheek, it would've appeared nothing out of the ordinary had happened. Josh sat down at the kitchen table. He scanned the area. Cracked bits of white ceramic on the floor. A piece of bread half hidden underneath the lip of the oven.

She put the omelette down in front of him and set the fork perfectly by its side. He reached up and touched her shoulder, wishing he knew what to say. He'd become an expert at covering for his father, but this, this was a hard one. What excuse could he give this time? He'd heard his mother and father arguing before, lots of times, but it had never come to this.

Divorce. It was inconceivable. After so many years of missing him when he was on the road nine months out of the year, when he finally came home for keeps, Josh was relieved. He felt guilty for being happy his father could no longer play baseball. Everyone else seemed to feel a loss, but not Josh. His world was opening up, large with possibilities—camping, fishing, hanging out at the park, or playing catch. His father would be there for his Little League games like all the other dads. It was a reason to celebrate. But his dad, he quickly learned, had no time to sit still. If he stayed still too long, the grief would attach to his body, leaving him paralyzed. Useless.

Josh had watched his friends' parents divorce over silly things, at least what he and his friends considered silly, like needs not being met, or not loving anymore.

Surely his parents would top the charts for having stupid reasons. *My mom is tired of my dad's crying. He cries all the time when he thinks no one is looking or listening, in the shower, watching TV, and sometimes when he's in my room. He just sits in there and cries. He doesn't play with none of my stuff. He just sits there and cries.*

He decided he wouldn't tell anyone, not even Elliot.

He looked up at his mother. The eggs had no taste, warm cotton in his mouth.

"I'm going now, Mom."

She turned around and hugged him. "Try and have a good day, baby." She pressed the good side of her face to his. She kissed him and patted him off.

He assumed she hadn't looked into the mirror yet. He worried that once she had a glimpse of herself she'd become angry, and the fighting would start all over again. His mother put a lot of energy into her appearance, always up-to-date with the latest hairstyle and clothing. Her skin brightened by a new shade of lip color, from deep burgundy to light bronze. Her hair color changed with the seasons. He wondered if the same people who made up the names he'd read on her discarded boxes were the same people in charge of the colors in his Crayola collection. Chestnut, black cherry, sienna. Whatever hair color she chose, his mother was the most beautiful. She was even prettier than the made-up ones on TV. In the area of Los Angeles where they lived, actresses roamed the hills like regular people, plain-faced and flat-haired, hoping no one would recognize them. He remembered seeing Vanessa Gaines, the TV mom who always kept her high heels on while cooking and cleaning, even reading on the couch. When they saw Vanessa Gaines in the grocery store, she looked completely different. It took the entire drive back home for his mother to explain the difference between TV makeup and the regular daytime stuff. Still, he couldn't believe it was her, Vanessa Gaines. And where were her high heels?

He blinked out the slap to his mother's cheek. He placed an imaginary shield on the welt and drew a smile around her raised skin. That was the picture he'd take to school with him. He'd never make it any other way. Bye, Mom. Have a happy day. He flew out the door, racing to the bus stop only seconds before the long yellow snail pulled up with its doors wide open.

chapter 5

LEAH DIALED THE numbers slowly, wishing she could think of a better solution before the call went through. She hesitated when the emergency operator answered.

I repeat, this is the 911 operator. What is your emergency?

My husband hit me.

Are you injured? Do you need medical attention?

No.

Is he still in the house with you?

Yes.

Is he threatening you in any way?

Leah looked up, catching her image in the bathroom mirror, moving her hand to the swollen area on her cheek and pressing it, almost not believing it was her face she was touching. Not believing Dell had hit her, not Dell.

"Ma'am, is he there now, threatening you?"

The tears muffled her answer. "No."

"Okay, ma'am. I've got an officer in route to your home. Are you at 5543 Winding Wind Road?"

"Yes."

"Where are you now? What part of the house are you in?"

"Downstairs. The bathroom."

"All right, I'm going to ask you to move to the front porch. Can you get outside without being stopped? Where is your husband, ma'am?"

"Upstairs."

"Okay, are you on a cordless phone, can it reach outside?"

"Yes."

"I'm going to stay on the line with you until the officer gets there. Do you have any children in the house with you?"

"No." Leah looked out the bathroom door and into the long corridor. She checked both directions, before dashing in her bare feet to the front door.

"I'm still with you, ma'am. What's your name?"

"Leah Fletcher."

"And your husband's name?"

"Dell Fletcher."

"Did you say Dell Fletcher, ma'am?"

Leah was now crouched on the porch. The cement still moist from last night's fog. She felt the wetness seep through her robe before the chill started permeating her skin. "Yes, I'm Mrs. Dell Fletcher." She and the operator sat in silence for a long period of time, listening to each other's shift in position.

"All right, Mrs. Fletcher. You should be seeing a patrol car in a few minutes. Just wave at the officer when he gets there so he knows there's no threatening situation."

Leah raised her hand as she saw the black-and-white patrol car pull up moments later.

"Okay, now, you realize we can't help you unless we have your full cooperation." The operator was tapping keys, probably typing Leah's acknowledgment. Yes, she agrees to send her husband to jail, perhaps, to make him even more miserable than he is right now. Most certainly. She agrees to feel angry and feel contempt so he can be locked up and penalized. She agrees to feel pity and shame for giving up on the only man she has ever loved. But this, this was unacceptable. God only gives you as much as you can handle, she remembered hearing that off and on, from faith riddlers, people who blamed every little thing that went wrong on the will of God.

Well, she couldn't handle this. As a child, she'd seen her father slap her mother hard across the face. One good whack. Leah stood frozen in the doorway of their bedroom. Her father, a large Black man, standing over her mother, a petite Chinese woman who believed silence was power, she did nothing but catch her tears as they mixed with red droplets of blood seeping from her nose. Even her sobs were undetectable, silent gasps for air.

Leah ran to her mother's side, her five-year-old fists swelled with anger. She became ten feet tall, matching her father's rage, challenging him with her tight lips and squinted eyes. He turned and left, wordless, out the door without a look back. Her mother still catching tears, diluted red tears. Leah remembered the relief she felt when her father left. At five years old, she only pretended to be able to stand up to him while the entire time she was thinking about the large black gun underneath her parents' bed, ready for an assault from any intruder, any person with intent to do harm. She'd stumbled upon it looking for hidden Christmas presents. She remembered pulling it out, holding it, pretending she'd caught a bad guy, "Freeze, stop or I'll shoot." She never expected that the person would be her own father, right there in their own home. That the enemy had poured her cereal that very morning and let her drink the excess milk out of the bowl with a straw. That the enemy had driven her to school and pressed his nose to hers before kissing her good-bye. She didn't want to shoot her father, but she would have if he'd touched her mother one more time.

Leah opened her eyes to see the patrol car idling in front of the house. She took in its presence. Acknowledged the shift of balance from what her life really was and what she thought it ought to be. The officer stayed in his car for a few extra minutes. She wondered if it was too late, if she could send him away. Go back, start again. See if she could say the words more carefully. I want you out of this house! She felt the sting of Dell's hand all over again.

The police officer walked up the brick pathway. His shiny black shoes and pinch-pleated pants landing in front of her. "That's a pretty mean bruise." He leaned toward her. Close enough that she read his gold-plated nametag, A. Lopez. Close enough that she smelled the coolness of his aftershave on his bare throat.

"Has this happened before?" He waited, then asked the question again, this time slower with more compassion. "Anything like this ever happen before, Mrs. Fletcher?"

"This is the first time." Leah squinted over the puffiness underneath her eye as she tried to look up at him. *And it will definitely be the last;* she looked away so he couldn't see the threat of redemption.

"What was it that got the Roadrunner so upset?"

"His name is Dell . . . Mr. Fletcher."

He looked at her cheek, "No disrespect intended, Mrs. Fletcher. It's just that I used to be a fan." He scribbled a couple of notes in the small pad in his hand. "Has he been drinking, or doing any kind of drugs that you know of?"

Leah looked past him to see her neighbor, Gail, doing a slow drive-by with her head twisted to see what was going on.

There hadn't been a frenzy of police activity at the Fletcher home since last year. Dell had been in a car accident that landed on every network, national and local, as a lead story. "Dellonzo Fletcher, one of our local baseball greats, lost control of his car Friday evening while driving on the Golden State Freeway, landing in the Los Angeles River. He's now in critical condition at Cedar Sinai Hospital." They'd just had an argument about his drinking and the overmedicating. Leah threatened to end the marriage if he didn't get help, she didn't want to, but she would, for his sake. No, that was unacceptable, he'd rather die first. Dell made that clear before he pulled off into the worst rainstorm Southern California had seen in twenty years.

She told herself and the children that it was an accident, but all the while in the back of her mind she knew the truth. Dell had given up, deciding there was nothing else to lose. She, Josh, and Kayla were the nothing.

Leah's head went down, pretending not to see her neighbor staring, making assessments and assumptions she had no business making. "No. No drugs, no alcohol," she told the police officer, putting a shaking hand over the swelling on her face.

"Okay, Mrs. Fletcher. Right now I'm going in to talk to your husband. I want you to wait out here." The officer stepped past her, making her feel small and helpless.

Dell would never forgive her. Her head fell forward to rest on her exposed knees. She bunched her robe closed and buried her face in the terry fabric. There was nothing worse than being exposed, allowing strangers in. The loss of control was degrading. The police officer sent in to referee, to make the right call. She started it... no, he started it, like children in need of guidance. But what other choice did she have?

Dell walked out the door first with the young officer casually behind him. Leah stood up and moved back. Her mouth dropped open. Handcuffs around Dell's wrists. His head hung low, his eyes watching her while he passed.

Wait. Wait a minute.

"Here's the case number if you want to call for information. You'll need it if you want to know his status." A. Lopez held out the card for what seemed like an eternity. "Take it, they won't release any information if you don't have that number." Leah finally dropped it into her robe pocket.

They drove off, leaving a bare spot on the street. An icy chill set around Leah's arms and shoulders. She rubbed for warmth and continued to stare into the street where Dell had disappeared. The weight of stillness, the pause button she'd just pushed on her life. She stood swaying, moving to the hum of trees feeding and growing. The echo of air passing through her ears. She closed her eyes, letting the sun heat her upturned face. What had she done? Unforgivable. She clutched the fabric around her chest, pulling, pulling. Where was her heart? That's your husband, she whispered to the sky, *what have you done?*

chapter 6

ANGEL LOPEZ GREW UP on baseball. It was life, sustenance, a way to survive the harsh reality of East Los Angeles, an area full of his Latin brothers and sisters, notorious for gang violence and drugs. But now here he was, a grown man watching his hero deteriorate before his very eyes. He'd admired the Roadrunner; Dellonzo Fletcher was a hero, superman with a baseball cap and cleats. Stealing bases at a blink of an eye. Sliding into the plate in a blaze of dust while the umpire flagged his hands, yelling, *SAFE.*

Watching the Roadrunner play was one of the few things Lopez looked forward to. He watched the games on the thirteen-inch TV that sat on the dining room table, because the big one wasn't working in the living room and had been covered with a white table cloth, which sat there till this day as part of the furniture.

There were nine of them in that tiny green house. Four brothers, three sisters, and his mother. But they all knew, when it was time for the game, the game took priority. Angel was the baby of the family and he always got what he wanted. His mother would turn the little television so that it would face only him, snarling at anyone who dared reach for the channel changer. "*Mijo,* you can be a baseball player, too, just like your father. You stay out of the streets and study hard, and practice. You have to practice," she'd tell him. But he didn't believe her. Superheroes were born, not made. He understood his place in this world. He knew that the Roadrunner had a gift, precious and real. It shocked him when he first walked into the upstairs bedroom, turning the doorknob and slowly hearing the hoarse sound of a man's crying, seeing him sitting there with his hands over his face. This was Dellonzo Fletcher, the one he'd watched on that tiny television, admiring his every nuance, his every move.

"What happened?" The voice came out of nowhere. Lopez even surprised himself. He was thinking it but hadn't meant for the words to come out. He turned his rearview mirror to focus directly on Dell Fletcher's face.

"You think this is funny?" Dell Fletcher asked, a look of incredulousness.

More like amazement. Astonishment. Disgust. Lopez wanted to tell him but thought better of it. The police officer adjusted the mirror so that Dell Fletcher could catch the roll of his eyes.

"Excuse me? You got something you want to say to me?" He turned his attention away and watched the houses one by one as they passed. Large, old, gated castles, fading in and out of view. The sun-breaks of the overhead trees sent blinding light inside the car. Lopez watched him close his eyes.

"I guess I just wanted to know what brought you to this point, how you got here?"

Dell Fletcher's feet went up together, surprising Lopez when he felt the kick hit the back of his seat. "Mind your own damned business," he groaned, rolling over and squeezing his legs closed.

"Your injury? Still hurts, huh? Wasn't that over a year ago?"

"Just drive and shut the hell up," Dell Fletcher barked. "I need to go back for my meds. Turn this car around so I can get my meds."

Lopez ignored the plea. He assumed that was part of his problem, the weight loss, the dark circles under his eyes.

"You know, I used to look up to you. I wanted to play professional ball. I guess every boy does, every man can see himself out there. It's got to be the ultimate ride to be thought of as a hero. My father played, my uncles, in Panama. It was in my blood. I had the potential, but it just wasn't my path. But you, you did it. You made it to where every man aspires to be. Then all of a sudden, you disappear. What happened? Guys get injured all the time, they come back. But you, gone, POOF.

"Hey, you still got the millions, right? Just because you can't play doesn't mean they cut you off, right?

"Nice Porsche sitting in the driveway. How much you pay for that?" Lopez's eyes darted back and forth between the rearview mirror and the road. "I bet you guys don't even pay for half the stuff you get? Car dealer sees you walk in, they're so happy to be graced with your presence, they just give you the keys. That's the way it is, the rich stay rich?" His voice faded off as if he were talking to himself.

They drove at a snail's pace. Traffic lights changed in full rotation before Lopez slowed to a complete stop. This time, he turned and faced Dell casually. "You know how many calls I respond to, some idiot putting his hands on a woman? I see it day in and day out. You go out slapping people on the street, you might get shot, but when you're at home nobody's bigger or badder than you, so it's okay. Right? Is that how it works—"

No matter how many times he asked, Dell wasn't falling into that trap, as if a woman could do anything to warrant being hit by a man. He knew it was a setup. Dell sat straight up trying to take his concentration off the pain. He needed the Vicodin, three or four of the tiny tablets would suffice. He'd swallow them dry, no need for a chaser to wash them down. He kept playing the pictures over in his head. It had been his hand that connected to Leah's face. His eyes squeezed tighter. If he could take it back, he would. He'd never hit rock bottom before, not with Leah. She was the one person he could count on. He should have been the person she could count on.

"Seriously though, what'd she do?" They started moving again.

"Son of a . . ." Dell kicked at the seat again, knowing the consequence of the pain, but he wanted to get at the smart-ass, shut him up, close him down.

"Relax back there. You see what I'm saying? You're too intense." The officer shook his head back and forth, doing a tisk, tisk. "You need to let go of some of that anger."

His thought exactly, and Dell knew right where he wanted to direct it, right in the square of the cop's jaw. His wire had been tripped all right, but at the moment, he could do nothing but seethe quietly in the confines of his handcuffs. "I guess we're here, Officer *Loco.*"

Dell found a concentration point on the young officer's face, the thin bone on the bridge of his nose. The sharp angle between his thick brows, right there, where his fist could connect and do serious damage.

"I'm not the one in handcuffs. So who's the crazy one?" The officer's grin was deep, showcasing a set of dimples that could land him on the cover of *Gentleman's Quarterly*. A cocky look. The boldness of his dark eyes made him look dangerous. Unpredictable.

"You are, you crazy son of a—"

"Let's not exchange insults." They pulled into the freshly paved parking lot with distinct thick white rows. Lopez put the car in park, then turned around. He leaned into the mesh gate, the skin of his face outlined with small octagons. The Hollywood Division was a small brick building, three stories high. Nothing like the huge, block-long, block-wide jail downtown. This was nothing more than a transient facility. Pimp and ho rest stop for the night. The officer reached over and turned the police radio down. His story was more important. "It's just that I take it personal when I see that kind of thing... like my sister, Mari. She lives with an ingrate who knocks her around. She won't let me do anything to him. If I wasn't on the good side of the law, I'd take him out like in *The Godfather*. You've seen that movie, right? Everyone's seen *The Godfather*. That was my favorite part, when James Caan took that guy out that was laying the hand to his sister." He lifted his hand and formed it in the shape of a gun, "Spsssh, just like that, I'd shoot him in the head. But she loves him, they got three cute little boys. Three little boys who're probably going to beat their wives when they grow up. That shit is hereditary." He quieted for a moment, staring out into the parking lot.

Dell looked out, too, seeing three police cars lined neatly in a row. Shiny, black-and-white cars waiting for their masters to drive them through neighborhoods where they weren't wanted. Officers doing their civic duty to serve, protect, and break a nigga's neck. The LAPD was over thirty thousand strong, and Dell had to end up with this lunatic.

"That's what happens, you know? You may not think your children are watching, but they are. They see and hear everything, next thing you know you got little clones running around mimicking you. You got me?" His wide blunt lips still in position to speak.

Dell cut him off. "Aren't we supposed to be inside taking mug shots or something?" How much more of this nightmare did he need to endure?

"I'm sorry, am I boring you?" The dark eyes shifted down, almost as a threat. "So, why'd you say you hit her, again?" The officer leaned back in his seat and pulled out his little notepad, posturing for all the time in the world, making it obvious, if he had to wait, he would, but he wanted an answer.

Dell's head rolled back against the seat. He stared up through the back window into the smog-layered sky. He wished he had an answer to give.

At this point, any answer would do. He wished he could tell his inquisitor that he'd been abused as a child, or maybe that he'd watched his father beat his mother. Legitimate excuses, but untrue. He'd been raised in Detroit by a single mother and a single father. Two parents who loved him adoringly but separately, keeping their distance from each other. He lived with his mother who was a nurse, his father was a . . . well, it depended on how you looked at it. Conservatives would see him as an out-of-work bum. More creative types would see him as an entrepreneur who lacked resources, a preacher without a congregation, a musician without an instrument, an artist without a brush. Always lacking something for the follow-through; still, he never made excuses. Dell didn't believe in them either. When you were wrong, you were wrong, period. He'd made a mistake, and it was obvious that he'd be a long time paying for it.

chapter 7

AS SOON AS he jumped off the school bus, Josh was moving at bullet speed. No time to waste with the other kids, talking about the new Nintendo 64 games or the new trading cards they'd just gotten.

"Josh!"

He pretended not to hear his name being called.

His friends Elliot, and Skeet, could have that freckle-faced Jessica. Girls were at the bottom of his list. His only concern was getting home to check on his dad, making sure he didn't have any more accidents. Josh knew the responsibility fell square on his shoulders. Since the accident, it had become an unspoken assignment.

With his sister, Kayla, losing her mind to boys, clothes, and gossip, Joshua C, as his grandmother called him, was left holding the bag. Mama Fletch would whisper in his ear, "You're the man of the house when your father's not well," all the while sliding a folded twenty-dollar bill into his back jeans pocket. Sometimes folded up so small, he'd feel it later and think it was an old gum wrapper before pulling it out to be pleasantly surprised. He'd kept every one of those twenties, flattened out and aligned neatly under his mattress. It was a reminder to take care of the family, especially since Mama Fletch had gotten sick. The last time they all went to visit her at the Sunburst Home, she couldn't move her lips to speak, but he knew what she was thinking. Take care of your father. Take care of the family.

He didn't have time to wait for Elliot and Skeet to catch up. He had to get home.

The house seemed too quiet. Josh dropped his backpack on the floor and began his search of the house.

His mother was lying across her bed when he found her, still wearing the yellow robe. Her arms hung loosely over the edge. A rush of fear enveloped him. Just as quickly, her head popped up.

"Come here, baby. How was school?"

"It was okay." Josh sat next to his mother. It was now three o'clock, and the swelling had gone down around her cheek. "How's Daddy?" He kissed her on the good side.

"Dad had to leave for a little while."

"Where'd he go?"

She sat up to meet his eyes. "He had to leave, Josh. You know the kind of problems he was having. We just thought it best for him to spend a few nights away. I'm not sure where he'll be staying, but as soon as he calls, I'll let you know." She kissed him on the bridge of his small nose, the center of his eyes.

It wasn't that he didn't believe her, but he had a natural propensity to question everything adults said, like they could never say what they meant. So when his mother said his father would be gone for a few days, he immediately interpreted it as "I kicked him out, but please don't blame me."

Josh went to his room, pushed the dirty clothes off his bed and made a spot to lie in. His head hurt. His eyes hurt. The ceiling reminded him of dried-out cottage cheese. He connected the dots and formed different pictures, an old man with wild hair, a Pegasus with spread wings, a snarling dinosaur.

If his dad was kicked out, where would he go? His father's friends had become distant acquaintances. The guys from the team used to come over, bring their kids, and watch the football games on the big screen. Their house was the gathering place, because some guy who lived here before them built a really cool room downstairs to watch movies in that made you feel like you were in an air-conditioned theater. It even had a real popcorn machine like at the concession stand that stayed lit up in the corner. But no one went down there anymore since the guys from the team stopped coming around, as if an injury were contagious.

Maybe he went to go see Mama Fletch. But his dad couldn't stay there. His dad was too big. Mama Fletch stayed in a small room with a thin hard bed that even Josh was constantly straining to sit on.

His father could be at a hotel, one of the big ones downtown with the mirrored windows and guys that wore big red coats and hats even when it was one hundred degrees outside.

He closed his eyes. He couldn't help his father if he didn't know where he was. He couldn't keep watch.

His mind succumbed to the darkness that had fallen under his heavy lids. It was safe to sleep in the daytime. There were no shadows.

Dinner was quiet. Nothing original about that. Leah rinsed off the plates and stacked them in the dishwasher. The solemn mood hung in the air long after they'd gone to bed. Josh had even offered to clean the kitchen. She declined quickly so that he wouldn't see her exhaustion.

Why had it all backfired? She was supposed to be doing the right thing. Isn't that what all the talk shows say, the psychiatrist, the therapist. End it. Never let it happen more than once. Well, she'd done that. She'd stopped him in his tracks. Dell would know that he could never touch her like that again, ever. She wasn't her meek Chinese mother who believed silence was golden, suffering quietly. She'd seen how it had gotten her nowhere. But look at all the damage in between. Kayla and Josh only knew one thing—it was her fault. Their dad was gone and in some way she was responsible.

She grabbed her stomach, feeling a sudden queasiness. Their North Hollywood neighborhood was a Who's Who list of rich but not so famous. A grapevine, like any other tree-lined suburb. Neighbors sharing what tidbit of information they could with others just to make conversation. What if Gail's son told Kayla? They went to school together. My mother saw the police at your house. Heard your dad got arrested. She blocked out the scenario. She needed to tell Josh and Kayla the truth, and she needed to do it now.

The halls of the house were dark and empty. Light showed underneath the bedroom doors. After knocking quietly, she entered the room. She tapped her on the shoulder and motioned for her to take off the headphones. "We need to talk."

Kayla looked bored, as usual. Her *how long is this gonna take* look. "I already know, Mom. Everybody does." She turned back to her homework.

Leah reached out and touched one of Kayla's braids, she played with the end of it, trying to figure out what to say. "Well, I had no other choice. He slapped me."

"You slapped me, did I call the police?" Kayla blinked slow, waiting for a response.

"It's not the same, Kayla."

"How is it not the same? You're bigger than me, you're older than me. I couldn't fight back." Kayla slipped her headphones back on and put her head in her geometry book.

Leah couldn't argue with that. She was talking about the incident months ago. A quiet Sunday afternoon that was spent shopping with her daughter, a perfect idea, but lousy implementation. Kayla had spent the entire time sulking and complaining, sucking her teeth and rolling her eyes at any suggestion of decency Leah made. By the time they'd arrived back home, Leah was a balloon waiting to pop. She told Kayla to help carry bags from the car (filled with crop tops, knit skirts, and belly-showing jeans that Leah disapproved of). Kayla turned around and told Leah, "Get 'em yourself," a tone so full of disdain she wondered if she was possessed. Leah slapped her hard across the mouth, no denying it, an involuntary reflex that held pure rage, anger, plain old-fashioned disgust. That's what lifted her hand. It happened and Kayla was right, no one went to jail.

Leah stood up, without a leg to stand on, so to speak. Kayla was right, on principle, but not on relativity. She'd hit her out of frustration, out of the need to control a child who had gotten out of hand. That was exactly the reason that it wasn't the same. Leah wasn't a child, especially not Dell's, to discipline as he saw fit. She touched Kayla's shoulder to signify that she was leaving. Kayla didn't bother to look up.

Her next stop was Josh. She knew he would still be up. Josh never slept soundly, like his little brain was circling the world while his body lay still.

She peeped into his dark room. "It's me, baby." She heard him move under the sheets. She felt her way to the center of his room not turning on any lights. She had been painted with a healthy dose of shame that she didn't want anyone else to see.

"You know where Dad is, Josh?"

She could see the shadow of his head move up and down.

"How long does he have to stay there?" His soft small voice tugged at her heart. She fought the need to cry in her hands and beg for forgiveness.

"Just one night. He'll be home tomorrow." She sniffed back and swallowed hard. "I'm sorry I didn't tell you the truth earlier. I didn't want you to worry."

He leaned into her and kissed her on the cheek. "It's okay, Mom."

That was enough, that's all it took. She held it long enough to get out of his room, but once the door was closed, she broke down in a wall of tears.

chapter 8

DELLONZO FLETCHER jumped up, remembering where he was. Starving. He'd tried to get someone's attention during the night, but no one responded. He was alone in his cell, unlike the other questionable guests he'd passed when he was first brought in. Criminals standing arm to arm against the wall with no place to sit except the piss-covered floor.

The ringing in his ears vibrated throughout his brain. Not a hangover, no possibility of that. Not after he'd suffered all night through a severe bout of chills and chattering teeth. He was in withdrawal. His stomach knotted in one large cramp. He'd called out for his meds, "Call my wife, please, somebody." He'd yelled until his voice went hoarse. Now it hurt to sit up. He rubbed the incision above his right knee, the scar where he'd had the surgery. The surgery that was supposed to make everything better. The doctor had told him there was no reason for the pain, everything had healed properly. All that was required was physical therapy, three weeks, six, perhaps, but the pain never went away, a chronic, nagging pull from his knee to his groin. It only infuriated him to hear that it was all in his head. How the hell could he create something so vile, how could his mind conjure up something so debilitating? He made them go in again, find the problem. The second surgery was simply exploratory, to make sure the torn ligaments had been rejoined properly. When he was closed up and healed, the pain came back twofold.

He began to think it was some kind of revenge. Some sort of what-you-do-comes-back-to-you cycle that he couldn't escape. Punishment for stealing someone's bubble gum in the third grade, or maligning a girl's good name in the eighth. Or the women while he was on the road. *The women.* He showed restraint when he could, but on occasion *resistance was futile.* Gorgeous streamlined bodies, sexy wide mouths promising to do anything he wanted. "No one will know, I'll never tell" was the catchall phrase, a pass code. Dell favored the married ones who had as much to lose as he did. He couldn't believe it when the wife of a Midwest mayor sought him out after a game in their fair town, sending a champagne and strawberry tray to his hotel room. When he opened the door, she was standing behind the room-service waiter wearing nothing but a full mink coat and dark sunglasses. "Special delivery," she said once inside, dropping the fur to the ground and exposing her rich sepia-toned body. They had a wild night doing things they both never wanted to speak of again. He'd awakened in bed, sore and tender, while she managed to be on the morning news cutting a ribbon with her husband before he'd had his Wheaties. He knew one day he would pay for those misdeeds.

Or maybe, and this was a long shot, maybe it was God trying to tell him to bow down. He'd gotten through life only giving *Him* partial credit. Thanking *Him* at award ceremonies or at the end of a spectacular game. *He* always had to be thanked first, it was customary and expected. But he'd never really had anything to say privately, just between old friends. Once he walked off that stage or out of the public eye, he thanked no one but himself; he'd been responsible for his successes and equally his failures. His days and nights had been filled with strategy, with maintaining control of his destination. He could only guess what had led him here; at some point he'd fallen asleep at the wheel.

"Let's go." The voice made him realize he wasn't dreaming. The jail cell slid open.

Dell had to do a double take to make sure it was the same man, the same one who'd tormented him less than twenty-four hours ago. He didn't look as menacing in jeans and a hooded sweatshirt. His hair was wet, soaked along with the top part of his gray sweatshirt. "It's raining out there," he responded to the questioning stare. "C'mon."

"I don't need your help." Dell pushed off of him. He hadn't forgotten about the earlier grilling. His head swam. "What time is it, anyway?" Out of habit he looked to his wrist for the watch he'd left behind before he was rushed out of his own home in handcuffs.

"It's 2:15."

"In the morning?"

"Yes sir."

They walked through the bare corridor. The officer stopped and waved a badge in front of a black box. A message ran across the screen in red digital letters, Have a nice evening, Officer Lopez. The double doors pushed themselves open. Rain fell heavy, splashing on the pavement in front of them.

"Don't I need to sign out, or something? You guys just let criminals walk out the back door, no problem?" Dell looked around for a sign of regiment.

"You a criminal?"

"No, I'm not. As a matter of fact, I'm innocent. How often do you hear that?" Dell worked to keep up with the hurrying officer.

The locks flipped open in the Taurus. Dell wanted out of the rain that exacerbated the chill working through his body. He slid into the passenger side. "No patrol car?"

"Just fasten up and stay quiet."

They rolled past the security gate, a friendly wave to the security attendant who looked like he was annoyed his sleep had been disturbed.

"So you're going to tell me what that was all about?" Dell's washed-out face was beaded with raindrops. The back of his T-shirt, wet.

"I never booked you." The officer's eyes were searching for the recognition. The pat on the back. "I felt bad for giving you such a hard time, wanted to make it up to you. Save you the embarrassment of an arrest and the media."

"Then why the hell was I sitting in that jail cell damn near all night? If I was never booked, why wasn't I sleeping in my own bed?"

"Hey, you were going to sit there all night whether I booked you or not. Thought you needed a little time to reflect on life. Understand the magnitude of what we talked about earlier."

"Are you crazy? Who the hell do you think you are? You think I need your help, some little playcop, probably don't even have a high-school diploma, slid in with a GED, and you're going to save me? Right, you got something to offer me, right? More advice on how to treat a lady, my lady. More self-righteous messages about how grateful I should be?" Dell looked out the window into the wet darkness of the street. They idled at a streetlight alone. Not another car in sight.

"You know what I think?"

"Nah, unh unh. I don't want to know what you think. Just take me home." He didn't want him starting in again. He couldn't take it. Not with an empty stomach. The clothes he had on, shorts and a T-shirt, smelled of the dank odor of a jail cell. He needed a shower, to sleep in his own bed. To hold his wife and ask for forgiveness. To pour a handful of happy and swallow them with one gulp.

The light turned green. Lopez steered with the precision of someone who'd been driving all his life. The boy who snuck out the window and took his mother's car keys. Maybe a joy ride or two in some unsuspecting victim's stolen car.

"You're no longer welcome there."

Dell couldn't help but turn and stare at the man.

The officer stared back at Dell. The stabbing intensity of his eyes said he could just as easily be a criminal as an officer of the law.

"What's that supposed to mean?" Dell inhaled with caution. His head was pounding, along with his racing heart.

"Your wife doesn't want you there," he repeated, his tone resolute.

"So now you know what my wife wants and doesn't want?" It took him a moment to understand the substantial part of what the officer had insinuated. "You talked to my wife?" Dell's voice shook in a low tremor. "I'm not handcuffed anymore. You play these games if you want to." His breath was damp, increasing the fog on the window in front of him. The rain was light but steady. A fine mist covered the window with each stroke of the wiper blades.

"Am I supposed to be afraid of you? What do you weigh now, about a buck fifty?" The officer snapped his gum, "You're not at your fighting weight, *Roadrunner*. Oh excuse me, Mr. Dellonzo Fletcher. So what hotel would you like me to drop you off at?" He steered with his left hand, the other resting by his side under the shadow on the car seat.

"Pull over, let me out right here. I'll walk," Dell said, realizing the man wasn't dealing with a full deck. The sooner they ended this rap session, the better.

"You know what, you're right, we should pull over." Something in the man's voice had shifted.

"The hotel is fine, man. Whatever. It's cool." Dell felt for the car door latch. He'd jump if he had to. He wasn't about to get caught up in a schizo cop's nightmare.

"That's a great idea. We can talk about the game you blew 'cause your hamstring hurt."

"That's it." The force that moved through Dell's arm landed squarely on the young officer's jaw. The car swerved along with the snap of his smug face. Only for a few seconds did Dell feel the satisfaction of finally shutting him up before the hand that had been riding incognito rose up out of the darkness. Dell now faced the shiny gleam of what looked like the barrel of a gun. He grabbed it, his eyes closed tight. If it went off, he didn't want to face it head-on. They struggled while the car zigzagged through the middle of the street. He could feel the hard shiny instrument in his hand but didn't have full control of it. The tires skidded and dragged on the wet surface. They fell into each other, back and forth like a roller coaster. "Stop! You're going to kill us. Let go, shit!" The panic rose; he couldn't choose between the probability of a car accident or a bullet to the forehead. The last thing Dell saw was the dashboard when the car careened into the telephone pole. His head flew forward, then back like a heavy lead ball connecting with the force of a bat, so strong and hard, he knew it was a home run, his brain feeling like it was being sent over the fence, past the bleachers and into the sky.

chapter 9

LEAH ROSE IN the middle of the night, feeling ill. Something she couldn't shake with an aspirin or a glass of Alka-Seltzer. The uneasy culprit of worry had consumed her. The image of Dell kept rising to the surface as he was being escorted to the police car in handcuffs. His face caught in the middle of anger and self-pity, staring her down. It had all been a terrible mistake. First Dell's, then hers. She'd tell the police that it was all a big misunderstanding, that she wanted her husband home, safe beside her. What married couples didn't have their fights? What husband, or wife, hasn't lost control, done something they regretted? Everything had moved so quickly. It was rash, idiotic. She'd tell them that she was on her way to pick him up. Dell didn't deserve to be locked up in a filthy jail cell, not with real criminals. The kind that may have still had blood on their hands, the kind that killed and murdered. Not her husband.

She pulled at her robe that laid at the foot of the bed. The card. She dug into the pocket and pulled it out. She picked up the phone and dialed the police station. She spoke slowly so that she wouldn't have to repeat herself. "My husband was arrested today; I want to come get him. His name is Dellonzo Fletcher. I don't want to file charges. It was all a mistake."

The clean honest voice responded, having no concern for the situation, no need for details, only the numbers on the bottom of the card written in the blue box. Leah read them slowly. 531661. She waited and listened to the keys being punched in.

"That was filed as a warning, Mrs. Fletcher. Mr. Fletcher was not charged or detained."

"What do you mean not charged? He's not there? Is that what you're saying?"

"Exactly."

"But he was taken from here in handcuffs. I saw him. The officer arrested him, and they drove off."

"That's not uncommon to remove someone from the premises who may be a threat, ma'am. Officers make that judgment call."

Leah's eyes trailed to the empty side of her bed. "But he's not here." Her voice quieted by the realization. He's not here.

"Is there anything else I can do for you?" the objective voice asked, ending the silence.

"No. Yes. Is there any way to contact the officer to find out where he took him, where he dropped him off?"

"You can inquire with a written request?"

"A written request! It's a simple question. Can't you just ask him where he took my husband?"

"Absolutely, but it has to be put in writing. Legally, we aren't allowed to give out any information unless it's documented."

Leah slammed the phone down. Her hand slid to the pillows that had gone unused all night, squeezing, inhaling, as if she could sense where Dell now lay his head. A soothing picture, hopefully, would be transmitted to her mind, and she'd see Dell safe. She sat quiet, sitting in the darkness. Waiting. Listening to the mist of rain as it blew against her bedroom window like sprinkles of sand. She waited holding the pillow tight.

A chill jolted her body. Then another. *Oh God, Dell. Where are you?*

She picked up the phone and dialed. The voice full of zest at two in the morning made Leah forget whose number she'd punched into the keypad. Making her forget why she'd picked up the phone in the first place. Who did she think could bring Dell back? The voice asked again, "Hello, who is this?"

"It's me, Elicia. I'm sorry."

"Hey." A more relaxed tone this time, the one reserved for friends. Elicia could control her voice like a volume knob, adjusting base and treble. As an anchorwoman, that was her best skill, right along with her sculpted beauty. She was a friend, but she also worked with the enemy. In all truth, she was the enemy. News, we bring it to you first, that was the Channel 8 slogan that appeared underneath her smiling face on the downtown billboard off the freeway. She was an evening sports anchor and also hosted her own weekend show. They'd become fast friends last year while she was doing a story on Dell. Nothing like the usual overmadeup airheads who had showed up for interviews. Elicia Silvas was a Cornell graduate in journalism, the daughter of a West African mother and a pale-skinned Dominican father. The producer sent her over after Dell's accident last year. See, I'm harmless, my skin is brown just like yours. I come in peace. She was humble but not stupid. She came straight out with the reason. Admitted that she'd been sent to find out whether it had been an accident or a suicide attempt and made it clear that whatever he said it was... it was.

That was the day Elicia was invited into the family. Leah appreciated honesty and had a profound respect for it living in the land of make-believe, where a good number of people put faces on to suit the mood; it became a rare commodity to deal with someone real. It'd been a long time since she could call someone a friend. So many past relationships had soured because of Dell's status, the fame. She didn't trust easily. And with, of all people, a news hound. "I was just thinking about you. How're you holding up?" she asked cautiously.

The silence was an indicator.

"Leah, we've already gone over this. It was something you had to do. Stop blaming yourself."

She grabbed the pillow to her chest. She inhaled the scent of sleeping Dell, the calm, loving Dell.

"Are you there?" Elicia asked.

"I just called the police station where Dell was supposed to be taken this morning, and he's not there."

"That was fast. They take domestic offense more seriously since the Nicole Simpson thing. Are you all right? Did he come back there? Were you two fighting again? I'll come over if you need me to."

"He's not here. I don't know where he is."

"I can come over and stay with you, Leah, if you're afraid."

Before Leah could offer a *no thank you,* the pitiful cause that she'd become sitting in the dark, imagining the worst possible scenario, she began to cry.

"Sweetie, what. What is it?"

Leah folded the pillow smaller, leaning into it to press away the bubbles and knots forming in her stomach. "I want him to come home. I'd give anything if he walked through the front door right now. I'm so scared something happened to him. If it has, I'll never make it. I won't."

This time the silence traveled from the other end of the line. Leah quieted her sobbing long enough to wonder if she was wallowing to herself. "Elicia?"

"I'm here."

"I guess I sound pretty ridiculous, right? After I sent him out of here in shackles, now I want him back?"

"You have no idea where he is?"

"Not a clue. The police station said I had to put it in writing, my request to know where Dell was dropped off. Can you believe that? I'm his wife, and they can't tell me anything. As if I'm the enemy, or the one who did the victimizing. In a way that's the way I feel, like the bad guy. Now I'm being punished, not knowing where he is, agonizing over where he could be. Why would he come home? I embarrassed him, humiliated him; I'm the last person he wants to see."

The silence again. Leah felt like she was sitting on a therapist's couch while she talked herself into conclusions, questioning, then answering. Carrying on a conversation with herself. What was the point of having someone listen if they had nothing to say? Leah knew the answer to that question as well. Or maybe she was being completely selfish, the way she'd felt many times after talking Elicia's ear off, realizing that she hadn't asked her one thing about her day, her life.

"You're not the bad guy, Leah," Elicia finally interjected, giving her a moment of calm, relief from her own badgering. "He's the one who hit you."

She wanted to hear that one more time but shifted her concern where it deserved to be. "If something bad happened to Dell, wouldn't it come over the wire? Wouldn't your station know before anyone else?"

"I haven't heard anything, sweetie. You know I would tell you." Her voice was so much softer than the one she used on television sitting next to Steve Humble, her weeknight coanchor. "I wish there was something I could say to make you feel better."

"I wish there was, too," Leah whispered in the dark.

"Call me tomorrow. And remember, you're not the guilty party here. He's probably fine, wherever he's hiding. All this worrying will have taken ten good years off your life for nothing."

Leah still held the receiver after the line was dead. She closed her eyes and slipped down into the bed, pulling the soft down comforter over her shoulders. The words played in her head, don't worry, he's probably fine. Don't worry . . . Leah felt it again, the raw chills rising along her legs and feet. Please be safe, Dell, she squeezed his pillow harder, using it to catch her tears.

chapter 10

AFTER THE ACCIDENT, Officer Lopez had been taking things slow. He reported to work the next morning as if nothing had happened. He sat in the first row during roll call and looked his sergeant directly in the eye to show he had nothing to hide. He was prepared for whatever punishment he deserved for driving a good citizen into a telephone pole. He was fully aware that he was a condemned man, not taking anything too seriously, the way a man works when he knows it's his last day. It was torture having that feeling of the inevitable, that something was in store, that something lay in wait.

He sat in his patrol car at the stoplight on Sunset, staring up at the tall palms swaying back and forth, demanding attention with each sudden jerk. His shoulder and neck were still bothering him. He wasn't out looking for any trouble. In fact, he tried to have as little contact with anyone as possible. It hurt to get in and out of the car. If he was stiff and sore, he could only imagine what shape Dell Fletcher was in. Lopez exercised daily, either running or lifting weights. His body could take the shock of an accident more easily than an ex-athlete who'd let himself go.

Sunset Avenue was dark and deserted, for which he was grateful. Without the college kids cruising in groups with no particular place to go, or couples holding hands in odd pairs and shapes, the street had lost all its appeal. Prostitutes closed shop for the day. Their long legs posed in stiletto heels were as much a part of this area as the buildings. Los Angelenos didn't know how to act if it wasn't seventy degrees with a mild breeze. This wind was moving through like it had taken over, a new sheriff in town. He drove slowly, taking time to peer through the dark business and community shop windows. Freeloaders took advantage of nights like these to come through and take what they pleased with no attention to dodge.

Movement through two buildings caught his eye. He stepped on the brake and backed up to get a better look down the small alleyway. He lifted his large flashlight, and an immediate flood of illumination took over the area. He could see clear down the alley, but there was nothing but a large dumpster and small round trash barrels stacked neatly by size. Probably just a cat jumping from base to base. Lopez released the trigger on the light and let his foot pat the gas slightly. This time the rearview mirror was the source of the movement. He backed up again and parallel parked on the wrong side of the street. The wind seemed to hold his door shut. He pushed hard against the force and stepped out slowly, zipping his black-issue bomber up around his ears.

Whatever ran across the street was bigger than a cat and definitely didn't want to be seen. Fearing he might be outnumbered by street riffraff, he slid back into his cruiser to contemplate calling into dispatch to see if another car was in the vicinity. Then again, it was probably the homeless folks looking for a warm dry place to bed down for the night. The Police Department had been sued by the ACLU more times than he could count for rousting homeless out of private property. "Sent them out to freeze to death. Murder that's what it was, first degree." Now there was a hands-off approach floating through the precinct. Unless they were committing an actual crime, they were free to spit and piss wherever they desired.

He shifted the idling cruiser into drive and decided he'd do his own surveillance down the other side of the alley, and that'd be it. Time to call it a night. He had a fresh new Slavic gem waiting for his call when he got off at eleven. She'd been watching him while he did the street markings of a hit-and-run from the sidewalk where a small tourist crowd had gathered. To the out-of-towners, yellow tape meant photos for back home, like they were on the set of a cop drama. Never mind that there might be real people sprawled out in the middle of the street dripping real blood. It didn't help matters that most of the Los Angeles force met the good-looking quotient. Officers with straight shoulders, lean waistlines, and power-bar diets. This was the land of make-believe. And to the little foreign cheerleader watching from the sideline, he was a star, a hero who chased bad guys.

The lips. Lopez grinned hard to himself thinking about those big juicy lips. Her bold red hair and pale skin were nothing but a frame for those Jessica Rabbit lips. The phone number she scribbled half-backward on his pad was tucked safely in his right pocket. She was only going to be here four more days, which was perfect. No phone calls and messages past the point of interest. He appreciated the international cuisine Los Angeles had to offer. The melting pot had a buffet of beauties from all over the world. He'd tasted Italian, French, German, East Indian, Brazilian, all interesting delicacies. He ran his fingers through his tightly curled hair and tilted the rearview mirror to see if he needed to waste precious time detouring for a shave.

The dispatch blasted through, chasing Jessica Rabbit from his thoughts.

"We have a 187 reported on Tenth and Olympic. Are you in the area, 214?"

"On my way." The exact address glowed with green light coming from the miniature computer screen in his console. He made an abrupt U-turn in the middle of the street, barely missing a parked sedan. The multicolored lights flashed silently as he sped down the deserted street, greeting each green traffic light with full force.

When he arrived at the scene, he recognized the cruiser already parked erratically at an angle. He took two steps at a time with his gun drawn and in position.

"LAPD," Lopez called out as he took a cautious step inside.

Janowitz came from the rear of the apartment stepping heavily. "Talk about vengeance is mine. This woman filled him with all six bullets." He slid his palm through his blonde highlighted hair, always the actor-in-training, strong straight teeth, square jaw and straight shoulders, ready for his big break in TV Land.

He followed Janowitz toward the other side of the room where two feet lay spread out beyond the tattered green sofa. The man's face had been spraypainted red with blood. He could see how some could start to believe it was all make-believe, like the movies.

Janowitz reached down and came up with the wallet, reading it out loud.

"Dellonzo Fletcher. 5543 Winding Wind Road. Hollywood Hills, California. Oh shit!" Janowitz yelped, like he'd won the grand prize.

Lopez stood still, feet unable to move.

"You know who this is, man?" Janowitz shifted his wild blue eyes back and forth from Lopez to the body. "Roadrunner, you know, from the Angels. Oooh shiittt."

Lopez swallowed hard, unable to breathe. The pounding in his ears made the words sound garbled. He could see Janowitz speaking into his left shoulder, radio dispatch. He was calling in the special homicide team for high visibility cases. LAPD had learned from past mistakes. Cases like this received special handling...no chance of misplacing evidence, or leaving anything in the wrong hands.

"They're going to have a field day with this one. You think he was doing her, had a little ghetto piece on the side?"

Lopez stood motionless. "Doing who?" He hadn't been able to force himself to look down again into the bloodied face.

"The woman who shot him."

No, it can't be. Those few crucial moments had led to this? He'd tried to eliminate the whole day, from beginning to end, from his mind. Picking up Dell Fletcher from his house, taunting him, careening into the telephone pole, the crash. He'd blacked out afterward. Woke and surprised himself when he was able to step out of the car. The car was pushed in deep around the pole. Lopez was standing outside of the car when it hit him that someone else had been riding alongside of him. He stuck his head through the crumpled window. No one. Only the empty seat where Dell Fletcher had been sitting. A splatter of blood on the dash, a tinged handprint on the door handle. He was gone. Lopez assumed he'd made it home somehow. Back to his precious wife, his snazzy Porsche, the Spanish-villa-style home worth more than a small country. A full day had passed while Lopez waited patiently for his sergeant to walk in with the yellow sheet, a signed affidavit and complaint about the young officer who'd overstepped his bounds. Put a civilian's life in jeopardy, threatened to kill him. He waited. At every turn, he expected to see Dell Fletcher standing behind Sergeant Carver's wide shoulders, smiling, smug—who's laughing now?—but it never happened. Dell Fletcher never came after him, and now he knew why.

He was dead.

Lopez followed Janowitz's eyes to the back room.

"She's in there. Says she caught him stealing from her. Can you believe this? Unbelievable! Get your game face on, man. By the time we walk out that door, we're going to be on every news channel in LA county, shit, the whole country." Lopez watched him pull out a small plastic comb from his front pocket.

"What the hell are you doing?" He grabbed Janowitz's hand, still dazed by what was happening around him.

"No shit, man. You're right." Janowitz's excitement slid a few notches down. "Wouldn't want them chasing any blonde suspects." He slipped the comb back in his pocket.

"I think we better get out front and run the tape. You know, first officers on the scene always get blamed if it's not clean." Janowitz took two large strides and was already pushing through the screen door.

Lopez purposely didn't look down, instead walking straight ahead, using the dirty walls in his peripheral vision for guidance. Cheaply framed art hung the length of the dark hall. Yellow light edged through the bottom rim of the door when he reached the end of the hall. He snapped on a plastic glove and turned the bedroom knob.

"LAPD, ma'am. Entering the room." Lopez quickly surveyed the square box, decorated to look like a bedroom. The raggedy dresser had several pictures taped haphazardly inside the mirror. The woman sat on the edge of the bed holding on to her three little children. They sat huddled together dressed in their pajamas, shaking and crying. Their small chests rose and fell in rhythm together, a chorus of moans and sobs.

"Did you get it out of here? Is it gone? I want it out of here!"

Lopez assumed she was talking about the body. "It's going to be a while before that happens, ma'am. I need to ask you a few questions. First of all, are you all right? Are your children harmed?"

She seemed to have found his shoes a focal point.

"Ma'am?"

"I already told that other policeman what happened. I can't keep talking about this in front of my kids."

"I understand. I do. But it helps to have it on record with two separate officers. It's easier to confirm the story was told right the first time." He scanned the room once again. Were there any answers hidden in the walls, the floor, the box that once held the dilapidated .22 revolver?

"No story. Only the truth. I woke up in the middle of the night to find that bastard sifting through my drawers." She heaved, and a flow of liquid broke through her already-strained eyes. "Like I wasn't even here, like my children weren't even here. I'm tired of these sons of bitches thinking they can come in my home and take whatever they want," she wiped more tears, "...from my babies mouths. I'm tired of it. And I'd shoot him again if I had to. I'd shoot him again."

"Tired. You mean this same person has been here before? Did you know him?"

"No, I didn't know him. What I did know is that these homeless creatures think they can come through here and take whatever they want, and nobody's gonna do nothing about it. I work hard for everything I have. Nobody's taking anything from here. I showed him." She swallowed another wave of salty tears as she rocked into the children's sobs. "I work too hard to feed my babies."

He took another all-encompassing look around the room, placing both feet underneath him in a wide stance to keep himself from wobbling. He felt sick. How did he get here? How had it come to this?

The door looked too far away. He didn't think he would make it. His head flew in first and leaned over the bathroom toilet. The wave followed by another only brought up moist air. He gasped, another wave. He'd never intended to do anyone harm, only to scare him, shake him up a little. Dell Fletcher was his idol, he'd admired him... at one time.

"It wasn't him." The bathroom door pushed open, "you all right, man?" Janowitz stood outside the door, disgusted more so by the state of the bathroom than Lopez's weak stomach.

Lopez stood up wiping his mouth with the back of his shaking hand. "What?"

"I don't know what he was doing with the Roadrunner's wallet, but it wasn't him. Coroner walked in and took two seconds to make that assessment." Janowitz walked away disappointed. His hopes dashed for being on the nightly news.

The small tiny apartment was overflowing with uniformed officers and detectives. Lopez pushed past the forensics team and stopped in front of the now-plastic-covered body. He grabbed the first jacket that he saw with Coroner printed on the back. A short pale woman with clear eyes faced him.

"What do you mean, that's not him? He just looks different. He's been sick, had some problems. I know this guy, I'm a friend of the family. That's him."

"Well, friend of the family, do you remember him having eight rotted out teeth and track marks in his neck and arms that were older than you?" She actually paused, waiting for an answer. "This guy's an old junkie. I don't know what he was doing with Dell Fletcher's wallet, but this ain't him."

Lopez took a deep breath and pulled down the zipper of the plastic body bag. The blood had dried around the man's face, blending in with his own dark skin. He didn't need a closer look. She was right, it wasn't him.

Someone reached around and zipped the body bag closed. The stretcher lifted and was carried briskly out the front door.

"A close friend, huh? That's deep. How long you guys been hanging out?" Janowitz was barely able to contain his sarcastic grin. "Next time you have the Roadrunner over for dinner, invite me, too. We can all hang out, watching the game, drinking a Bud." He slapped a stunned Lopez on the back before walking away.

chapter 11

LEAH PLACED A KISS between Josh's eyes. He didn't want the light off. She pushed the blankets up around his ears. She knew what he wanted to ask, he knew she didn't have an answer. So they stayed silent. She stepped out of his bedroom and reached into her robe pocket. She pulled the card out, Officer A. Lopez, Hollywood Division, Los Angeles Police Department. She'd already dialed the number several times more, hanging up before there was an answer. She wanted to confront the officer personally, find out if it was true, that Dellonzo Fletcher had never been arrested, that he'd never spent one night in jail. She wanted to leave him a personal message, but embarrassment stopped her. The joke was on her. They'd probably fallen out laughing once they'd cleared the corner, stopped off for a couple of beers. All for show, exclusively for her the pathetic scene, the handcuffs, the look of pity.

She made her way down the hall, stopping with a sudden panic when she heard the doorbell. Fear crept around her heart. It was far too late for it to be good news. The police car's hood underneath the yellow streetlamp shone, sending a ray of light through the front doors. She took two more steps, catching the olive skin and thick dark hair. She swung the door open before he rested his finger on the chime a second time.

"Mrs. Fletcher."

"Officer... Lopez, I've been wanting to talk to you." She looked behind him, expecting Dell to miraculously appear. "What's going on?" The first prayer had been said as she took the walk down the stairs. Now she was begging. All the other prayers that came before this one had to count for something, like stock invested over time, waiting for the day of true need to cash out. "Has something happened to Dell?"

He watched her face. "There was an accident tonight, a man found dead. A homeless thug trying to rob a family was shot and killed. At first we thought it was your husband, but it wasn't. He had your husband's wallet."

She stepped back, letting him in.

"I don't know how this guy got a hold of your husband's wallet." He grabbed her arm as she began tumbling backward. "Mrs. Fletcher."

She felt a hundred years old, like she'd lived twenty lifetimes, as if she'd lived through this moment over and over before now. How many times had Dell died in her nightmares? How many times had death knocked on the door, message for Leah Fletcher? Her husband wanted it enough to will it to happen. But what about her and the children?

When Leah opened her eyes, he was kneeling over her with the phone in his hand. She interrupted his call for an ambulance. "I don't need that." She stood up, as if just recovering from a stumble in her step. She tightened the robe around her chest, closed it around her legs. She touched her face and took a few seconds to inventory her surroundings.

Yes, she was here, living this nightmare.

"Why did you say you felt responsible?" She studied the officer's face looking for errors in his story.

He paused as if he didn't remember admitting such a thing, but she'd heard him. Her eyes were closed, her legs and arms limp, but she could hear, feel all that was going on around her. He whispered the words over her while he touched her cheek... *it's my fault, shit, this is all my fault.* She heard him say it.

"I just meant, I felt like if I hadn't arrested him, that he wouldn't have ever been in the situation he was in."

"What situation? How does he go from leaving his home in handcuffs with you, to being mugged?" Her lips were quivering. "Tell me what happened. I called the station and they never had a Dell Fletcher booked in jail. Tell me everything." Her eyes turned into small slits. "What happened? Where did you take him?"

"Mom." She looked up to see her son staring down at what must've looked like a frightening sight. She and the policeman in a standoff, her face filled with terror, ready to claw at whatever story he'd conjured up.

Josh unsteadily moved down the stairs holding the banister with both hands. "Did something happen to Dad?"

"No, he's fine." Her voice shook with determination. "We just don't know where he is exactly." She folded her arms over her chest and put her accusing eyes back on Officer Lopez.

"Then how do you know he's fine?" Josh stopped between the two of them. Leah focused on the baseball jersey that hung well past his thighs. It was Dell's.

"I'm here to let your mom know the details."

"Where is he?" Josh would not be easily thwarted.

Leah knew better than to lie to him, but what was the alternative? She didn't know the truth. "He's in a safe place, Josh. He's dealing with his issues. When he's better and ready to talk to us, he'll call."

"Then why are all those guys parked out front?"

Leah rushed to the small window. The circus had come to town. News vans parked along the length of the curb. It wasn't a shock to Leah. She'd been down this road before, many times in fact. She wiped the budding tears away long enough to focus, but the haze returned instantly. Her arm was being held, pulled, guided. She stopped. "I can't talk to them. Not now." Her greatest fear and loathing of her husband's fame, the news media, the exposure. She always tried to stay out of sight, always a few steps behind so the camera never slipped to her.

"I'll tell them what I know, okay. Just go back inside." Lopez took the first steps to the edge of the brick walkway. She watched as the group descended upon him. The lights illuminated his face, making him appear lighter than his soft beige tone. He tried to refrain from squinting. He spoke to no one in particular.

"I'm Officer Angel Lopez of the Los Angeles Police Department, Hollywood Division. I was given permission to speak on the Fletcher family's behalf."

"Where is the Roadrunner? Why was his wallet found on a dead man?" A voice beyond the lights.

"At this time we're not sure of his whereabouts. The family is just grateful that the man found dead was not Dellonzo Fletcher. If any further information comes up, you'll be the first to know." He turned back around and went inside.

Leah Fletcher stood directly behind the door, her arms around the boy and a teenaged girl. All three, their eyes filled with fear and worry. His conscience was yelling at him, that he may have screwed up their entire lives, this sweet family without a father because of one act of stupidity.

Playing games. He'd always been good at that. Teasing. When he was in school he was the king, they called it the dozens. He could get under the other guy's skin the deepest... yo mama, yo sister, wherever the weakness, you went for it. He'd found Dell Fletcher's immediately. His wife. *She doesn't want to see you.* He could see the Roadrunner's flash, the heat and anger in his face. He was only playing around.

"Thank you." She suddenly had a different tone from the accusatory one moments ago. She took a deep shaky breath, "If you hear anything, anything at all, please call me first." She was being held up by her children, an anchor on each side.

"I'm sorry." He bit his lip hard. That's all he could think to say. He'd be sorry for the rest of his life if something had really happened to Dell Fletcher. The look on her face, her children. *I'm sorry.*

He reached in his chest pocket and pulled out his card. This time he scribbled another number, his home phone, on the back. "I know you want to talk. Call me." He looked hard at her so she would know, I'll tell you everything.

Lopez started the squad car and rode through the news crews and watched them scatter like vultures being disrupted from a carcass feeding. He rode south on the Hollywood Freeway, back to the scene of the accident. Maybe Dell was still lying out there somewhere, wobbling around with a head injury. He made that assessment based on the amount of blood that he'd cleaned from his dashboard.

He turned onto Western Avenue. Looped the patrol car around, cutting an illegal U-turn in the middle of the street, heading in the direction where it all took place. The street was lined with old dilapidated buildings, some windows broken out and boarded up. Hollywood's rebirth hadn't made it to this part of the district yet. The city had structured a plan to rebuild the town but ran out of money on the first block.

The pole stood erect without a dent. Wish he could say the same for his car. After cleaning the inside with ammonia to remove the blood, he took it to the autobody shop. Six thousand dollars straight out of his pocket. If he filed an insurance claim, it would go on his driving record. Police officers had to have spotless records. A collision without anyone to blame didn't look good. What, were you drunk?

A homeless woman wearing skates and pushing a shopping cart watched him park underneath the street lamp and get out of the car. She wasn't shy, pulling in next to him as if the shopping cart had brakes and a gear for park. She smiled and winked. "You sure are a cutie. Anything I can do for ya?" She left the basket and skated in front of him. She fluttered her sparse dry eyelashes to remind herself she was still a looker.

"As a matter of fact, there is. A few nights ago, did you see a guy running around with his nose busted up, maybe his forehead a little bloody. Wearing shorts and a T-shirt?"

She looked past Lopez over his shoulder. "Maybe." Her mouth was watering. "What's it worth to you?"

He tried to remember if he was carrying any cash. "That's what I thought." He turned to get back in his squad car.

"No, really. I saw him. It was raining, and he was standing out here looking like some zombie. Lost. That's the guy, right, he was wearing khaki shorts and a T-shirt?"

He turned around and followed her eyes to the corner. "You're just repeating what I already told you. How do I know you really saw him?"

"You didn't tell me it was raining. Did'cha? No. I saw him standing in the rain with blood coming down his face. That's why I paid him any attention at all because I was going to show him the shelter, see if he wanted to get in out of the rain. And it wasn't a few nights ago, it was just yesterday," she added for confirmation.

Lopez dug into his pocket but left his hand there as bait.

"So what happened? He was standing out here, then what?"

A happy-face smile creased her dry lips like this was an easy one. "Right before I was gonna ask him if he wanted to follow me to the shelter, a car came and got him."

"What kind of car?"

"A nice car." She rocked on her worn-out skate wheels, bonus round.

"All right, look. Here." He pulled out his wallet and flipped it open to a single twenty. He reluctantly peeled it out.

Her hand, remarkably smooth with long eloquent fingers, didn't fit with the mussed dirty hair and oversized sweatshirt. She took the bill from him and quickly pushed it down her bra. "A Mercedes, dark, couldn't make out the color, but it was one of those cute little ones. Probably an E200 series, something like that, I used to have one myself." She smiled a perfect set of teeth, a little stained, but perfect nonetheless.

"Who was driving?"

"I didn't see all that. The windows were tinted. He bent over and got in. Wasn't no conversating."

"No conversation?"

"It wasn't a ho exchange. The guy knew whoever it was, no conversating. He hopped right in the car and they took off." She batted those long wispy lashes again.

"Thanks." Lopez put his wallet back in his pocket.

"Any time, good looking. Hey, what time's your shift over?" She had a new sensibility, a new outlook with a flat new twenty pressed against her skin. Pulling her sweater down neater over her thick stomach, her smile now open to show an even set of yellow teeth, "Okay, well you know where to find me if you need me. A prime catch like me won't be standing around for long."

Lopez left her standing under the harsh street lamp. He drove off with a sense of calm. At least the Roadrunner was still alive. Leah would want to know that; he corrected himself, Mrs. Fletcher. She would want to know that her husband was still alive. Somewhere. At least he wasn't lying in a gutter with his head bashed in.

It didn't take Lopez long to weave back up the steep hill of Mulholland Drive. Even in the dark where the road seemed like an unending death trail, he drove with a mission. The landscape at the top of the hill made him feel like he'd escaped and found his way into paradise. Million-dollar homes. The air up here was less dense, the sky brighter, filled with sparkling dots and moving shapes. The smog couldn't reach this high. Too expensive. The cityscape of Los Angles, the lights of downtown high-rises presented a picturesque view that made one believe the smog, traffic, and violence were a figment of the imagination.

Lopez was glad to see most of the news crews had moved on. There was one lone van with the Channel 8 emblem standing out in yellow and blue. Before he rang the doorbell, he moistened his finger with his tongue and smoothed his silky eyebrows. The house had light seeping into the hallway. He could see the ficus tree Leah Fletcher had almost fallen into when she'd fainted. He pressed the bell.

The solid wood door pulled open slowly. At first he thought it was Leah, Mrs. Fletcher, but quickly realized it was the girl. Her expression, blank and stoic.

"Is your mother home?" He waited for her to respond. She didn't move.

"Can I come in?" Lopez looked past her into the expansiveness of the house.

"What did you find out?" The panicked voice came out of the darkness from behind the girl. "It's okay, Kayla, I got it."

"I'm Officer Angel Lopez," he whispered to the teenager as he moved past her and into the foyer. "Remember, I was here earlier?"

She sucked her teeth and rolled her eyes before walking away.

Leah called her back, "Please don't be rude." She introduced them properly.

"Can I go now?" Kayla was already headed up the stairs.

"You have a beautiful family." A family that was no longer whole, largely due to him. "I'm sorry." He said it twice before he noticed she'd backed away from him. "I think I should start from the beginning, so all of this will make sense." He looked around, making it obvious it was going to be a long story. The modest styling of the house was nothing like a millionaire's home. Where were the gaudy gold chandeliers, thick Persian rugs, and the heavy satin curtains? Here there were just simple wood trimmings and streamlined furniture. Techno modern came to mind.

"We can go in here." She escorted him through the center of the house. He tried not to act impressed. The rich didn't comprehend how rich they were until someone came through lavishing praise. He almost made it through without a word until she led him past an octagon-shaped atrium with tropical plants and a rock-stacked waterfall that poured into an illuminated blue pond. She stopped when she realized he'd stopped.

"That's nice. Those are beautiful fish." Bold reds and golds zigzagged their swimming bodies as they moved from one end of the pond to the other.

"They weren't supposed to get that big. One day we looked and they were huge, like full-grown trout." She was on the side of him, not really looking where he was looking. Her attention was somewhere else.

He followed her into a room. He knew before she flicked the light switch that it was hers. The scent, a woman's space, filled with soft things, pillows, candles, and potted plants. The chair and desk where she sat, a soft light hung over it. No clutter or papers, just a small laptop computer, closed. The pictures on the wall, sea and sunsets. He sat down next to her on the sofa.

"This is going to be hard to explain." He looked around again. Mauve. The walls were soothing. He drew out the word in his mind. Lengthening, stretching it like salt water taffy, soothing. He knew the color codes: reds and yellows were warm, blues and greens were cool and *sooothing*. He wasn't ashamed of having his own monthly subscriptions to all the home decorating magazines. He had the latest issue of *Metropolitan Home* in his patrol car right now, like a shiny new toy waiting to be opened. When his time came (and it would come) to buy his own home, a house wide and airy like this one, he was going to be ready. The plants, the colors, the framed art. Nothing like the small green box with rusty security bars on the windows that he'd grown up in, a house that made him feel like a captive of East Los Angeles.

His eyes fell back onto her. She was attentive, waiting patiently for his next word. He guessed she was part Asian, part Black. Her look wasn't unique in the melting pot of Los Angeles, but there was something different about her, a quiet self-confidence, that had nothing to do with knowing she was beautiful, or rich for that matter.

"When I drove off with your husband, I had every intention of putting him in jail and letting the system take its course. Then I started thinking, what point is it going to serve? He's a good guy, he's the Roadrunner. Maybe he just needed to talk to someone. Maybe get things off his chest." His eyes roamed again, this time landing on a framed photograph of the happy couple, the two of them enjoying the life they'd made for themselves. Her hair was lifted by a light breeze, her smile could light up a room.

"...so I offered to talk or in this case to just listen. He needed to get some things off his chest. We stopped at Highland Park and had some coffee and donuts." He looked around, past her eyes. Intense brown eyes hanging on his every word. "After a while he admitted how wrong he was for hitting you, so I figured my work was done. He asked me to take him to the Beverly Hills Inn and that's exactly what I did. He got out of the car and I watched him walk inside those big glass double doors." He leaned forward on his knees, holding her full attention. His black pupils locked on hers. "I'm going to do everything in my power to get to the bottom of this. I already backtracked and questioned a few people at the hotel. No one could recall anything."

By the time Lopez had finished, he'd forgotten the other story, the true story. The one where he and Dell Fletcher struggled. The one where he crashed into a telephone pole, shattering his car, and probably a few bones in the Roadrunner's face. The one where he looked up and couldn't figure out where an injured man would run, or how he could've with as much blood as he'd had to clean up.

This story was much more logical. There had to be a degree of reasonability to his actions, otherwise they were interpreted as malicious. It was never his intention to alter the path of Dell Fletcher, his wife, and his children. But he was here now. Everything in life happened for a reason, some things were meant to be.

"Did you try the hospitals? Was there any evidence on the man who was shot, any sign that he might have hurt Dell?" She sat with her body rigid and tense, her bare arms not quite resting on her side. He was still noticing the honey wood color of her skin, her neck, the smooth cleavage of her chest while she sat waiting for his answer.

"I...did. No record of him at all. As far as the dead man, he was a crackhead, nothing but a malnourished drug addict. He couldn't have harmed a flea." The muscles in his jaw tightened. He kept his eyes from blinking too often, concentrating to stay focused on hers. The academy had taught him to watch a person's eyes. Downcast to the left, the perpetrator was lying. Downcast to the right, trying to remember. Incessant blinking, searching for answers as they went along.

"That man was a threat to someone. Someone thought he was a threat or they wouldn't have shot him. Did he have a gun, a knife?" She stood up and walked around the back of the sofa. She wrapped her arms around herself. "My husband wouldn't let someone take his wallet, no matter what shape he was in. He'd fight." She turned away. "Did you at least look for him? He could be somewhere bleeding to death. You don't know."

"He's famous, he's a legend. The whole force cares. Nobody is taking this lightly. I think we should just be thankful it wasn't him found in that apartment, dead."

It took Lopez a minute to realize she was crying. A silent pang strong enough to send waves of guilt through his gut. *Please don't cry, no.* He came to her side, touched her shoulder. She didn't jerk away. He turned her around and held her tight against his chest, tight as he reasonably could. What he really wanted was to bury himself in her. It took all the control that he could muster not to do so. *I'm sorry.*

She pulled away as if it had just occurred to her that she was being comforted by the man responsible, the arresting officer. She wiped at her eyes. "Did you look absolutely everywhere? You've got to keep looking."

"I swear, I'll do everything I can."

She watched him carefully, cautious, wanting to trust what he said as the truth.

"If you need anything, don't hesitate to call. Anything at all." He paused. "Even if you just want to talk. You still have the card I gave you earlier?" She nodded. "My home number is on the back. Whatever you need, if there's anything I can do for you, I will." He wanted to say it again, knowing one more *I'm sorry* would be one too many. But he wanted her to believe him. Her eyes were pushing him out the door... do something, find him.

He let himself out into the cool night, closing the door behind him. Stomach acids were pumping, churning into sharp jabs. As soon as he got inside his patrol car, he cracked a bottle of spring water and chugged it to the last drop.

Shit. He'd lied. Why'd he do that?

If Dell Fletcher turned up telling his version of the events, his career, his life, would be over. Lopez wasn't prepared for that to happen. Things were different now. He had a glimpse into the future. He looked up at the tall palatial home. The lights went out one at a time in a trail leading upward, until the final light went out in her bedroom. He knew that part of the house. That was where he'd read Dell Fletcher his rights, explained to him that every man had equal representation under the law. But it wasn't true. Someone like Dell Fletcher could buy his way out of most anything. He could also make sure a police officer choked on his own story, filing assault charges, or kidnapping, the list was too long and scary to contemplate. Dell Fletcher could make Lopez's life difficult, he was sure of that.

Don't just sit there... find him. Indeed. But what would he do with him once he did?

chapter 12

THE LIGHT ON his answering machine was blinking when Lopez walked into his apartment. He pushed skip until the third message, knowing the first two were from Maria a couple of nights ago. He let it play while he kicked off his shoes and shed his uniform.

"Thought we were getting together tonight. Give me a call when you get in." Tanya Valasquez was his steady backup, always available for a late night bite, and he wasn't referring to food. They met in the police academy, six years ago. Both had grown up in East Los Angeles; he went to Garfield High and she went to Belmont. Archrivals. They both entered the academy to get off the streets, get away from the stray bullets and ten-year-olds wielding knives. Most would say he and Tanya were made for each other, tight Latino bodies, same age, same wit, but who wanted to spend every waking moment with themselves?

He tossed the black uniform into the mesh laundry bag behind the bathroom door.

"Angel, it's Maria." He walked to the kitchen where his sister's voice followed. He pulled open the refrigerator and grabbed one of the Moosehead beers standing at attention like good soldiers. He used his undershirt to palm the spiky bottle cap before twisting it off. He took a sip of the ice cold beer. "I want to make sure you're helping out with Mama's birthday party."

He nearly choked on his laughter, spitting out the cool suds. "Helping out." He shook his head at the ridiculousness of the message. Translation, helping out meant paying for everything because the rest of his siblings were useless bums, living with their mama.

The next message was soft, pleasant, and easy, the Slavic cheerleader drawing out her English words, but still not the voice that he wanted to hear.

Leah Fletcher hadn't called. Did he really think she would? Maybe she didn't believe his story. Maybe right now she was on the phone to his sergeant repeating what she'd told him and looking for someone to be held responsible. In the back of his mind, he really didn't care where Dell Fletcher had run off to... who had picked him up, where he'd gone. What concerned him was the family that was left behind. *Su esposa.* A woman that beautiful, how could a man just walk away?

He grabbed the remote control and pushed the button. The CD player shifted to disc 3. A light tremor of music sailed into the air. A smooth compilation of earthy tones that reminded him of being on a beach, quiet, relaxing. He wanted to clear his head, stop thinking about Leah and Dell Fletcher. For all he knew, this was the norm. Married people operated on a different set of rules, a skewed standard of normal in their own little worlds. Dell Fletcher running off, disappearing for a few days, might be the spice in an otherwise dull union. He recalled the wife who tried to hit him over the head with a lamp while he was arresting the husband who'd just blackened her eye and sent two teeth down her throat. Sick.

Lopez took another long swallow of his beer. Leah Fletcher didn't fit into that scenario. She had class and attitude. Smart. This could be a real case of disappearance. The kind where the husband isn't found for twenty years, maybe more. Maybe never. If that were the case, Leah Fletcher would be a lonely widow. A rich, beautiful, lonely widow—he closed his eyes, letting the beer work its subtle magic.

It could happen. It wasn't impossible, he and Leah Fletcher, together. How many disparities had he overcome in his lifetime? Barriers so large and real, his life could have been categorized as Horror. While everyone else in his neighborhood was being arrested or killed, he'd made a decision that he was going to be the one doing the arresting. He'd seen Ebeneezer, his friend since second grade, lying in a pool of his own blood. The broken-off knife rising and falling with each breath he fought to take. He died the summer they'd decided to stop smoking, both only thirteen years old. That same year, Gertie, the girl every boy on the street had sex with at least once, was found dead in her bed. Lopez watched her body as it was carried out of the small pink stucco house. No one ever brought up the fact that she was pregnant. The shape of her belly protruding above the sheet that covered her. That meant whoever sliced her throat was a babykiller as well.

His old neighborhood bred doubt and fear. No one could succeed with those two traits implanted in the psyche. He stopped running with Gino and Sammy and started hitting the books. His brothers called him pansy, sissy, faggot, anything to get him back out there. Stealing hubcaps, bicycles, whatever could be rolled away.

"No thanks, that's aw'ight, you guys go ahead." He'd stand on the other side of the screen door and watch their sagging khakis dip and slink away. He wasn't going to jail and he wasn't going to die.

When he finished high school, he had two options, two more than every other Vato fiend in the neighborhood. Military or the police academy. He didn't see any vast differences between the two; one was preparing for war in foreign countries, and the other for the war right here in the streets of Los Angeles. Nineteen years old, never been arrested, passed all the drug tests, passed all the exams, and he was on his way to becoming an officer of the law. Sometimes he'd have to contain himself from laughing out loud. What a gig.

As he lay in his top bunk at the academy, the laughing fit would hit him, the irony. Pillows would get thrown at him, balled-up paper, pencils, open water bottles, "Shut up, Lopez." He couldn't help it, it was too funny. "Officer Angel Lopez, L-A-P-D. Yes sir!" What a joke.

He knew there was no obstacle he couldn't overcome if he put his mind to it. Certainly winning the love of a beautiful woman fell under the list of his easiest accomplishments.

chapter 13

THE PHONE RANG IN the darkness. Leah fumbled around looking for the loud intrusion that was disrupting the sleep she'd fought hard for.

"Yes," she said, still groggy.

"Are you awake?"

"Elicia," Leah sat up. "You heard?"

"Well of course, I was shocked. I didn't want to ring you in the middle of the night and give you this news. I couldn't believe it when they said it was Dell's body lying in that woman's apartment, then two seconds later, the story changed. I was thinking, thank God, thank you..."

"Have you heard anything new?"

"No."

"It's just bizarre. Do you think he's still in a rehab now? After hearing this, what's your theory?"

Elicia didn't speak.

"I'm not being sarcastic. I just want to know what you think," Leah said, honestly wanting her to respond.

"I think he's fine." Elicia said it with an unveiled confidence. "He's going to show up on your doorstep good as new and you're going to say... what took you so long?"

"You really think so?"

"I do."

Leah wiped at her face and was surprised to find there were no tears. Her eyes stung and burned, dry and irritated. She'd cried all night into her pillow, tossing and turning, imagining the worst. "I'll try to hold on to that," Leah cleared her throat. "Somewhere deep inside of me, I know he's all right, too."

• • •

It had been a solid week and still no sign of Dell Fletcher. Everyone was waiting for the same thing, the big news break. Dell Fletcher showing up a little worn, but with a sensational tale, kidnapped by monkeys, living in a commune, but in fact, a new man. It struck Lopez the same way every time he thought of it... why hadn't Dell Fletcher beelined it straight to his little slice of paradise? Crawling or walking, Lopez would have made it back to a woman like Leah Fletcher, this house, this life.

He drove by 5543 Winding Wind Road three or four times a day, taking note of which lights were on, guessing what she was doing, how she was getting through this tough time. The news vans constantly sitting out front, nearly blockading her driveway. Lopez threatened them with a ticket or tow, sending them off momentarily until they thought he was gone, but soon enough he would be back, harassing them as they harassed Leah.

He had just sent the camera crew from Channel 2 packing when Leah pulled out of her driveway. She slowed her car next to his.

"Thank you. I saw what you did."

He quieted the desire to smile, he put on his professional policeman face, straight eyes, square jaw, "My pleasure. Those guys are vultures."

"They've been following me everywhere I go. This time I'll get there with some peace of mind."

"That's my job, to keep the peace." He still resisted the urge to smile. He was maintaining objectivity. Keeping the lines invisible, the ground clear of threat. He wanted to be her friend, and the easiest way to make a woman drop her guard was to make her think she was of no interest. She'd question herself eventually, wondering why he didn't find her attractive. Whatever she summed up as the answer, it would spell SAFE. He wanted her to know she could trust him. He wasn't the bad guy.

Lopez waved her a good-bye and went about his business. He watched her turn the corner. wondering where she was heading off to, what she did with her days.

Right behind her was a news van. The same guy he'd chased off a little while ago was following Leah. Lopez swerved around, flashing his patrol lights. He pulled the van over with a warning siren. Leah was a few blocks ahead, oblivious, he assumed, to the entire scene. It was okay, he didn't expect a medal for every good deed. The payoff would come with time. The reward sweet.

If nothing else, he was a patient man.

chapter 14

DELL'S EYES FLEW OPEN, assuming he'd find whoever had fiercely shaken him awake. Whoever's voice he'd heard in his ear. No one was there.

The room was empty or seemed that way. The sheer curtains hung by a single chrome rod. The flat white walls stretched high, meeting in angles above his head. He sat up, shoving the white down comforter to the side, revealing brown sticks.

He didn't recognize these as his legs, but when he put his hands to them, it was his own touch he felt. His hands felt all around his body and up the sides of his cheeks. Gauze taped to his forehead. Swelling. His jawline felt uneven, but more shocking was that he could feel the bones underneath his skin. A tomb. He was dead and this was his resting place. Finally.

On his attempt to stand, his legs gave out underneath him. His butt hit the hard wood floor, cold moving through him like lightning rods, stiffening him with pain. He felt like the scarecrow in the Wizard of Oz. He didn't have the strength in his arms to rise and pull himself up. With one burst of determination, he picked himself up and rolled back on the bed. The act itself shut him down. He pulled the thick cover back over his shoulders and drifted back into a deep sleep.

Josh rushed home every day after school. Even knowing that his father wasn't going to be there.

The intention was to get to the phone before Kayla. If she got to it first, he couldn't check the caller ID right away. He'd have to stand around listening to her inane conversations, waiting for a break. There was a crisis going on and all Kayla was concerned about was herself, who said what about her, or her stupid boyfriend Virgil. Her high-school reputation mattered more than their father being gone.

Josh was grateful the house was silent when he stepped in. The phone sat untouched on the cradle. He picked it up and carried it to the kitchen table. The red spiral notebook that was supposed to be used as his journal had become his Call log book. He pulled it out of his backpack, placing it on the table. The last entry page was bookmarked with his Pokemon pen. The date, he always started off with the date. Then the time, he wrote this down to cross-reference with the other pages. His class was learning about number patterns in school. No one else seemed to take it as seriously as he, graphing and plotting. Probability.

For him, it applied to his life. Everything, every second, minute, and hour of the day, applied to his life. He didn't take anything for granted, afraid he might miss something, a clue.

Only five calls today. He dialed the first one holding his breath. An automatic prompt in Spanish . . . telemarketer. He hung up and dialed the next one.

"Happy Maid Service, we're here to help."

"I'm sorry, wrong number." He pressed the talk button to start again.

The next, "Hello, hello, well, don't call back, you loser!"

Josh hung up, recognizing the voice, hoping his sister's friend didn't know which loser she was talking to. He noted the call at 12:03 P.M., the time when she should have been in school. Maybe her friend Clementine was at home sick today. He put a check next to the number, his code for suspicious activity.

He dialed the fourth number, holding his breath. A message machine picked up, crackling before the voice settled in, "You've reached Angel, don't hang up, I want to hear why you called me today. And remember, I can't call you back if you don't leave the number." Josh put another check. Who was Angel? A man named Angel, now that was suspicious.

The last number was long distance, an area code he didn't recognize, a city he didn't know. His father always called from wherever he was, a two-minute call from his hotel room right around the time Josh would be getting home from school. San Antonio, Dallas, Cincinnati, Minnesota, New York. This one wasn't familiar.

He pressed the 1 and put in the rest of the numbers.

The phone rang, four times, felt like ten. "Hello."

Josh stayed quiet.

The female voice sang out again, "Helllooo."

"Hi."

"Hi." She answered back as if it were a game of Simon Says.

"Who is this?"

"Who is this?"

"Ummm, what city are you in?"

"What city are you in?"

Josh was growing frustrated, even though he was the intruder.

"Do you know my dad?"

The silence surprised him.

"I was wondering if you knew my dad," he said again.

"Who's your dad?" That was more like it; he circled the number on his log sheet.

"The Roadrunner, Dell Fletcher."

"Never heard of him." The voice sounded like it was stretching, growing in distance.

"But you called my house. That's how I got your number. Who did you call for?"

"Well, if you tell me your phone number, it might come back to me."

Josh gave it to her. "Does it ring a bell?"

"Can't say that it does. I could have dialed a wrong number. My sister lives out there in LaLa Land."

"What?"

"That's what we call Los Angeles?"

"We?"

"Yeah, everybody out here. I live in Yuma, Arizona. So, Roadrunner—is that some kind of nickname?"

"My dad's. He was a baseball player. They gave him that nickname because he stole bases faster than anyone ever, disappearing from one base to the next before your very eyes." Josh remembered his father reading the newspaper out loud, the article that first gave him his name.

"Sounds like he did it again, huh?"

"Did what?"

"Disappeared. Why else would you be looking for him?"

Josh swallowed hard, again and again, trying to push the balled knot out of his throat. She was sounding more like his sister. Hard and unfeeling. He wanted to ask her how old she was so he could be sure it could all be justified by hormones like Mrs. Felding explained in health class. He hung up feeling a swell of anger. The word kicked hard in his chest. Disappeared. He wiped the wetness from his eyes.

No, his father was coming back. He always came back.

He put a dark line through the number. The wrong number. He closed the notebook and stuck it in his backpack. The English book was calling him, two pages of adverbs and conjunctions. He kicked the bag and watched it slide to the other side of the kitchen, stopping in front of Kayla's feet.

"Hey." She seemed in wonder that someone besides her could be in a sour mood. She picked up his backpack and brought it back over to him. Kayla's dark eyes, darker by the settled eyeliner, "What's going on?" She was still dressed in her cheer practice sweats.

"Nothing, just don't feel like doing my homework."

"Join the club, and it's only going to get worse." She walked away without another word, carrying the phone with her.

Didn't she know how to get past the "nothing" answer? Didn't she know how to prod and pry? *Nothing* meant, ask me again. He put his head down on the table and finished what he'd started, letting the tears soak his sleeve. *Please come home, Dad.*

Lopez wasn't surprised to find himself back up the hill, perusing the blocks of the rich and famous like he belonged there, slowly working his way back to Winding Wind Road. The area had its own security service. The rolling hills were like a private universe; once you entered the first block with large cypress trees and sprawling estates, each home built independently, having nothing in common but largeness, it was obvious you were in another sphere. Some of the homes looked like tropical villas, Georgian southern mansions, adobe, and resort styles from the Hollywood types who built in the 1950s and 1960s. A few looked like something stationed in outer space with large dome-shaped roofs and solar panels. These were the homes that only the seriously rich could afford.

The decadence left a nasty taste in his mouth when he thought about the waste, how his family and millions like them lived annually on what these people paid for lawn and pool maintenance. But then again, he'd be more than happy to trade living arrangements. Had he hated Dell for having this life, the life every man would want, and not being grateful for it? Who made Angel Lopez the judge and jury to hand down punishment?

No one. It was simply fate.

That was something he tried to accept. Fate had an awful way of ensuring that we never knew the answers to questions, no matter how much we replayed the moments in our head. He'd intervened in Dell Fletcher's life and now he was here, riding down Winding Wind Road, doing a noble cause by keeping an eye out on the young family who needed his help, his protection and attention. Who would have thought the rewards would be so great? Every day he woke like he had something to look forward to. Sometimes things just worked out for the best. But today, the closer he drove to the Fletcher home, the faster his heart skipped. He couldn't figure out the anxiety. Maybe seeing Leah again wearing that nearly sheer blouse and the slim beige skirt that hugged her hips as if it were drawn on. He nearly blew it when he saw her earlier getting into her car. She looked like soft cotton candy. He didn't want to ponder that thought too long. The oxygen needed for his brain to function properly would be detoured. Couldn't have that while operating a moving vehicle. A ton of steel and him behind the wheel feeling like silly putty on a stick.

He pulled into the curved driveway and parked. He usually didn't feel the need to actually get out of the car. He parked his cruiser in the half-moon driveway. He knocked and rang the doorbell at the same time.

The door pulled open and stopped, with only one eye and a partial nose staring back at him.

"How's it going? Is your mom here?"

The face turned side to side. "Do you remember me? I'm Officer Lopez." He pointed to his gold nameplate, then stuck his hand out. The boy took hold for a millisecond.

"My mom isn't here."

"Is your sister here? I wanted to make sure you and your sister were all right."

"We're fine." Josh looked to the ground.

"You don't look fine to me." Lopez dropped to the boy's height. "When I was your age, I spent a lot of time outside playing. My friends and I played kickball, football, baseball, you name it. Do you like any of those games?"

Josh raised his shoulders and let them fall.

"You know what, I've got like a half an hour and I wouldn't mind tossing the ball around with you, what do you say?"

The boy's face visibly lightened up. He turned around as if he needed to consult with someone before making the decision, but there was no one there. "Okay," he mumbled.

"Great."

Lopez entered the house feeling right at home. "Looks like this guy needs some water." He stood in front of the hulking ficus near the door. "You go find us a couple of balls and gloves and I'll give this guy a hand."

"Someone comes to take care of our plants."

"I'm sure they do, but I don't think this one can wait." He pulled a dry leave off and let it fall into the wide clay pot.

"Okay." Josh backed away, "I'll get the baseball." He turned and ran.

Most young Black men had an immediate distrust of the police. At some point, the boy would pick up on the running theme, that the guys with badges were a threat to his survival. He was glad that Josh had not learned this yet. He stood up and took a deep breath, inhaling fresh clean air, the kind that money could buy. He walked to the kitchen and filled a glass with tap water. The open arched windows over the sink looked out to a pristine lawn with a hilly forest area as a backdrop. A paved swerving walkway led to a redwood gazebo sitting area tucked off to the side of a lima bean-shaped swimming pool. For a moment he was watching a scene made in heaven, he and Leah sipping on lemonade, dressed in cool cotton and lazy sandals as the kids played, splashing about.

"I got it." Josh stood behind him, holding up the gloves.

Lopez turned around holding the glass; he took a sip, then walked back to the pet tree. He poured the glass on it, knowing that it wouldn't put a dent in its thirst. "All right, let's play ball."

He took the mitt being handed to him. He slid it over his left hand. "Perfect fit."

"It was my dad's." Josh said the words then quickly tried to retrieve them. "I mean, it *is* my dad's."

"Well, I'm sure he won't mind me borrowing it." Lopez unfastened his utility belt, setting it on a chair. He looked at the gun snapped neatly in the holster and thought better of it. "Is there a closet I can hang this in?"

Josh led him a few feet down the hall to a shutter-style door. He opened it, "You can put it in here."

A closet? This was the size of Lopez's bedroom. He hung the belt by the buckle on a wood hook next to a few jackets and umbrellas.

"Can I see it?"

Lopez was surprised the request took as long as it had. He pulled the .45-caliber pistol out and removed the cartridge. "Very dangerous piece of equipment. The thing about equipment is that you have to have a license to operate it. Just like a car, or a motorcycle." He turned it over. "But for you I will make an exception."

Josh opened his hands, letting Lopez place the weight of the gun. "It's heavy."

"And it's dangerous."

He replaced the cartridge and snapped it back into the holster. They moved out of the closet one at a time, Lopez closing the door. "Now are we going to toss the ball around or what? I want to see what you got."

"I got plenty, but I think I'm a better hitter than an outfielder."

Aren't we all? Lopez thought back to the ball games on his street, the fights that ensued when a team didn't get first up. Knock down dragouts because the quarter landed on heads instead of tails. You cheated... nah, you cheated.

The police car sat in her driveway like a red flag blowing in the wind. It sent her adrenaline soaring. She parked in back of it because it was blocking the garage entrance. She moved quickly, her heels sending a sharp echo with each step, opening the door without much effort since it was left ajar. The coolness from the house greeted her. She paused at the first sound she heard. Leah followed the wind shifting laughter, quiet, followed by talking. Laughter. It was Josh. She looked out the kitchen window, prepared to speak, then speechless.

She marched to the French doors, pulling on the brass knobs, not quickly enough.

"What's going on?"

She looked to the police officer, who suddenly looked younger, less authoritative than his uniform called for with his shirt unbuttoned to a white T-shirt. His dark wild hair matched his thick dark eyebrows and lashes, giving him an exotic mussed look. He smiled, then it disappeared. He read her face, he understood that she was fighting to hold back her tongue. Josh turned around with a full smile, something Leah hadn't seen in days, weeks. "We're playing catch, Mom."

"I see that, I was just wondering what Officer Lopez was doing here... playing catch?" Leah unfolded her arms and waited for Josh to find his way to her. "Where's Kayla?" she whispered in the top of his head, moist from perspiration.

Josh looked up, clearly understanding he'd made a mistake. "She's in her room, I guess, on the phone. We were just playing catch."

"Okay, I want to talk to the officer—"

"Angel." The officer called out from the center of the grass, now walking toward her and Josh.

"Go inside, Josh. I want to talk to *Angel.*"

The first thing out of his mother's mouth was, "Who do you think you are?"

She started most of her scoldings with those words, hand on hip, one leg bent while the other foot tapped to the beat of her words.

Josh closed the double-paned doors and watched from the kitchen window. He didn't need to hear anything else; his mother's head working from side to side, her hand on her hip while the other whirled around the face of *Angel,* was plenty enough information.

He would be next. He knew better than to let someone in the house when his mother wasn't home. She'd told him a million times, "I don't care if Jesus Christ himself knocks... you do not open that door."

He was in trouble.

Because of *Angel.*

It was he who'd called. Then why was his mother so mad? They'd obviously had other conversations; he'd called.

Josh rested his head on his hands, still watching. It was Angel's turn to talk. He held up both his hands like he was under arrest, pleading guilty. His mother's arms fell back across her rib cage. Angel put his hands together as a martial-arts student bowing in respect. He was talking his way out of it. "Don't forget to save me, too," Josh whispered to himself.

The two of them came inside. Josh stood up, prepared for his admonishment.

"Josh, I think you know what I'm going to say, so I don't need to say it. But let me warn you, if I ever have to have this conversation with you again, there will be some major hell to pay."

Angel stood slightly in the foreground and tilted his shoulders up and his head sideways, a prompt that nearly made Josh break out in laughter.

"Okay," he managed to squeak out. "I'm going to my room. Bye—"

"Angel," he added. They were friends now.

Josh waved and made a fast safe exit.

"Can we start over?" he asked, trying to retain what ground he had left.

"Don't you have better things to do with your time, like finding my husband?"

"Mrs. Fletcher, that's my main focus right now. That's why I came here today. I wanted to ask Josh a few questions. Sometimes kids know more than they let on. He could have some insight that you and I don't."

"I think it's time for you to go."

"My belt." He moved past her, lingering slightly. "I hung it up in here."

She followed him, her heels clicking on the clay tiled floor. She waited outside of the closet while he gathered his things.

"I'm sorry," he said as he was leaving.

"Me, too." She slammed the door and locked it.

chapter 15

THE PHONE WAS RINGING when she finally made it up the stairs, lucky for Josh. She ran to her bedroom and picked up the phone, hurried and out of breath. "Hello."

"So how'd it go? I tried your office and they said you were no longer taking calls there."

"There's your answer. Just as expected, I walked out. I'd already made the decision before I sat down to talk to Squire. It just seemed like the right thing to do. The kids need me here." Leah kicked off the right shoe and let the coolness of the floor soothe the ache at the ball of her foot. That's what she got for not wanting to move half a size up. "Besides, I can't think about anything, except Dell. What good am I going to do? I'm supposed to be writing about some mindless teenagers who have nothing better to do except grope each other."

Elicia let out a sigh. "I agree. It's not like you need the job anyway."

"I know, but it's more than a job, it's something I love, just like you and broadcasting." Leah's voice turned grave. "By the way, how's the news world?"

"Leah, you know I would tell you if I knew anything. I really don't think you should be this completely stressed out. Dell is probably fine."

"You sound like Squire. He had the nerve to say Dell was probably out drinking and laying up with some groupie." Her earring was in the way of the phone. She threw it next to the keys on the half-moon table near the arched entryway, then climbed on the large chaise, pulling her feet underneath her.

The silence on the other end of the phone was speak no evil.

"Elicia, you can't possibly believe that?"

"No. Of course not. It's possible for him to be getting the help that he needs though. He's sick, being addicted to painkillers is real. It's dangerous."

"But I called every hospital, every exclusive celebrity hole, and he's not there."

"Leah, would he be there under his real name?"

"No." Logically, no. She sniffed back, she could feel it again, the unbelievable sadness. "I don't know…"

"Leah—"

She was waving at the kids. Kayla had promised to take Josh with her to one of the high-school basketball games. "Have fun," she whispered with her hand over the mouthpiece.

"What's going on?"

"The kids, they're leaving."

"Well, there's your chance. You need a break. While they're gone, go out and spend the rest of the day at Milan's, get a massage, sit in the hot tub. Even if it's a few minutes of sanity, it's got to be better than what you're putting yourself through, worrying yourself to death."

"I can soak in a hot tub at home."

"The point is, you need to stop thinking about Dell. Sitting in the midst of everything that reminds you of him doesn't help."

"You're probably right." But the truth was, Leah didn't want to stop thinking of Dell, for fear that she'd lose him if she did. As long as his name was on her lips, his face etched in her mind, she had a link. An invisible direct line that told her he was all right. That was the part that made her angry, infuriated her at odd moments of the day. Out of nowhere, she was sure Dell was smiling, alive, and working at surviving without her.

After hanging up with Elicia, she went straight to her master bath. Elicia had one thing right, a good soak was in order. When Dell offered to remodel their entire house, the only request Leah made was the large sunken tub with Jacuzzi jets. He was willing to spend an endless amount, but she talked him into adding small details that only the trained eye would notice, such as the sculpted birchwood moldings and skylight windows. Dell had signed one of the largest playing contracts in baseball history, but all she wanted was a private sanctuary where she could light her candles, meditate, and relax. She didn't see any point in spending money on a lavish redecorating plan. All she'd ever wanted, she already had. Truly, what she needed from Dell money couldn't buy.

While the water filled, she pinned up her hair. The sheer blouse she was wearing floated to her feet, followed by her skirt. She climbed into the bubbling water and sank deeply enough for the water to fill her ears. The low hum of the whirlpool quieted her thoughts. She drifted off to a semiconscious sleep. Her head was cradled by a soft vinyl pillow, while the rest of her body was immersed in the pulsating bubbles.

Why did you have to leave me, Dell? She soaked a small towel with the hot water, then squeezed it over her face.

Before Dell started playing professionally, he and Leah spent most of their free time in parks and beaches where money was not a factor. Leah would bring home food from the professor's lounge where she was a hostess. Movies were the late-night Turner Classics on channel 27. Their favorite, *Carmen Jones* starring Harry Belefonte and Dorothy Dandridge, would cause Leah to jump up, dance on top of the bed in her sleeping T-shirt with no bottoms, miming Carmen's seduction song until Dell couldn't stand it anymore, pulling her down on top of him. The strength in his arms, the power, always surprised her.

She drifted into a quiet dream. The two of them sitting on the edge of the Santa Monica Pier with the sun above their heads, the glare off the ocean forcing them to talk with their eyes closed.

"In the order of importance. You go first."

"No, you."

"Okay, to be a mother, live in a nice house, write plays that open on Broadway, own a restaurant, eat whatever I want and never gain weight. Stop laughing. Okay, say yours."

"I didn't have five, I only have two."

"That's no fair; okay, go."

"To play major league baseball, and marry Leah Willow."

She'd opened her sun-warmed eyes; her vision had to adjust to the black velvet box he held in front of her.

"I love you" was his only reply to her questioning stare.

"Is this what I think it is?" She wiped the tear forming in the corner of her eye. "If it's not, you better be a good swimmer."

"Open it."

She pulled the box open slowly. "This is so beautiful, Dell." She slid the tiny diamond on her ring finger. "It fits perfectly." She fingered it, twisting it side to side, letting the small gem dance with color. She let out a sigh of relief. "So you're going to make an honest woman of me?"

"You're already an honest woman, this gives you license to be a freak mama and a promise from me not to tell." His wide smile melted into an intense line across the center of his mouth. "Just don't change, Leah. That's all I ask. I love everything about you, every little thing. I don't expect you to give up one single dream you have to be my wife. You're talented, smart, sexy, and crazy fine; those are the things I love about you."

"In that order?" Her hand was wrapped in his.

"You'll have to keep guessing in what order, it changes like a deck of cards. Sometimes you deal me a heap of knowledge that makes me check myself, some days it's a healthy serving of good loving," he said while nuzzling her ear. "But none would be right without the other. So I can't say in what order. You're everything I've ever wanted. I don't ever want to be without you."

What sounded like glass breaking shook Leah awake.

She kicked from under the weight of the water. She stood up, feeling the immediate cold on her dripping skin. The sun had settled on the other side of the house, making the bathroom dim with grayness. Her robe was an arm's distance away. She grabbed it and pulled it tight around her waist. Stepping cautiously to her bathroom doorway, she peeked out. The bedroom was empty, but the door was wide open. She knew she'd closed it. Her eyes swept the room once again; the bedroom window was open, a slight breeze blowing the sheer curtains.

A large gulf of silence surrounded her. "Kayla, Josh." She waited for a response. She called out again, this time louder. She stopped breathing to listen. Only the sound of the downstairs clock, its pendulum swaying, side to side, ticking with each second that went by without her breathing. She slowly stepped to the bedroom door. An unmistakable presence of someone in her home. Her legs were wobbly by the time she reached her bedroom door. But she still had enough strength to close it. She pressed herself against the door and reached for the telephone. That's when she saw the broken glass on her bureau. One of the perfume bottles from her eighteenth-century collection had been knocked over. Delicate shards glittered against the polished maple wood dresser.

The operator answered. She whispered into the phone, "I think someone is in my house." Remembering that the kids could be on their way home and could walk into a bad situation, she asked the dispatcher, "What time is it?" not really looking for an answer, but fumbling in her nightstand drawer looking for her bracelet watch. The one she never wore because of the loose clasp. Kneeling over the open drawer, she held the phone tight against her face.

A hesitant response, "It's 6:30, Mrs. Fletcher."

Okay, now she was crazy. The noise of her pushing pens, old birthday cards, and loose change around in the drawer probably didn't help. The watch was missing. It sat in that drawer for the past year like a fixture and now it was missing.

"Can you send someone over quickly? My kids are due home soon and I don't want them stepping into a bad situation. I'm upstairs. I'm afraid to come out of my room."

"Yes, right away, Mrs. Fletcher. Don't panic, someone is on the way."

The watch wasn't worth much, but it was gone. She stayed quiet listening to her own airway, inhale slow, exhale slow. After crouching in the same position for too long, numbness crawled up from her feet to her ankles. She realized she'd have to change position soon or she wouldn't be able to run, let alone walk. She stayed still, taking short, shallow breaths. Who would take a worthless watch? She could almost feel it in her palm, the weight of it. Maybe she'd misplaced it, maybe she'd really thrown it out. She'd given it quite a bit of thought, tossing it, pitching it hard as she could, the watch Dell had given her after they'd only been dating a few months. It was packaged in pinched plastic, with a "Made in China" stamp on it, but it was her birthday and no one else had gotten her anything. Not her dorm-mate, not Squire, who claimed he still cared, not her own mother who had remarried by then to a doctor who owned ten Laser Eye Centers in Southern California. No one but Dell. So she'd cherished the cheap little timepiece. But now it was gone.

This was ridiculous. She'd been crouched down hiding, imagining the worst. She stood up, almost falling forward, unstable without circulation in her limbs. Enough of this. She swung the bedroom door open and stomped sloppily down the stairs, partly because her feet were warped with the numbing sting of sleep and partly out of contempt. *You want me, come and get me.*

She walked unsteadily through the house, checking the locks of the French doors. She pushed on the windows; they were secure, too. Room by room, she checked to make sure everything was locked as it should have been. The rhythm of her heart returned. The wind of her open bedroom window could have knocked the perfume bottle over. Her mind raced with a million logical explanations. Just as she had put herself at ease, she turned around and screamed at the top of her lungs.

"Mom!" Josh screamed because she screamed.

They hugged each other.

"What happened?" he asked with his face crushed in her chest.

She hugged him harder and tried to extinguish the last of her doubts. The wind could've knocked over the bottle. Her bedroom window was open. But the wind couldn't open drawers and take away her watch. "I thought I heard something." She kissed the top of his head.

"Where's Kayla?"

"She dropped me off. Her and Virgil went to Starbucks for mocha shakes. I didn't want to go."

She kissed him again. Her bodyguard.

chapter 16

SOMETIMES THE MOST TRIVIAL detail can go unnoticed. The Jacky Wu show was the perfect example. The eleven-year-old Nickelodeon sleuth never left the house without her pocket-sized magnified glass. How many times had a piece of evidence been left behind by the big cops, only to be found after careful, thorough inspection? Josh wouldn't let a single piece of evidence get left behind. He moved slowly behind the white shirt and black polyester pants that swished when the security guard walked.

"Does this gate have a key?" The security guard turned to face the determined wide-eyed youngster who took his responsibility as the man of the house seriously. He asked again impatiently, "Does it?"

"Yeah." Josh stayed put, knowing where this conversation was headed.

"Will you be a big help and go get the key from your mom?"

"Why do you need the key? If somebody was back here, they would have hopped the fence. We should check for strips of fabric, follow the route they would've gone, we'll miss clues if we use a key." Josh stepped around the girth of the security guard who could easily pass for a Mike Tyson look-alike. He pulled himself to the rise of the fence, struggling, unable to get completely over. He shook his leg, only to find it being held by the security guard's sausage-colored fingers.

"Look, kid, I know you're trying to be a big help, but right now I need you to come down from there, and just chill. I got this thing covered."

"Let go. Let go of my leg." Josh kicked at him but couldn't shake the thick fingers that held onto his ankle. Josh kicked and writhed until his arms gave out and could no longer support his wiry body. He let out an exasperating grunt when he hit the brick walkway below, landing on his butt. He rose up ready to fight. If only he were five inches taller. Still, no competition for this Tyson look-alike. The thick neck and shoulders melding into one form made Josh think twice about swinging the dried-out tree branch that found its way into his hand.

Strike! He wanted to hit something, or someone. It would be worth it. One good hit!

"Joshua Fletcher, get into the house right now. What do you think you're doing? You are in the way." Josh felt the tug of his shirt collar and was partly relieved his mother had saved him.

"He doesn't know what he's doing. Why didn't you call the real police?" he pleaded. "Angel said he'd be here if we needed anything. I heard him say it."

"Sweetie, we can't keep calling the police for every little thing. Let the man do his job. If he finds anything suspicious, then he'll make the call." Josh knew his mother didn't want to involve the police because the other people, the news scavengers, had scanners and would know all her business. She was afraid of them.

His light brown eyes watered up.

She hugged her son, cradling his clean-cut head in her hands. "Everything is going to be all right, Josh. I know you don't believe me right now. I know it looks impossible, but we're all going to get through this." With her words, he let out a muffled moan and buried his face deep in her chest. She swayed his body in conjunction with hers, side to side. Since his father had been gone nothing had gone right. Jessica told everybody that she liked him, so now Elliot and Skeet didn't want to be his friends.

Mr. Flannigan made him stand up and do an impossible math problem on the board. And now this.

"Mrs. Fletcher. I found something."

He swiped the tears out of his way to get a good look at whatever evidence had been found.

"Do you have a cat?" Leah shook her head no. He moved around some dry leaves and bark with the large stick Josh had used only minutes ago as his sword of honor. "Cat poo, now look at this," he lifted the stick up as a pointer, "see the scratch lines on this tree. Cat probably climbed up here and went in through your open window, then slid down when it got spooked."

Likely story. Josh held onto his mother's hand, better than making the fists that wanted to creep up.

"I thought so. I knew it had to be a simple explanation." She turned to Josh, "See, baby, I told you it was nothing."

He looked directly into the woods, as if he could see beyond the thick marsh of leaves and ivy. He hadn't ventured into that part of their property because of the snake stories his sister had been teasing him with. He suddenly wished there was a huge brick fence to separate the unknown.

She and Josh followed the security guard around to the side yard. The crackle of dried leaves under their feet and the swishing sound of the guy's thighs rubbing together in his polyester pants were the only sounds coming from the search crew. Josh pondered the thought that it could have been a cat, but then again, what if it wasn't? The look on his mom's face when he walked in from behind. She was scared. Frightened like the horror movies where the woman comes running and screaming out of the house. That was the part that bothered him most... that his mother was afraid. That he wasn't doing his job to protect her and the household.

The security guard wrote down the name and number of someone who could spray around the house to ward off certain unwelcome animals: cats, raccoons, and beavers. "Don't be embarrassed, you're not the only one with this problem. This kind of area with the woods so close, you're just lucky it wasn't a skunk." His thick fingers handed the card over. "Give him a call, he's good people. He won't try to take advantage of you like most people when they know there's no man around." His mother took the card and waved him good-bye.

But he is around, Josh thought and wanted to say out loud. His father wouldn't leave them alone, not like this.

He sat outside and watched the security guard drive off, then went back to work sleuthing. The critical key was motive. Who would want to break into their home? What exactly were they looking for?

"Hey, buddy, why's the door open?"

Josh nearly jumped out of his skin, turning around with his eyes in wide circles. "Angel!" A swift step and he was in the center of Lopez's chest, holding on. He was about to tell his version of the story when Leah came down the hall. She had a bewildered look on her face.

Lopez felt a need to explain. "The door was open."

"What made you stop by, *again?*" She folded her arms over her chest as she walked toward him.

"I don't know, but I guess it's a good thing I did." Lopez watched their faces feeling he was the one who should be asking the questions. "What's going on?"

"Somebody broke in our house."

"No one broke into the house." Leah wrapped a graceful arm around Josh's shoulder, her hand patted over his face. "Josh, please don't repeat that again."

"What happened?" His tone was shaky, not his usual just-the-facts-ma'am voice. Leah unconvincingly explained about the perfume bottle breaking… a cat, the wind. Then Josh, ignoring his mother's reprimand, filled in the blanks with his skeptical side of the story.

Lopez leaned on one knee, making himself shorter than the boy. His round face was full of apprehension. "Let's take a look around together. We'll get to the bottom of this."

Lopez rose up. Leah was standing directly in front of him. "Don't feed into his fear. Just let it go."

He leaned into her ear, "He needs to see for himself... you know that. He's a boy." He turned to Josh, who was already ahead of him. "Be right there," he called out. "I'll follow you back."

Lopez turned back to Leah. "He's not going to take your word for it, or mine. He's convinced something went afoul here. He's too smart to fall for any excuse that's handed to him. I'll talk to him, gradually...." Don't worry, he mouthed, before following the boy through the long hallway and out the back door.

"Guess who has tickets to the Lakers' game Thursday night?" Lopez told him while Josh led the way to the side gate of the backyard. Josh loosened up immediately. "Front row seats. Think you might want to go?"

Josh stopped and turned around, a smile bright and open. "My dad used to take me to the Lakers' games all the time. He knew most of the players, and afterward, I could go in the locker room and shake their hands. Do you know how big Shaq's hand is?" He held up both of his hands in a shoulder width, "like this big, huge." He turned back around. "But my mom probably won't let me go."

"I bet she'll let you. You just let her know how bad you want to go, I'll do the rest."

They never made it upstairs to the actual scene of the hypothetical crime. Within a few minutes, Josh was standing in front of his mother, practically begging. "Can I go?"

"I don't think so, Josh."

"Please, Mom." His voice softened, creating something enormous in her eyes. What Lopez remembered seeing in his own mother's eyes. Love.

"I'm really not comfortable with the idea."

"Mommmm," he pleaded.

"All right, but you have to be home early because it's a school night, and I don't want you eating a lot of junk."

"Yeah!" Josh jumped up and down, giving a high five to Lopez before he ran off with a new mission. He seemed to have forgotten about the broken glass, the security guard, and his need to hit someone over the head with a stick.

"Your date might not be happy about being nixed by a nine-year-old." Leah's arms seemed to always be folded over each other. Lopez knew about body language. The defensive stance that said she was not going to let her guard down.

"I didn't have a date. Got a buddy who gets tickets by arresting scalpers. No problem . . . front row seats just like that." He added a snap with his fingers.

"That's nice," she said in a forced voice. "Please keep an eye on him . . . at all times."

"Scout's honor." He stood erect and lifted up his hand.

"I mean it."

He turned serious, heeding her plea. "I will guard him with my life, I promise. Scout's honor."

She pressed her fingers into his wrist and assisted him, putting down the left hand and lifting the right. "Scouts use the right hand." He could still feel the indentation of her slender fingers. The touch pressed into his pulse. He prayed that she missed it, the throbbing of his blood pressure, elevating with her closeness. She'd unfolded herself, just like magic. He looked again to make sure her arms didn't go back into guard's position.

"I've still got four hours on my shift. I better get moving." He didn't want to leave, he forced himself out the door. "Don't forget to lock it this time."

She lifted up a hand and did a child's wave good-bye.

He wanted to blow her a kiss. Corny fool. He turned around and waved again. She was still standing there. "I'll call you about Thursday's game." He tried to sound nonchalant.

Lopez walked to his patrol car on a balance beam, drunk with anticipation, hope, and a sincere wish to carry her off into the sunset. Stay steady, he breathed out, knowing she was still watching. Things were coming together, coming along quite nicely.

He started the car and immediately turned the volume of the dispatch down to its lowest setting. He wanted to savor this moment, this small victory.

chapter 17

LEAH HADN'T INTENDED to watch him walk all the way back to his car. She closed the door, glad to get back to her project of finding the watch. It bothered her. She looked feverishly, everywhere her eyes and hands could take her, stumbling across other things she thought she'd lost for good, which made her feel even more foolish. The gold hoop earring she'd wanted to wear to the ESPY awards with Dell but ended up wearing the dangly silver swirls that didn't match her dress. The video of Josh's first day in kindergarten. The bent and scratched pictures of her mother as a teenager, looking like a refugee standing over her younger brother and sisters. The pinky ring with the missing amethyst stone.

It was becoming a pattern, losing the precious things in her life. Losing pieces of Dell. What next, her own wedding ring? She stopped the incessant search for a moment and looked down at the sparkling pear-shaped diamond on her finger. He'd given it to her on their tenth anniversary. He told her he was embarrassed for her to be wearing the original dot-sized diamond when he could afford so much more. You're worth it, he'd said when he slid it on her finger.

She pulled out one more box from the top of her closet. The corners of the box were frayed and withered. *Candies*... the shoes were long gone. Size 8. This one was truly old. She stopped fitting this size when Kayla was born.

She used a towel to wipe off the dust. She laid the top by her side on the floor. Inside the cardboard box were tattered envelopes, ripped at the seams from when she'd received them and couldn't wait to read what Dell had to say. How could she have forgotten about the letters? Her fingers dug until they were wrapped around every card and piece of paper. She spread them out, looking at the faded postmarks. His first year away at spring training when he was drafted by the Texas Rangers... he'd kept his promise to write every day. Sometimes she'd receive two in one day. A card and a letter, or two cards, one romantic and mystical, the other funny and wisecracking. She reached in and pulled out the worn sheet of notebook paper. His handwriting heavy enough to make lines on the other side of the page. This letter, she remembered this one.

> Leah,
>
> I miss you enough to cry. I miss our beautiful baby. I miss the way the two of you look when she's nursing at your breast. Do you realize this is the life I've always dreamed of? I don't think you truly know how much you mean to me, you and Kayla. Do you know? It hit me today, struck me over the head like rain. I can't breathe without you. I can't think straight. I can't talk or walk straight. You're my left hand and my right. The only way I can make it is by looking at the picture of the two of you. I got a family. This is my purpose. Everything I do, I do because of you.
>
> Don't laugh, but, I snuck something of yours here with me. I figured it would be a while before you needed it again. The red thong panties, the ones that drive me crazy, cut between your tight brown buns, yes, those. Guess where I keep them. I'm not going to tell you, but I know you're going to guess. Right there, for five seconds, any

time of day, I'm there between you, pushing those red panties to the side, reaching in to feel what's mine.

I can't wait to come home... that's how I'm able to bear being away from you, planning how we'll celebrate.

I love you,

Dell

She hugged the letter to her heart.

She remembered Dell coming home. Kayla smiled her first smile when her daddy came into the room. She was a chubby baby with round cheeks and fat knees. His voice sent her legs kicking out like a trampoline artist. "Where's that precious girl, there she is, there's my precious girl." After he held her and rocked her to sleep, he came for Leah. Woke her from her nap with nudging kisses. "Did you save any sweet milk for me, baby?"

Leah put the letter to her lips, hearing his words loud and vivid in her head. She could feel him making good on his promises. Their lovemaking had been intense, rich and full. He savored her. Tasted every part of her body. He took his time searching for spots he may have forgotten. Making up for lost time. Homecomings. They would make love all day, into the night, until their need was satisfied, until it was time for him to leave again.

Leah opened up more of the letters, the cards. She was in each and every moment, revisited. He had to leave again, and again. Short bursts of time. He resorted to calling, always a stream of voices in the background, "We won, baby." In some cases, if his team lost, he didn't bother to call at all. She understood. Winning meant everything to Dell. It was never about the money; with him, all that mattered was the game. She'd heard him cry two thousand miles away, "It was up to me, baby, and I blew it." Voices in the background, sad mutterings of his own. "Don't worry about it," she'd say, "you'll get 'em next time." What else could she say. Pretty soon, she stopped caring who won, who lost. Are you coming home? would be her final words of the conversation.

"Not for another couple of days, baby. You know the schedule."

Leah would look on the calendar he'd given her, the one that said when she could start thinking and feeling again. When he was gone, she shut down, not allowing herself to find emotion. Staring down in her daughter's bright unknowing face, she'd kiss her eyes, her nose, her parted mouth, but it wasn't enough. The enveloping depression of being alone could not be defeated by the proof of love she held in her arms.

Her mother advised her to go with Dell when he played for the Texas Rangers. Move to Texas. What did she have so precious in California that she couldn't follow her husband? Nothing. What would she have in Texas? Nothing. More of nothing. The career of sport required him to be gone days at a time, stretches of time that knew no state, city, or place. She would have had to get on every plane, train, or automobile to keep up with Dell.

She knew some wives who followed their husbands everywhere, sitting in the stands of every game, watchdogs, afraid some fresh hottie was going to steal their man. She was more than *Dell Fletcher's wife.* She wasn't the type who'd set out to marry a professional athlete, it hadn't been listed as one of her goals to achieve. Although she knew plenty of women who did. Jamie, Sharon, Bridgette. They'd all talked about the business of *scouting.* Explaining to Leah how they would follow a player's career, then begin following him, literally. Going to every game, every after-party, staying in certain circles to get close to the target. Finding out his likes, dislikes, the good the bad and the ugly.

Jamie, a petite cocoa-brown beauty with long wavy black hair, bragged about the pro athletes from the NBA to the NFL whom she'd fought hard to snag before she settled for Barry. Settled, she'd called it, because the baseball player's life wasn't as exciting, and, in most instances, he didn't get paid NBA money and didn't receive as much hype from the press. But the benefit was a baseball player's career was more secure, longer years in the dugout. Less chance of injury. "By the time he's through playing, I'll be through, too," Jamie had coughed out while downing her fifth mimosa, her silicone-enhanced breasts pushing up through her low-cut blouse. She admitted she had better things to do than sit around waiting for her man to get off the road. Everyone understood what her *better thang* entailed. As they sat on the veranda during the charity golf tournament, the wives on the team lifted their champagne flutes to toast to the truth as they saw it. "A woman's gotta do what a woman's gotta do," they'd chanted, the glasses clinking together in salute. All of them except Leah. She never did fit in. Unlike the women gathered around that table, she wanted more than shopping and getting her hair and nails done. She didn't want to sit at home baking cookies, either. She just wanted to know she was worth something.

She'd never forget the day she told Dell that she would be working, starting her own career. Hadn't she received her degree on the same day as he? Hadn't they walked across that stage together, both last names Fletcher, hers called right after his? Then why was she sitting here with her chin on her knees?

"Squire's going to give me a job as an assistant writer," she blurted out. Nothing would get under his skin more than she and Squire, her ex-boyfriend, being in the same building day in and day out. Maybe then he'd understand how she felt while he toured the country with women throwing themselves at his feet.

"An assistant writer? What the hell is that, like fetching coffee and making copies? My wife..." the words faded in and out with his movement. He was in Boston. He and a few of the guys from the team were headed out to dinner to celebrate their win. "And with Squire... hell nah... whose idea was this?"

She listened intently, trying to fill in the blanks. Eventually, she hung up, pretending that she couldn't hear him anymore. "Call me back, sweetie, you're breaking up."

Which he did, promptly. She listened to the phone ring, then his own voice asking the caller to leave a message. With each try he became more agitated, his voice unable to hold the cool front. The last call, she noticed, there were no voices in the background, no air between them. He'd gone somewhere private to beg. "Leah, baby, just hold off on this decision till I get home. I know it's hard being there alone, taking care of Kayla all by yourself. You don't have any friends right now who're in your shoes, but you will. Lots of wives are staying home to raise their kids; I'll help you find one of those mommy groups. One of the guys on the team was telling me, his wife and baby go to some kind of Gymborree. We can work it out, whatever's bothering you. But this... working with Squire... I don't think that's a good idea. Please, um, just hold off a minute on that. Okay. I'll be home soon so we can talk about it. I love you. You know that, okay."

The machine had cut off, out of tape, out of time. Whichever was most appropriate. Squire wasn't a threat, but she was intent on making Dell feel the way that she felt, day in and day out. The apartment they lived in had tightened around her throat, the quiet rhythm of her own thoughts driving her mad. She hadn't signed on for this. When Dell had asked her to marry him, he said he never wanted her to change. To be the loving, vivacious woman that he'd fallen in love with, and there she was, makeup-less, clothes ill fitting, her mind taxed with heavy decisions about Huggies or Pampers. Anger at herself for letting it happen. How does one come into second place? Letting the opponent forge ahead, racing past, better, quicker, or smarter. She would never know how it happened. When. She may have been second all along, trailing behind like a quiet breeze. Propelling the one in front even closer to his goal while she floated in constant transition.

Leah grabbed the letters and put them back in the box. They didn't mean anything anymore. As far as she was concerned, they were a pack of lies, broken promises. *Everything I do, I do because of you.*

She tore at the folded cards, ripping into the brittle letters. "Liar, damned liar! It was never about me, only you and your baseball." Her arms tightened into muscle while she grabbed thicker stacks, tearing multiple pages at a time. "You never loved me. I was always second, Dell. It was always more important than me, than Kayla... than Josh." When she was done, she pushed herself back to lean on the closet door. She saw the mess through her blurry tears. A pile of chunked confetti, a stack of good intentions. And here she was again, sitting with her knees tucked under her chin, wondering what to do with herself. What was her life without Dell? As hard as it was, and as much as she hated to admit it, Dell was her life.

chapter 18

"TRY THIS."

He felt the pressure of her body back by his side, pushing down the edge of the bed.

He opened his mouth as wide as he could and let the cool sweet flavor melt on his tongue. He hadn't tasted Jell-O since he was a child. He remembered being a child. Like it was yesterday, but that was all. He could see his mother and father watching from a distance. He was wearing a T-ball uniform. His father had enrolled him when he was five so they'd have something to do on the alternate Saturdays they spent together.

Dell played his heart out, content with the notion he had somewhere to go that removed him from both his parents long enough to have a clear thought of his own. The ball would sit on the plastic T like a sitting duck. He didn't need more than one try. When he swung his miniature steel bat, the ball would fly past all the thumb-suckers, over their heads, landing in the dusty outfield. He'd look up and see his father smiling, sometimes his mother, too, sitting on opposite sides of the bleachers like strangers. Both inhabiting the same wishes and dreams for their boy, the same anticipation washed across their faces when he was up at bat. The same proud grin when his bat connected with the ball. But that was the extent of their commonalities, their divorce still not final. They agreed on one thing only, that their boy was gifted.

He lived with his mother on the west side of Detroit, where half the area was being torn down to build a freeway. His father was a preacher, a man of faith. "All things will come, son, just trust in the Lord." By the third time they'd been threatened with eviction, his mother had given up on his father's faith and his promises and decided she could do better by herself. Going to school to become a registered nurse in two years while still working full-time to support her son was a rigorous ride. Getting home briefly long enough to check his homework, then drop him off at baseball practice after scarfing down Swanson TV dinners and not quite sweet enough Kool-Aid.

His father helped out when he could, giving thirty or forty dollars in scraggly bills and coins straight from his Promised Land Church collection plate. His mother would peel open the crinkled bills, hoping just once there would be a twenty or a ten buried under the tattered one-dollar bills. She would give Dell all the loose coins out of disgust. Spending all night counting nickels, dimes, and quarters wasn't worth her loss of sleep. She'd listen to the click of coins going from one side of the table to the other. He would leave a neatly written note with the exact amount accounted to the penny. She'd respond on the bottom, "Thanks sweetie, keep it for yourself."

Sure enough, when his mother would get in a financial pinch, he'd wobble out of his bed wearing his flannel plaid pajama bottoms that were cropped nearly to his shins, with a plastic bag full of neatly wrapped coins, just enough to keep the lights on or solve whatever the crisis was at the moment. How could a baby be so smart, she'd wonder, taking note of the smooth berry-brown cheeks pressed against her face? She'd cup his woolly head in her hands and ask, "What did I ever do to deserve the best boy in the world? You're all I got, did you know that?" She'd pull out the cool clear bowl of red Jell-O, his treat for being the best boy in the world. For always saving the day.

He wasn't a boy anymore. He was a grown man being fed by a woman. He swallowed another spoonful of the cherry sweet flavor. Her hand worked at the last contents of the bowl. "I can't believe you finished it all." She looked proud, another kiss. He would thank her if he knew how. If he knew whether to call her *my love, my friend,* or *my wife.* Maybe she was all three. For now, it didn't matter. He closed his eye. He loved her scent.

chapter 19

WHEN LOPEZ ARRIVED, JOSH WAS STANDING at the front door, his baseball cap pulled low over his head, jacket zipped up to his neck, ready to go. He was excited. Had probably been standing there for the entire two days since Lopez had invited him to the basketball game.

He touched the boy's shoulder, "Where's your mom?" He looked into the house, up and down the spacious entryway. Light seemed to be flooding in from all angles.

"She's in her office." Josh dug in his pocket. "She said to have a good time at the game. She gave me $20." He held up the money. "She told me to buy you anything you wanted, within reason, of course."

Great, now he was a paid baby-sitter. Lopez moved past Josh. "I'll be right back." He went directly to the room she'd taken him to the first night. The one with the soft pillows and the probably lit candles right now. He stopped at the door and could hear her typing, moving at bullet speed on her keys. He backed away.

Josh was still waiting, not as bubbly as when Lopez first arrived, but he could easily make up for the delay.

"Hey, what's your favorite pizza?"

"Who's paying?"

"I am."

Josh stuck his twenty back in his jacket pocket. "Well, in that case, a double deluxe with pepperoni, sausage, and extra cheese."

"Wise choice." Lopez pushed the bib of Josh's hat lower. "Little man after my own heart."

The pizzeria was crowded for a weeknight. They were pressed for time since the game started at seven. Lopez looked at the vinyl booths filled with families, moms and dads, their kids, divvying up the slices and pouring the pitchers of soda. Voices tried to compete with the music playing on the jukebox, a constant thick beat that Lopez would've bobbed his head to if he wasn't so nervous. He and Josh sat at a table, looking like a case of orphan and Big Brother assignment.

It could've been possible that Josh was his son, if he'd gotten a girl pregnant and had a baby when he was fourteen or fifteen, like some of the guys he grew up with had done. Not just some of the guys, him too, but Lettie was smart enough to have an abortion. What would his kid be like right now? Nothing like Josh, 'cause Lettie would've raised him, kept him in that gutter of a neighborhood. Taught him how to cut rock and sell it for twenty bucks a bag.

The waitress brought over their tray. The hot pizza still bubbling, fresh out of the oven. Josh wasted no time grabbing the first slice. He dropped it on his plate and shook his hand, blowing on the burn.

"Usually when you see steam, that means it's hot." Lopez used the knife and fork to deliver the next slice to his plate. He poured the pitcher of cola in the plastic glass, as he'd seen another father do a few settings away.

"Thanks."

"No problem. Glad we could hang out." Lopez used the knife and fork to set a couple of slices on his own plate. "Did your mom say anything… about us hanging out? I mean, she's glad, right?"

"Ahuh." His mouth was now full.

"Good. I hope we can do more stuff together. I know it's rough not having a dad around. That's how I grew up, it's no fun."

Oops. Fumble. Lopez saw Josh's immediate downturned eyes, his jaws working in less exuberance on the pizza than a minute ago. Good dinner conversation… good job. He had to resurrect the mood. "So do you have a girlfriend at school?"

"Uh uh." He mumbled between lazy chews.

"What? Good-looking young man such as yourself not macking no hotties?"

"Uh uh," he said between his smile. Good recovery.

"You're saying, out of all those little cuties at your school, not one's caught your eye? I find that hard to believe. I know you got game. Good-looking fello such as yourself. Look at cha. Let me hear your best Mack Daddy line." Lopez took a bite of his pizza.

"I don't have one." A full grin and a case of the giggles.

"Well, there lies our problem. You gotta have a Mack Daddy line. Like, 'hey baby, those cupcakes are looking mighty tasty.' Or, 'I want you to be the cream that goes in my coffee.' "

Josh was shaking his head, *no,* still with his wide-mouth grin. His eyes had disappeared under his eyelids, laughing.

"Come on, let me hear you."

"If we talk like that, we get suspended."

"Suspended? What kind of school makes mackin' honeys a federal offense? That's sacrilege."

"My school. My friend Elliot got sent home for telling a girl that she had a nice butt."

"Get out of here." Lopez slapped the table. "Well, did she?"

"Did she what?"

He whispered in a conspirator's tone, "Have a nice butt?"

They both took sips of their cola at the same time. Josh wiped his mouth with the back of his hand; leaning back in his chair, he was in the spirit. A slow nod of the boy's head in serious assessment, "Very nice."

Lopez lifted his hand over the table, Josh instinctively moved his where they met in the middle, slapping across each other in a celebratory shake. "That's half the battle, my good man. You gotta know what's worth taking a hit for. A little appreciation can go a long way." They chuckled through the rest of their pizza. Lopez had saved the day. He wouldn't go down that road again, talking about the boy's father. After all, it was his goal to make him forget.

Josh woke up still excited from the rush of the basketball game. It was the most fun he'd had, since... ever. The Lakers won by one point over the San Antonio Spurs in the last four seconds of the game. When the last shot was sent up by Shaq, over David Robinson's head, the whole arena of fans jumped to their feet, screaming at the top of their lungs. Josh screamed until he couldn't hear his own voice. "Yea! Shaq!"

"You must've had a good time. You're still smiling from ear to ear."

Josh picked up the fork and dove right into the stack of pancakes his mother made for him.

She walked over to the kitchen entrance and yelled up the stairs. "Kayla, your breakfast is getting cold."

"Mom, you would've liked the game. Next time, Angel said he was going to get tickets for all of us to go."

"Well, count me out." Kayla came in and dropped her backpack near Josh's feet and pulled the chair out. She sat down with a thud.

"You can't keep skipping meals, Kay. That's why you don't have any energy." Leah put the plate down in front of her. Four pancakes, scrambled eggs, and two slices of turkey bacon.

"What do I look like, a linebacker? I'm not eating all of this." She picked up her plate and slid half the food onto Josh's.

He welcomed it without a word, pouring fresh syrup on his new bounty.

"Kayla, you gotta go to a Lakers' game. It's way better than that high-school stuff you cheer for." Josh shoved half a piece of bacon in his mouth. He chewed noisily. "And we had soooo much fun."

"No thanks." Kayla stood up over her untouched food, sliding her arms through her backpack straps. "Mom, Virgil is giving me a ride." She kissed her on the cheek. "See you later alligator." She touched Josh on top of his head where the hair had thickened and curled past three haircuts. She didn't mention it since no one else seemed to mind.

"Later."

When the door closed, Josh felt a shift, from feeling on top of the world to a sudden case of guilt. While his mother was still lamenting his missing dad, he had been out sharing a pizza and having guy talk. It wasn't that he'd let it go so easily himself. He still checked the caller ID every day when he got home from school. Calling back numbers he didn't recognize, just in case his father's voice picked up on the other end. He still waited for the sound of the garage door to rise in the middle of the night. And in the mornings, he still expected to find him sitting at the kitchen table with a full cup of coffee.

Worst of all, he felt torn right down the middle for enjoying the time he spent with Angel. Hanging out with him seemed like the ultimate betrayal. He felt weak and dishonest. But he couldn't deny the other feelings, either, like someone finally cared about what he had to say. Finally.

He got up and tucked himself under his mother's arm. He wrapped his arm around her waist. "Thanks for breakfast."

"You're quite welcome."

He wanted to tell her that everything was going to be all right, but he knew that was something she hated, when people offered what they didn't have to give, or made promises that they couldn't keep. He'd heard his mother tell his dad, "I hate when you build up everybody's expectations just to let them down." It had been his birthday. The cake had six candles and was frosted to look like a baseball field. Home plate had the number six drawn in gel. The party was nearly over when the phone rang. He followed his mother into her office where she took the call. He could tell it was his father by the way she listened to his excuses. "Yeah, ahuh, yeah, whatever." When they were done, she slammed the phone down. He ran back to his two guests who hadn't been picked up by their parents yet. He watched the tense, strained smile on her face and knew where she was headed. She picked up the big butcher knife.

"You guys want to split the last of the cake?" His mother sliced into the number six that he was saving for his dad before he could stop her, splitting it in three small pieces. Josh took his piece on the plastic plate and wrapped it in a napkin. He saved it for his dad because he knew he would come home, eventually.

That's exactly how he felt now. Eventually, his father was coming home. He wished his mother knew it, too, then she wouldn't be so sad all the time. It was like she had taken over where his dad had left off, sitting alone, staring into space, tears falling like rain sheeting down a window pane.

"I love you, Mom."

"I love you, too, baby. The bus is coming, you better go." She turned around and gave him a full-sized hug. His heart filled, swelled, and wanted to leap out of his chest.

chapter 20

THE SOUND OF THE TOILET flushing jogged him awake. His back was facing the bathroom door; he didn't bother to turn over when he heard the bare feet tracing back to the bed. He could feel the warm naked body slide under the cover close to him. A hand moved, massaging his back, then the edge of his body, around to his thighs. He squeezed his eyes shut, determined not to stir.

"Angel, are you awake?" The soft whisper vibrated through his spine. She nuzzled his ear, then lay back down.

When he was sure she had fallen back to sleep, his eyes opened wide. He balled some of the sheet into his fist. He was starting to feel like things were taking too long. Even though he was digging the time spent with Josh; they'd had fun last night at the ball game.

But it was still bugging him. He'd been hanging around the house like a newfound puppy. A cute little brown-nosed puppy that the family had decided to keep and give some milk, a few toys, and a bone. But what the puppy really wanted was to be inside, sleeping in the warm bed, lying by his new master's side, and getting a soft stroke every now and then. Not to be played with all day then kicked outdoors when the lights went down.

The warm body asked him again, sensing his stress, "Angel, you awake?"

"Yeah, good morning," he said, while turning around to greet his ever-ready, but no-need-for-commitment partner.

Tanya propped herself up on one elbow and started twirling his curly hair around her finger. She was ready for round two. The morning sex was always the best, both of them full of energy from a good night's sleep. But he'd had enough. He was still exhausted from his evening playing daddy. Although he had to admit, he had a good time. A great time.

"You were doing some acrobatics over there. How'd you sleep?"

"Fine."

"I don't think so; you sounded like you were ready to put a cap in somebody's ass."

Lopez recalled now, the dream, the nightmare. He'd shot Dell Fletcher six times in the face, and he still wouldn't die. He was still alive in the Fletcher heart and mind. Leah couldn't stop dreaming of him, the kids couldn't stop wishing for him. Dell Fletcher was still alive, somewhere.

"Did I scare you?" he asked, staring into her ample bronze bosom.

"Not a bit," she said while climbing on top of his shoulders, pinning him down. She straddled his face with her smooth thighs, not really caring what the root of his anguish had been during the night. She knew that was why she had been summoned at nearly one in the morning, to help him work it out. And by the fierceness of his lovemaking, she assumed the frustration would be diffused by the time she headed out the door. "Everything is going to be fine," she mumbled into the air.

He closed his eyes, feeling the weight of her body slide toward his face. She tasted honest and sweet. The smoothness and strength of her rhythm sent shivers down his spine. He kissed the open mouth, whispering between love-tasting, "Leah."

Tanya struggled to remove herself. "That's where I draw the line. Let go."

He held on tight to her aerobic-built thighs. She pinched his neck until he relinquished his grip.

"Ouch, shit." Conceding with the pain. He rubbed the red spot, feeling the moisture of blood.

"I don't give a damn if you're thinking about some other woman, but don't you ever forget where you're getting it from." She was standing at the edge of the bed with her hands directing the chorus, her naked body taut with anger. "I don't ask anything of you, Angel, only that you respect me. Do you hear me? I'm not playing that shit."

He smiled apologetically, reaching out for her solid waist. "I'm sorry. Please." He could feel her muscles soften under his touch. "Please."

"You know I don't play that, Angel." Her tone softened, following where her body was being led.

He started the dance over again. He prompted her to slide over his face. He'd get it right this time. No mistakes.

* * *

Leah was tired of feeling sorry for herself. She sat at her desk and waited while her computer flicked on. A glimmer of her reflection startled her before the blue screen appeared. A basic case of the blues, her hair was parted down the middle with black roots growing out of place in her auburn mix. The eyebrows that usually blended with a fine line looked woolly in comparison. She flipped the computer screen down and pushed herself away from her desk. This was a job for D. B. Hill.

She pushed the note underneath the picture-frame magnet of Kayla with pigtails. It was the way she preferred to remember her daughter, even though now she was more of a woman than Leah would like to acknowledge. *Went to the hair salon. Will be back late, start dinner.*

Under Josh's magnet, his picture just as cute, standing on the edge of the beach with his bucket of shells, she wrote, "Help Kayla with dinner, do your homework." She slipped XO's in the corner.

The drive in itself was relaxing. She couldn't believe how many days she had stayed in the house, especially after the broken perfume bottle and missing-watch incident. A changing of the guards was necessary. Today she was free.

The sun was shining as usual in Los Angeles, but the difference was, she could actually see it. It was a yellow hue with a light-blue backdrop, not the usual blinding haze, illuminating the sky. Days like this only came after a gust of hard wind blew the smog east, toward San Bernardino and Riverside. Unfortunate for the Inland Empire since the smog never went away, essentially only shifting from one set of mountains to the other.

The salon sat on the busy corner of Beverly and La Cienega. A valet standing in the dry California heat with a long-sleeve white shirt and tie opened Leah's door when she pulled up. There were certain perks that came along with being Mrs. Dellonzo Fletcher that she would always be grateful for. Then again, there was the downside. She pushed up her dark Persol sunglasses so as not to be recognized.

D. B. was walking toward the front of the salon as she entered the double-glass doors framed in heavy brass. "Let me look at you." He turned Leah around by the tips of her fingers. He turned to the receptionist. "Oh, and the nails, too. Jennifer, put Ms. Leah down for nails at two o'clock. I should be halfway done by then." D. B. turned back to his customer, who had a nasty habit of trying to do her own dye jobs. "I know you put this color on when I wasn't looking. What is this?" He put his fingers in her mop and fussed around.

"I don't even remember."

"I swear." As if he abhorred the thought.

She concentrated on the top of his shaved bald head as he led the way to his chair. She sat down. He swirled her around to face the mirror. "You know I canceled someone who is never going to forgive me, just to fit you in this chair right here. And see how you do me, always putting this supermarket bonanza in your hair."

"Just fix me, D. B."

Leah's sad drained eyes must've touched a nerve, a sudden pity nerve. Everyone knew about Dell being gone. At least anyone who had a television. The story was a brief caption, the trailer before each commercial, but nothing more than a sentence or two in the last hour… "Dell Fletcher has still not been located, friends and family are hopeful for his return."

"You know I love to hear myself talk." D. B. rubbed her shoulders. "Pay me no mind." He pulled his fingers from her temple to the back of her neck and started massaging. He rubbed and stroked until she forgot her own name, who she was, and what kind of problems awaited her outside that door. The scalp massage was D. B.'s trademark. He could have stopped right there and she would have paid him the full amount.

After he finished the massage, he made her look up to the mirror. "Smile or I can't save you."

Leah didn't have to force it. The heavy worn look of stress had been replaced with a light smile. The crease above her brow now a smooth pat of skin.

"There's my girl. I'm seeing a pixie cut, something spicy, full of color, lots of lipstick and a sassy wardrobe full of minis, what do you think?"

She concurred. She was feeling him and all his high hopes. If miracles could happen, D. B. was the one to do it. He was the master stylist of Beverly Drive. He had a customer list that bragged Mary J. Blige, Angela Bassett, and Lela Rochon, just to name a few.

The next time she opened her eyes, she was the *Essence* woman. Her eyebrows were waxed and lightened a shade to match her new deeply hued mane. The color seemed to come back to her face with the soft shade of raisin on her glossy lips. The cut was shorter than she'd worn before, the length rising on the top no higher than a pinky finger. It was good to recognize herself again. She sighed with appreciation.

"Now for the nails."

"Oh, no, D. B., I think I'll save that for another day." Leah stood up. It wasn't that she didn't need it, but life was calling. She had a new do and a budding attitude to match. She had a mental list in her head, errands to run, a house to put in order. She straightened her clothes, pulled down the crotch of her jeans from sitting too long, and threw her purse over her shoulder. "Thanks for everything."

"Anytime, Ms. Leah." There was still a real malady that even the best haircut couldn't cure. He recognized it, heartache; it was a common disease of the rich and famous. He brushed off any lingering hairs around her shoulders. "You look absolutely stunning." He tried to loosen up the strings around her heart. "Don't do anything I wouldn't do out there."

Finally a full smile, "Now you know that would take a lot of doing."

The weight that she carried on her shoulders seemed a lot lighter. She was near living, near breathing. The bustle of tourist shoppers had begun by the time she stepped out of the Beverly Hills salon. Leah stood next to the valet podium, people-watching as she waited for her car. Guessing what the conversation of an older woman with the same features and shading as the younger woman next to her was about. The older one was doing most of the talking, planting ideas and wishes, arms entwined. She bet they were planning a wedding.

She turned and watched another subject, a tall shapely model type strutting with the intensity of having only one goal, to get her man right where she wanted him, but first she had to have the right dress for tonight. The next, an affable group of men in suits, glad they got the contract signed, ready for the day to end that for most hadn't even started. Leah focused on their huge grins when the busty model type walked by.

She stepped off the curb when the valet pulled up with her car, the stern-faced boy intent on looking like he could handle the responsibility of the wealthy's expensive cars. He kept the car door open while she got in. She handed him the tip. "Thank you."

He pushed a half-smile to his cheeks.

"You can do better than that, can't you. If I double that, will you smile?" She simply wanted to pass it on. Leah felt better, she wanted the rest of the world to feel better, too.

He let a genuine gapped grin appear. "You don't have to." Now he was blushing, reminding her of Josh, what he'd be like as a teenager, sweet, honest.

She drove off, her music loud. Even if it was temporary, she wanted to enjoy it. One day without tears, one day without doubt and worry. One afternoon not sitting by the phone waiting for news of Dell's whereabouts. She felt like she'd exhausted every resource. Dell's associates, his family far removed, all said they would keep her in their prayers. For a minute, she wanted to take them at their word and pass the candle and let someone else hold it while she took a long deep breath.

She let the sound of music pull her away. She drove without a destination, going with the flow of whatever lane she found herself in. The windows rolled up, blocking out the street sounds. Only the tranquil horns of Kenny G flowing through the speakers and the cool air circulating through the vents.

The peace ended when she looked up and thought she saw *him* walking across the street. *Dell.* She threw the gear in park, fumbled with the door handle before jumping out of the car, her heel still stuck in the crevice between the brake pedal and leather car mat.

"Dell!" She grabbed his arm. The horns of the stalled drivers, along with the realization that it wasn't him, sent her soaring over the edge. "I'm sorry," she said to no one in particular before her head hit the asphalt.

She felt the hands pressing down on her neck, searching for a pulse, then the lift of her body. She was a child being carried off to bed after falling asleep. Someone big and strong like her father making sure she was safe.

"Leah, can you hear me?"

The sound of traffic and concerned voices resonated in her mind. It wasn't her father. She wasn't home.

The arms lowered her to the sidewalk, the hands traced the side of her face. "C'mon, wake up."

She was too tired. There were so many reasons not to ever open her eyes again. She'd lost her life, the only one she'd known. The only man she'd ever truly loved. She'd lost her ability to get through the day and sometimes the night.

"C'mon, Leah." The voice, the hands.

She opened her eyes to see Angel staring down on her. He pulled her close. "That-a-girl." He called out over her head, "Please, clear out so she can get some air."

He helped her sit up, propping her with his chest. She felt the sharp edge of his badge in her back but felt powerless to do anything about it.

"Here's some water." A petite Asian woman managed to squirm through the crowd with an Evian bottle. Angel clicked the top off and put it to Leah's mouth.

"I've got it" were her first words. She held the bottle loosely and sipped.

"You need anything else, my store's right over there." The woman scooted out the way she came. Soon the others left, somewhat disappointed that it was anticlimactic. No blood, no shouting or panic.

Leah stood up with Angel's help.

"You all right?"

"I don't know what happened, I just lost it, like the carpet was pulled from under me." She looked around, seeing her car still parked in the middle of the street with traffic slowly getting by. "I better move my car." She took a staggering step before he grabbed her.

"Oh, no, no. You're not driving anywhere."

His face was the first one she'd seen when she'd awakened. Twice, now, he'd been leaning over her, like a guardian angel. How appropriate, she thought. He was an Angel.

He guided her to his patrol car parked directly behind hers, opening the door while she got inside. He trotted back and started her Range Rover, pulling it slowly out of the lane with the hazard lights on. He pulled into the Asian woman's little market parking lot.

"It'll be safe there until I get a tow for it. I'll have it delivered to your front door," he said while he started his patrol car.

They drove in silence. Her head leaned back against the headrest. He wanted to reach out and smooth her beautiful hair. Her silky, shining tresses in a new style. Short. He liked the way it defined her face, the sharpness of her features. She must've just come from the beauty salon before all this happened. He wanted to tell her how beautiful she looked but knew how shallow it would sound. He'd just scooped her off the pavement, and now he was giving compliments.

Good thing he was following her. He knew why she'd jumped out of the car, he was thinking the exact same thing. The man looked and walked like Dell Fletcher, when he was a whole man. But not now. The Dell Fletcher now would have walked with his head down, his shoulders slumped. Not nearly man enough for her now.

"How you feeling, you sure you don't want to drop in the hospital and have that knot on your head looked at?"

She reached up and rubbed the back of her head. "Just need some ice on it. I'll be fine."

"What happened?" he asked, making conversation.

Leah took a deep breath, continued staring out the window. Her shoulders rose, then fell, then rose in jagged bursts, then down again. She was crying.

He had to turn away.

"We're here." He put the car in park and ran around to her side to open the door. He reached in and took her hand, helping her out. The sun was high over their heads, shimmering with intensity.

She stood up and they were face to face, closer than he'd been to her since the first night Dell disappeared. She smelled like fresh coconut and soft oils. He could kiss her right now. Her lips moist and tender.

"You haven't found him yet."

Her words threw him; he backed away, moving to her side to continue escorting her to the front door. Her eyes remained closed from the glare of the sunlight.

"You said you were going to do everything in your power, and you haven't found him." She stood facing the door, making no attempt to retrieve her keys.

Lopez unzipped her purse and stuck his hand in. He felt the metal edge of her giant cursive A. A for the Angels, he assumed, Dell Fletcher's team. He tried two different keys before the third one worked. He opened the door, escorting her inside.

"You're going to find him?" she asked again. "You have to."

He touched her face. "You need to lie down."

This, he concluded, was the beginning of her breakdown. He'd seen people fall into shock, first the glazed eyes, then the spontaneous working of the mind shutting down before things became too difficult to understand. She didn't realize that tomorrow would be a better day. That all things passed and that all things happened for a reason. He was here, now. Dell Fletcher was gone.

"I just don't understand why you haven't found him. Why someone hasn't found him? Do you think he's dead?" She looked him straight in the eye. "Tell me, do you? Everyone thinks he's dead, but no one wants to say it. They think I won't be able to take it, but do you? Do you think he's dead?"

Lopez put his head down.

"Answer me!"

He reached out and pulled her close. He held her while she pushed and swung. She cried, each breath filled with a wail of hurt, of pain. This will pass, he thought while he held her gently. "Shhhh," he whispered in her ear.

He helped her up the stairs and tucked her into bed. She rolled over and sobbed herself to sleep.

* * *

He had a good swing. Lopez wondered if he came by it honestly, or if it was something his father had hammered out of him in his young life. The sun was moving directly behind his small form, preparing to disappear behind the mountains.

"All right, Josh. One more pitch and we gotta pack it in."

"Okay, no more lopsided strudel things." Josh held the bat perfectly, trained. His miniature muscles flexed as he gripped it, preparing for the pitch. His baseball cap was pulled low over his forehead, giving him an eagle-eye appearance.

Lopez wound his arm up like this was the big one, sending the kid into a fit of giggles.

"No, wait." All the preparation down the drain. "I'm not ready." Josh was trying to regain his stance. "Wait..." He couldn't help the strum of laughter that was beating out of his body. The harder he tried to stop, the more would come.

"All right, c'mon. The sun's going to set waiting for you. Here it comes, ready or not." Lopez wound up again. "I call this my Spin-o-rama Special." He looked silly wiggling his body, shaking his hips wildly.

Josh recuperated long enough to stand straight and take a deep breath. He swung hard.

Lopez watched as the fresh new baseball went flying over the outer edge of the trees. He mouthed the words, "Oh shit," as he watched it disappear. It didn't matter if it was natural or taught, the kid had major skills.

He trotted to where Josh stood staring off into the plot of hills and trees. "I think that one may have actually made it to heaven, li'l man." Lopez gave him a solid welcome-to-manhood pat on the boy's shoulder.

"I learned watching my dad."

"Well, I'm impressed." He gave him another squeeze, a polite smile, all the while wishing the kid would stop paying homage. It made forgetting about Dell Fletcher that much harder, constantly reminding him of his dastardly deed. "Maybe you can play pro one day."

Josh dropped the bat where he stood. "Nah. I don't think I could ever be that good." He rolled the bat around with his foot. "My dad says it takes a lot of skill to be a baseball player. You have to practice every day, all day. I don't have time for that, 'cause of school, and being the man of the house."

Angel knelt down to meet Josh's downcast gaze. He picked up the bat and put it back in the boy's hand. "Well, I think it's more than practice. I think it's something you're born with, and guess what... you've already got it. And besides, now that I'm around, I'll watch the house for you. What do you think about that? Then you'd have time to play and do some fun things for a change. We could sign you up for the Little League team. I'll even help you practice. How about that?"

Lopez was taken off guard when the tears sprang out of the boy like a suppressed leak. He'd been relieved of duty. It was obvious it had been weighing on him for some time. Josh wanted to be the strong man, the one to take charge of the family and not let everybody down, but for some time it had been too much. Lopez held him while he restored himself back to a child, one who didn't have the weight of the world on his shoulders, one who could rely on the strength of an adult. He nestled closer in the crook of Lopez's neck. Maybe he'd get a good night's sleep. Maybe, for once, the sun would beat him rising.

* * *

The sound of laughter had awakened her. She stood in her bedroom window, watching. First they were playing ball, then, in the next instant, Josh was huddled up next to Angel. It broke her heart to see how much Josh was hurting. He tried hard to be strong. Children were in fact resilient, more so than adults. Durable and able to adapt to any situation in order to survive. They could survive, but eventually the product of the environment would take shape, take over, mutating into a new life form. A man. A woman. No longer that child but always carrying the hurt of what they'd become.

She watched Angel holding him, letting him cry on his shoulder. He needed to depend on someone instead of always feeling like he had to be the rock. Leah used to warn Dell that he was only a baby. No matter how Josh tried to stand like a man. Yet, here she was guilty of the same misjudgment. She'd expected Josh to get through this while she carried on in her own dim light. And what about Kayla? It hadn't occurred to her that she might be walking in the same darkness.

She rushed around, splashing water to her face, changing clothes. She met them as they were coming in through the kitchen.

"Hey." Angel followed Josh inside, his hand still on his shoulder.

Leah didn't want to embarrass Josh by making it obvious she'd witnessed their friendship take hold, so she turned and busied herself making tea. She filled the steel decanter with tap water, not paying attention when it overflowed. Angel came and stood next to her, facing the sink. Shoulder and arm pinned against each other. "You ever thought about recessed lighting instead of these hanging kind."

Leah looked up. "No, can't say I have."

"It would give this room, the whole house a crisp new feel."

"I like the authenticity. Makes me feel like there are stories to tell."

"But they're old stories. Sometimes you've got to start over, rewrite a new one for yourself."

She moved her hand that was somehow pressed near his. "Thank you for stepping in while I pulled myself together. It was sort of amazing that you just happened to be there when I hit the ground. Is that your area as well, your route?"

"Yeah, I was covering for somebody else this afternoon, had their route as well."

"That's definitely what I call divine intervention. These people out here would run over Jesus himself if he got in the way of moving traffic. No telling what they would've done to me."

She turned to face Josh, whose head was now in his book doing homework. "Looks like you were having fun out there."

Josh looked up, his eyes still glossed with the remnant of tears. He blinked two times for "yes."

"Oh, no. I completely forgot, I've got to pick up Kayla."

"Your car's right out front. It made it here safely, but I don't think you need to be driving. I'll pick her up. Where is she?"

"Angel, you've done enough already." She threw the towel over the long steel bar in front of the sink.

"No... it's not a problem. Where is she? I'll leave right now." He waited. "I have to know where she is if I'm going to pick her up."

"She's at school. They had a game this evening."

"Right, the cheer thing." He jumped up and tumbled his hands like pom-poms. "Go team!" Pulling one more smile out of Josh. "You know what, I probably should change out of uniform. I got some regular clothes in the squad car."

"But aren't you still on duty?"

He looked at his thick wristwatch, "Not since about eleven this morning."

He came back holding a pair of jeans and a T-shirt, tennis shoes.

"You can change in there." Leah pointed to the bathroom. When he was gone, she came back and sat next to Josh. She brushed her hand across his cheek.

"I guess you really like him?"

Josh tilted his head in the other direction.

"It's okay, Josh. I like him, too. He's not out to take your daddy's place, nor could he." She nudged, putting her hand on his. "It's okay to have a friend, someone to talk to."

He looked up, still the sad eyes.

"I love you, Josh."

"I love you, too, Mom."

"You know everything is going to be all right."

He shook his head up and down. "I know, I know, I still miss him."

She kissed him on the side of his head and held him under the crook of her arm. He smelled of boy musk, a mixture of outdoors and schoolyard sand. Seemed he was getting taller every day, changing, maturing, but his heart was that of a child's, her baby.

Angel walked back in. "Oh, oh, I'm sorry."

"Not a problem. Just giving each other some much-needed love." She smiled down on Josh as she stood up. He reached up and grabbed her hand.

"You guys are so . . . I wish I had a family like this one. Josh, my man, you know how lucky you are? Your mom is awesome."

"You should probably get going. Kayla gets a little testy if she has to wait. Take my car, she'll be looking for me."

"Right. Good idea."

"Thanks again," she said with a concerted effort not to look him in the eye.

He touched her shoulder. "My pleasure. Go rest."

Repetition was the best way to kill spirit, will, and drive. Kayla floated through her days and nights with rules weighing down on her like a sack of bricks. Repeat after me, appropriate behavior for others, always give respect and compassion. She was tired of being told what to feel, how to act and react. She wanted to be free of this school, her family, especially her mother. Days felt like counting to infinity. She couldn't wait to be eighteen to leave and get away from everyone's rules.

"How you doing, Kayla?"

"Hi." She looked up, exasperated. Another rule-maker.

"Did your mom tell you I called last night?"

"Of course not. My mother doesn't like you anymore. Remember?" Kayla slammed her locker shut and adjusted the twenty-pound book bag across her back while she maneuvered her overstuffed pom-poms in one hand.

"Well, the last few times I called she was real nice."

"She's just being polite. She still doesn't like you." Kayla walked away with her ponytail bouncing behind.

"You want me to carry that for you?" Virgil reached out for her backpack.

"No, thanks. I got it."

He walked backward in front of her while he studied her bronze muscular legs striding boldly underneath the short pleated skirt.

"So I guess you don't like me either, huh?" His light blue eyes squinted as they came out into the bright sunlight.

"I like you." An unconvincing reply while she kept her eyes in the opposite direction.

"Then why is it you don't have anything to say? And how come I saw you talking to Tyrel?" They both stopped to look at the tall all-star basketball player surrounded by four idolizing sophomore girls.

"Don't even go there. I will talk to whomever, whenever I want, including Tyrel." She started walking again, the scowl still prominent.

"It's cool. I just needed to know what's going on. It's not like I need to be sweating you."

"Oh," she laughed with genuine amusement. "Fine honeys falling at your feet, right? That's what you said, 'I got honeys falling all over me. It's raining hoochies,'" she mocked as she'd overheard, giving her head a little wiggle and her hands a little shake like the rappers did on the videos.

"What was I supposed to say, you dissin' me in front of everybody like that?"

She smiled, enjoying the power she had somehow accumulated. The strength, like superwoman, able to make a man, a boy, jealous at her whim, fall to his knees in agony. Please, baby, baby, please.

"I'm sorry, all right, Kayla. Just ease up talking to guys like Tyrel Daine. He's no good. You being seen talking to him is the same as doing the do. He'll tell everybody he did, even if he didn't. Don't play yourself." He stopped walking backward and moved to her side. "I just care about you." His silkened lashes blinked slowly. He caught her looking. He moved in closer thinking he had softened up her edges.

Virgil had been the gatekeeper of Kayla's chastity belt for years before he realized he was the one carrying the key. He was two years older and had seen Kayla only as a baby sister type, having grown up with each other since she was seven and he, nine years old. That is, until she showed up as a freshman in the fall with thick shapely legs, a thin waist, and every guy's attention on the team. *Yo man, I got that,* he'd told them all while they ogled her.

"You think I care what Tyrel says?" Her tone was still sharp, slicing quick and immediate. "... what anybody at this stupid school says? I don't. I've got too much on my mind to care about what anyone has to say or think. I am so beyond all of this."

He watched her walk away, slightly off-balance from the weight of her books. He jogged to catch up, easing the bag from her strained shoulders. He slung it over his own. "I'll give you a ride."

"That's all right, my mom should be here any minute." She kept her focus straight ahead.

"Ride with me. We practically live next door to each other. Damn, why're you tripping? Let me take you home. Call your mother and tell her I'm bringing you."

She ignored his order. He'd been trying to boss her around since she set foot on the high school campus. Telling her who to talk to, who not.

They walked in silence through the last hallway lined with lockers and school banners. Painted words dripped with cheers and school spirit, GO JAGS!

The sun was already setting over the Hollywood mountain sign. He dropped the bag next to her white Converse that had tiny matching pompoms on the shoelace. Virgil took a seat on the edge of the stucco planter filled with blooming azaleas. He dropped his hand into the cool soil and played with the dirt. He didn't know what else to say. She continued to look straight ahead.

"How is everybody doing, anyway, with . . . your dad and all?" He kept his fingers in the dirt, then snapped one of the stems nearby.

"As good as everybody can be, I guess."

He put the flower in front of her. "I'm sorry about everything I said that day. I was inconsiderate, just like you said."

"Thank you." She took the yellow daisy, not bothering to sniff it. Everybody knows daisies have no smell.

He rubbed the California Invitational ring, the championship his team won last year. He pushed it around and between his fingers. He slipped it off and twirled it on his index finger. "Kayla, would you wear this, if I gave it to you?"

She looked down at his wide smooth hands, "I don't think that's a good idea. There's a lot going on in my household right now. I might lose it or something, and I know it means a lot to you." She sucked on her teeth, the way she did when she was nervous. "Can I take a rain check?" She wanted to leave him with a small light of hope. It wouldn't be any fun if he gave up completely.

"Yeah. Sure, whatever." He pushed the ring back on his long finger.

Kayla stood up, grabbing her bag when she saw her mother's car pull into the parking lot. She stopped in her tracks when she saw the man behind the wheel.

"Who's he?"

Good question, she thought to herself before heading to the car. Virgil stayed, watching the car pull away. Kayla didn't bother to say goodbye.

* * *

"What are you staring at?" Kayla asked impatiently.

"You tell me?" Angel smiled and adjusted himself under the seatbelt to eyeball her comfortably while he drove.

She rolled her eyes and stared out the window. "Is my mom paying you for bodyguard services? Why didn't she come?"

The houses were so much smaller over here. She took note of the elderly white-haired woman being pulled by her young peppy poodle. The yards were small squares sectioned off like a plaid blanket of green and various pinks and reds indicating rows of flowers. Strange how she'd never noticed all this before after almost an entire year of riding down this very street.

"No. Of course not. I'm her friend, yours, too. Your mom thought you might want to talk to someone besides her."

He was driving too slow. She felt her right foot pushing down, as if she could will him to go faster.

"Was that your boyfriend?"

"None of your business," she snapped.

"I see."

She hoped that kept him quiet the rest of the way, and it did until he pulled into the driveway and put the car in park. She could feel his eyes burning through her as she looked out in the opposite direction.

He grabbed her shoulder strap when she tried to get out of the car. "There's a lot of responsibility with having a boyfriend. You ready for all that, Kayla?"

"Are you kidding?" She shrugged his hand away and stomped into the house. Who do you think you are? Just one more rule-maker. She went in the house directly to her mother's office. The door was closed. She knocked and listened.

Nothing.

"She's upstairs resting." Angel leaned against the wall in the hallway. "You need something."

"No, nothing." Not from you, she wanted to scream. It was the way his eyes speared through her, like there was no hiding. The way he reached in and pulled something out of her and walked away with it, making her feel something had been confiscated. "Nothing," she said it again.

She went to her room and closed the door. She looked up, saw her father's baseball poster, and began to cry.

chapter 21

THE DAYS WERE GETTING LONGER. The restlessness was beginning to win. Dell tried to ignore it like a nagging itch he so desperately wanted to scratch. Counting days was something he no longer did, but reasonably, how many days could a man lounge around in silk pajamas? Six o'clock and the sun was still high above his head. He pushed the chair back from the patio table and stood up for a long stretch. His muscles and bones cracked in unison. The tightness was better than the sore tenderness. He didn't know what had caused the damage, the cut between his eyes, the thick lump on the back of his head. All he knew was that he was healing, and it felt good. He inhaled the crisp clean air high above the smog that encapsulated the rest of Los Angeles.

"There you are."

His stretch and yawn were cut off in the middle. He let his arms fall around the woman's soft shoulders. He was reminded of the other reason he'd stopped counting. This woman.

She kissed him underneath his chin. "I have to go now." Her full lips moved toward his Adam's apple, then came to a close. The moistness was still there when she pulled away to look at him. "I'll be back late, so you don't have to wait up."

Closing in on him was something he couldn't quite pinpoint. Indeed, he wanted to get out. See more than this deck and the cityscape of Los Angeles over the hills. Something he couldn't quite name, or put his finger on. Whatever it was, he knew it was wrong. The yearning, the desire, whatever it was called, he knew was something he'd needed in the past but couldn't seem to get a grasp on. What he had here was good, this woman who served him, hand and foot, food and constant attention. It didn't hurt that she was beautiful.

The phone rang just as he heard the door close. He thought about picking it up just to have contact with the outside world but remembered the warning. She asked him, begged him not to leave. It was safer that way. People were after him, she'd said. "It's dangerous." And for some reason he believed her. How else did he get the bruises, the feeling as though he'd been in a fight? A hell of a beat down, was more like it.

The voice called out after the beep, "If you're there, I need to talk to you. This is Leah, please call me when you get in. Doesn't matter what time."

He was hoping for some kind of an answer. The caller didn't ask for anyone, didn't call anyone by name. This Leah person gave him no answers. He needed to know who was taking care of him. Who held his hand while they ate toast and drank coffee. He knew nothing about her; it was embarrassing to say, "Excuse me. I realize you've been taking care of me for the last couple of weeks, and I was just wondering, who the hell are you?"

Worst of all, he didn't remember anything about himself, not about being a man. It was as if he'd been dropped from a time shuttle and skipped over the last twenty years of his life. He remembered going to the prom with Sandee Sorensen. 1981. The black tuxedo that was too tight on his arms and the pants too snug around his muscular thighs. He remembered the way Sandee looked when he arrived on her porch, the cream dress that showed a footlong line of cleavage. The shiny red lipstick that seemed to get brighter when she smiled. He remembered kissing Sandee's thick red lips and then dropping the bomb on her that he was going away to college. But where? What school did he go to? He could see his mama waving good-bye. He picked up the phone to dial her number. His own mother, the number wouldn't come. Lost, buried in a fog, a mixture of events, dates, and places, in his head.

He slammed the phone down. It rang at the same time. He stepped away and let the machine pick it up.

"It's Leah again. Cancel that last call. I don't want you panicking over nothing... I'm just... I wanted to see if you'd heard anything. If there were any leads."

He grabbed the phone as the woman was hanging up. Leah. Why did he know that name, her voice? He wanted to ask her if she knew him. His name was Dell.

Do you want something else to eat, Dell?

How are you feeling, Dell?

Dell, I love you.

His name was Dell. He grew up in Detroit. His mother's name was Kay. His father's name... "What's wrong with me? Why can't I remember?" The phone flew against the wall with the thrust of his hand. A plastic piece popped back in his direction. He sobbed like a baby or, worse, like a grown man. Thick pitiful tears purging out of him. He started moving through the house, first pulling open drawers in the kitchen, then in her bedroom. Just a name. That's all he needed, an electric bill, phone, gas, anything to identify who she was.

Did this woman who took care of him understand that he knew nothing, remembered nothing about this love she claimed as her own?

The house felt like a large open glass filled with nothingness. Clear and precise, windows for walls, sparse white furniture and white floors. He found himself in an office, the only sure sign of that was the slim desk in the corner with a thin anonymous chair. The room was like all the others, empty, unfeeling, unknowing. He turned to leave when he spotted a tall slender cabinet that matched the desk. A file cabinet that looked deceptively like nothing more than a lingerie bureau. He pulled on the locked drawers, one after the other, shaking them with what little strength he had. He was suddenly feeling weary. The lightheadedness, the shift of the room underneath him.

He fell into a heap of himself on the cool floor, letting the sudden numbness overtake his mind.

chapter 22

AFTER A RESTLESS NIGHT, Leah slept past getting the kids off to school. Her eyes opened to a silence and harsh blanket of sunshine that made it clear she was well into midmorning. Her first thought was to close her eyes again, fall into an uneasy sleep. Make room for the flood of memories, sectioning them off in time. Compartmentalizing Dell like a photo album, keeping the dates that were important and casting off the ones that weren't.

Careful, she thought. It wasn't good to pay pilgrimage, ignoring the hard times, the difficult and sometimes regretful times. Her life with Dell had been far from perfect, but it was her life. The only one she'd ever wanted to know. Yes, he'd had other women, slept with, made love to, she'd known about a few from unpacking his suitcase. Finding the note on Dell's hotel stationery, "call me whenever you're back in town," lip prints to seal the meaning on the bottom of the page. The heavy scent of perfume on his shirts and occasionally in the crotch of his pants. If you seek, you shall find.

She'd sought, checking pockets, taking whatever shred of evidence she could find, holding on to it for the day of reckoning. Though it never came. She never had the nerve to present her case. Bringing to the surface what was common knowledge, a way of the professional athlete's world. Money plus power equaled women. It was simple math.

Leah closed her eyes, sealing out the light with her forearms crisscrossed overhead.

And then there was the one he'd fallen in love with. The one he began comparing her to. The one he'd measured her against with his eyes, with his judgments. "Why can't you just accept me? Why are you always judging me? A woman is supposed to take care of her man, unconditionally. If you loved me, you'd do this."

Dell's measuring stick grew larger by the days and nights. Whoever she was, she'd convinced him that what Leah had been doing for the last decade wasn't enough. Wasn't right. Physically as well as mentally.

Quiet. Shhh, no more.

She'd tormented herself enough. The many nights he was supposed to be there, but wasn't. The nights she'd paged Dell endlessly with no response. Then, finally arriving as if the sun always shone and she would always be waiting.

She sat up, kicking the covers off. She rose up and stretched, instructing herself to breathe. It was a new day, full of potential. Each and every day after this one, she would no longer take for granted.

For some, cleaning was a chore, an awful regimen, and a necessary evil. Leah didn't see it that way; inhaling the fresh warmth of sheets coming out of the dryer did more for her than a full body massage. She snapped the flat sheet over the bed and began tucking in the sides, smoothing her hand over the center, then back again over the square corners, all while singing old Motown songs in her head. She slipped the pillows in the long cases, plumping them as she went.

The doorbell rang. She paused for a moment, then picked up right where she left off, ignoring the intrusion. *Could it be I'm falling in love... with you... with you?* She snapped the second set of pillowcases one at a time, dropping the fluffy cushions inside.

The bell again. Middle of the day, who knew she was home? Had to be a salesperson. Los Angeles had to be the only place in the country where people still sold things door to door. The breezy sunny afternoons lent themselves to easy foot travel carrying vacuums, candy, or samples of fresh dairy and meat. Some of her best finds were parlayed from afternoon door-knocking: maid service, gardening and lawn care.

Leah had no desire to find out what was being peddled today, but the ringing and knocking were persistent. She stepped lightly down the stairs and tried to peer from the edge without being seen through the arched glass. The dark hair and wide square shoulders could only belong to one person.

She opened the door, squinting in the sunlight. He held up the brown bags with oil spots.

"Thought you might be hungry. You look nice, very nice."

Her hand went up, stroking the precision cut of her hair. "I guess I didn't do it justice when I was flat out on the asphalt."

"Nah, I noticed it then, but I didn't want to seem shallow, talking about your new do while you were half-conscious. Did I interrupt anything?"

She stepped back, pulling the door with her. "No. C'mon in." She led the way to the kitchen. He sat down as if he belonged there, as if he'd sat in her kitchen a million times before, relaxed in his faded jeans, the denim lighter where the muscle of his thighs made an imprint. She tried not to notice the frayed edges, the way they hung over his boots. She concentrated on not seeing the shape of his chest through the thin T-shirt. If he looked at her right now, she would only be guilty of blinking. She unloaded the bag.

"You did buy some of everything." She carried two plates back to the table and scooped out the chow mein, broccoli and beef, almond chicken, and fried rice. She sat adjacent to him, their knees bumped for a second, then not.

"That was pretty presumptuous of you." She stuck a forkful of food in her mouth, not really tasting, only trying to exhibit normalcy, as if this were the most typical day of her life. Same as any other, a man showing up at her door, freshly showered, with shiny black curls still moist, arms glistening from body oil, and carrying Chinese food.

"Presumptuous by assuming you might be hungry?" Angel smiled, putting something extra with it. She was sure it was extra, the deeper tone in his voice, the lowered lashes.

Leah twisted the chow mein around her fork. "No, that I would be home with nothing better to do than have lunch with you." It'd been a long time since she felt like playing the coy game. The dumbfounded behavior of a girl hanging around the gorgeous hunk, stunned that he'd chosen her to talk to in the first place. She tried to shake it off. It was silly, this feeling, this stupid girly feeling. It didn't make sense.

He leaned in close, putting his fork in her plate. "Everybody's got to eat, Leah."

She'd never noticed the way he said her name before, a lilt, a wave, at the end. She'd never heard him say it at all, and yet it sounded as if he'd said it over and over.

Leah opened her mouth as he lifted the fork to meet her lips. The food slid in. He guided the fork out slowly. Her heart was beating unsteadily. Chew, she commanded. She swallowed before the fork returned. She opened her mouth again. Silly girl, stupid girl. She reached up and took the fork from his hand.

"I think I can take it from here."

He took it back. "That one's mine."

"Oh . . . right." She picked up her fork and tried to eat, taste, chew, and swallow at the same time. It may as well have been cow's hay for all that her brain was working. The synapses had closed down, leaving a hollow mix of irrational scenarios.

They ate quietly for the next few minutes, both feeling awkward. When they had decided the silence was unbearable, they attempted to speak at the same time.

"Thank you." Both voices fell into one another.

"Why are you thanking me?"

"Probably for the same reason you're thanking me." He smiled softly.

"I'm thanking you for spending time with Josh... and bringing me lunch."

"My pleasure on both counts. You know why I'm thanking you?"

Leah shook her head, no.

"I know you have no reason to trust me, no reason to let me in your life, but you did. That means more to me than you'll ever know. I like being around you, Josh, and Kayla. I especially like being around you."

The air caught in her throat. Leah turned to the wide encased clock with the swinging pendulum perched against the wall. It was safer to look there.

"I guess I better go." Angel stood up.

"You have to go to work?"

"Not for another four hours. I just don't want to wear out my welcome."

"You're not." She rubbed the sweat from her palm on her jean-covered thighs. She looked around, trying to figure what harm would come if he stayed. A warm buzz wrapped around her ears, working its way through her body. What harm would come if he held her, if she found her way to his arms? They shared an undeniable bond. An immediate link between them formed the first day he showed up on her porch. She was the accuser. He was the punisher. Neither would admit the connection, as if the silence made them clean and absolved.

"Leah." There it was again, the wave at the end. He touched her hand long enough for the tenseness to subside. "I better go. I can tell you're not comfortable."

"It's not you. I mean it is you, but not in a negative way. I've always been good about..."

"Staying faithful."

She looked up at him still standing, prepared to leave. She stood up. She felt herself being pulled into his grasp. She closed her eyes, giving consent. He held her there, his hands cupping the sides of her face. Tears rolled down, moistening his thumbs. He slid them away from each cheek. She wanted to be held. She wanted to cry.

"I know what you're thinking, Leah. It's not your fault. None of this. You called the police; you made sure that your husband understood that hitting, violence of any kind, would not be tolerated. You did what you were supposed to do." He lifted her face to his. "You didn't do anything wrong. No man should ever hit a woman, ever. It's not right. For your children alone, it was the right thing to do, calling the police. The chain of events that happened after that were out of your control, something like fate. I showed up at your door. I took him away—everything that happened after that happened because it was meant to. Maybe it was a wakeup call. I can't explain it any other way."

He held her chin, touched her cheek with his finger. "I'm here for a reason, Leah. Everything happens for a reason." He directed her face, closer. When his lips touched hers, she was already spinning. His lips flush, hot, sweet. His hand held the back of her head, pushing her deeper against his mouth. The absorption was quick, she felt like she was caught in a tornado, being twirled and thrown upside down. If he let go she would have fallen off the edge, disappeared into something small and invaluable. The colors danced behind her closed lids while he held her tight, made her see hope, gave her something to cling to.

A dizzying heat swept around her body. From head to toe she craved whatever he had to give. Her mouth opened wider, sucking his tongue, tasting his thoughts. He needed her, too, for reasons she couldn't understand. She kept her eyes closed, seeing herself in his touch, tender and caring. She was fragile, the words handle with care stamped on her breast, her stomach, and thighs, everywhere his hand ventured.

Let me love you.

Did she hear that or read his mind? She pulled back and studied his face. His eyes closed, his lashes fluttered. He opened them long enough to sweep her back into his kiss.

Silly girl, silly stupid girl. She should end this now. Her tongue slid around his bottom lip, sucking, pulling, wanting so much more, needing so much more.

"It's wrong." Leah spread her fingers open around his neck, tracing the back of his hairline. "It's so wrong." She kissed him harder. He was soft, sweet candy and toys on Easter Sunday. He was the basket of goodies, each thing wrapped in shiny pastel colors. Her hands smoothed around his brows and down his face.

He worked himself back into the chair, pulling her to sit on top of him. He pushed her T-shirt up all the while massaging her back, walking the line of her spine. Her respiration couldn't keep up with her heart. She repeated the words in her head, it's wrong. With every movement of his tongue, every grip of his hand, she told herself it was wrong. The heat stretched the length of her body, simmering near the folds of her labia, moistness percolating. "Please." She whispered in his open mouth, she wanted him to make this life go away, the sadness, the unknowing.

He did as he was directed, leaving wet kisses, his face pressed into the arch of her rib cage.

"Please," she moaned. She felt him push her bra aside, squeezing her breast out to be bathed by his tongue. Her head falling back, she felt him lick across the tip of her nipple. A wave passed through her belly, a quiver before the quake.

She held onto his neck, afraid of what the next wave would be. His mouth played around the edges of her nipple, then closed in; she shuddered. She could feel herself falling through locked doors, spinning in darkness where she couldn't breathe. Leah's mind and body shook with confusion. *It's wrong.*

She jumped up, insecure in her footing. Her eyes telling the story of remorse. If she spoke, her words would only contradict what her body had already confirmed.

"It's okay, Leah." He reached out and held her hands. Pulling her back toward him, kissing her mouth lightly.

She shook her head back and forth like a naughty child, guilty but unwilling to take responsibility or blame.

He stood up and held her tight, kissing her sweetly on the forehead.

She buried her face in his chest, still trembling. It seemed the fog was getting thicker, heavier around her soul. A sudden depth beyond rescue.

"You better go." She breathed the words into his chest. His hard beating chest. She pressed her face into the center. "I'll be fine." Her voice was barely there. She was still recuperating from the betrayal of her body, her need to be touched, held.

He smoothed a quiet thumb under her eye, capturing the last trace of regret. He searched her eyes. She held up long enough to get him out the door. The minute she heard it close behind him, she let out an exhausted wail.

* * *

As much as he wanted her, it would do him no good to make it happen quickly. Fast returns yielded even faster losses. He wanted her to need him, to ache without his presence. It took a bold amount of strength to walk out with Leah's eyes wet and vulnerable. He could've taken her upstairs and done whatever he pleased, at that moment, he knew it to be true.

He sat in the car in front of the house, her breath still in his ear. The radio played low—he wasn't listening. The taste of her breasts still on his tongue. He had to walk away . . . wasn't part of the plan. Still he sat in the car, unable to drive away. Was he waiting for her to run out behind him . . . *don't go. I need you.* Between the heat trapped in his parked car and his not being able to come down off the high, he was light-headed.

He got out and stood for a moment, taking a few deep breaths. A car was coming up the street and slowed down in front of the house. A woman got out of a dark green Mercedes. She walked up the staired pathway.

She beelined toward him. "Hello," which came out more as a question than a statement.

"How ya doin'?" Lopez leaned against his car with his arms folded across his chest. He recognized her when she came closer, the newswoman. Though she wasn't as stiff-looking. Much younger in real life, too. Her dark hair was softer, pulled back in a clip, and hanging loosely down her neck.

"Is Leah home? Mrs. Fletcher," she corrected herself. He may have been the help. One more domestic in Southern Cali, right? Her eyes were surfing the outside of the house, his car, him.

He looked toward the front door, giving himself a moment to think. "I believe she is." He didn't trust her type, pretty and smart. Too pretty. Too smart.

"Elicia Silvas," her painted nails were extended. "And you are?"

"Angel Lopez. Nice to meet someone famous."

She blushed immediately. Smart, but still a *woman.*

"I wouldn't say famous." Her skin was flawless, it wasn't just the television makeup. Her brows tilted up, giving her a vampy innocence. He guessed twenty something but wise in her own right.

"So, you're here for an interview?" He thought they'd given up on Dell Fletcher, old news.

"I'm a friend."

Before the inquiry could start, he excused himself, telling her how nice it was to meet her, but he had to go. She stood puzzled that she knew no more about him than when she pulled up. He got into his car and started it up. "Have a good day." He backed out of the driveway, taking note of her license plate, 234LTY, the make and model of her car as he passed by. It was only out of habit, the policing side of his brain.

He would love to be a fly on that wall, the moment Leah answered the door with her face flush with an undeniable telltale sign, the imprint of a man all over her.

That was another side he had to prepare for, the outsiders looking in. The ones who would tell Leah that a relationship was improper. Something not right about being with the man responsible for her husband's disappearance. Inexplicably wrong. He knew that was coming. A good long-term plan always considered the pitfalls and booby traps. The newswoman would be a definite problem with her natural inclination to poke holes in someone else's story. Looking for the angle at all times. He made a mental note to be on guard with Elicia Silvas. But she was small potatoes compared with the real threat. The one he knew was eventually coming. The truth.

"Who's the watchdog parked out front?"

Elicia hadn't stepped in the door completely before she was asking the question. "Umh, umh ummmph." She breezed in, her signature scent trailing behind. "Talk about easy on the eyes." She knew her way in and walked straight into the living room. She put her sleek pale-leather bag down on the couch and slipped out of her suit jacket. "Don't tell me, the pool boy." Elicia smiled but cut it short when she took a close look at Leah's face. "Are you all right?"

"Fine. Tired," she added to explain whatever misshapen lot she was in. "He's a police officer, still asking questions, trying to get an idea of where Dell might be." Leah kept her eyes down.

"Okay, that's not going to work, now the real story." She crossed her legs, slipping off one heel at a time.

Leah tried to rub the chill off her arms, the coldness that she couldn't shake the moment he'd stepped out of her space. "He's actually the officer who arrested Dell."

"What do you mean who arrested Dell? He never took him to jail, right, that's the story?"

"I know, that's the thing. He... Angel—"

"Angel?"

"Yes, that's his name. I guess they ended up having this male powwow, some male bonding experience, and he didn't want to take him in. He wanted to spare him the embarrassment of going to jail, so he took him to a hotel instead and dropped him off. That was the last he saw of Dell. He's only hanging around because he feels guilty, like if he'd done what he was supposed to, taken him to jail instead of leaving him to his own devices while he wasn't in a stable mind, none of this would be happening."

"I have no doubt about that."

Leah picked up on the suspicious vibe in Elicia's words. "He was the first person over here when that man was found dead with Dell's wallet. He didn't want me and the kids hearing about it on the news."

"That's a mean case of guilt, Leah. Think about it, the LAPD are known for coming up with their own convenient sequence of events, next thing you know, some innocent man of color is in jail, beaten to death, but it was all an accident." She enclosed the last word with finger quotations. "The code of silence is real. I mean, really, this officer's story should have at least been investigated. The last man who can actually be traced to Dell, physically seen with him, and nobody has asked one single question." Elicia's eyebrow lifted. "And don't you think it's strange that he would want to hang around you . . . I mean it looks kind of strange, the guy responsible for your husband's disappearance is all of a sudden your new best friend. I could make a sensational story out of that and I wouldn't have to try very hard."

"I wouldn't care what it was pasted into. He's a friend. Josh absolutely adores him. He's been here for him when I could barely keep my head up. I think it helps Josh to have someone to talk to who knows what's going on, another male." Leah tried to sound logical, as if the words coming out of her mouth were spoken by someone on an even keel, as if her head wasn't spinning like a bottle on its side. "Everyone else has been treating us like a leper colony. Not one of the guys from the team has called to ask how we're holding up. Even before all this happened, we were dealing with Dell's problems on our own. There was no one to say, man, I know how you feel, I've been there. No. Because they're all too worried about being exposed. Getting hooked on these painkillers is part of the program, but nobody wants to talk about it, or do anything about it. If someone starts bringing bad attention to himself, they don't want to be anywhere near, as if it has nothing to do with them. Left out in the cold. Now I know how he felt. I know how Dell felt, alone, feeling helpless, grasping for anything not to feel this way."

Leah realized she'd done it again. Ran off with the ball, playing her own game while Elicia sat in the square waiting for her turn. "He's just a friend," Leah said, trying to get back to the subject.

"So I guess this person fills a pretty big void?"

Leah turned away. It was coming back, the kiss on her lips, the heat of his chest. "Like I said, a friend."

"Well, be careful. We really don't know the whole story. If he did something to Dell—"

"What do you mean . . . if he did something to Dell? He didn't do anything to him. It wasn't Angel who was found with Dell's wallet. I mean, what are you saying? Why in the world would he do something to Dell?"

"Wait a minute. All I'm saying is that you don't know. You need to be cautious. If you get into a relationship with this man—"

"A relationship? He's a friend, Elicia. That's it!"

"He's too good-looking to be a friend, sweetie." She stood up and grabbed her purse. "Don't pretend you haven't noticed."

What Leah took notice of was the innuendo. She was coming down fast, a crash landing.

"It's kind of written all over your face . . . you're flustered, which is understandable. How long is a woman supposed to wait?"

This time it was Josh who came to the rescue, preventing Leah from lashing out, saying something she knew she'd regret, just as she'd rescued him from an inevitable beat down if he'd struck the security guard with that stick. He walked in and threw his arms around Elicia's neck.

She kissed him on the cheek. "Well, look at you. You haven't traded me in yet, have you? Replaced me with some chickadee with pink ribbons on the end of her long pigtails?"

Josh blushed, "Nah."

"Okay," she warned, "I don't want to come around here and find out some little teenybopper has stolen my favorite boy."

That got a rise out of Josh. He laughed hard, "I don't like any girls."

"Just checking. We women can sense when some other girl's trying to move in on our territory, but occasionally we just have to ask." She leaned into him as if that were a trade secret. She reached into her purse and pulled out a white plastic bag with FAO Swartz printed in large letters. "What did I promise I was going to get for you last time I was here?"

Josh scooted closer on his knees, lapping up Elicia's charm like a lovesick puppy. His smile rendered his eyeballs invisible.

She handed him the bag and watched him tear it open. "Here he is."

"Goku!" It was the last action figure he needed to complete his collection. "Thank you."

"You are forever welcome." She turned back to Leah, "Wish all men were that easy." She stood up and tossed her jacket over her arm, slipping her feet back in her heels. She kissed Leah on the forehead. "Get some rest."

Leah closed the door behind her, glad she was gone. She watched Elicia's buoyant step down the walkway. Leah wasn't the only one glowing. She wished she'd had the energy to point that fact out to her as well. A new pep in her step, a new song in her words. She was definitely floating on her own magic carpet, but at least Elicia was single, so floating on someone else's magic carpet wasn't purgatory.

chapter 23

HIS MOTHER STILL LIVED in the third house from the corner. The green one. That was the way everyone referred to the house he grew up in. The color of a ripe avocado, with black blotches on the siding indicating the need for a new coat of paint. There was no way he was going to tell his mother to have it done, since he'd be the one footing the bill. Maria's car, Jose's and Gino's, too, parked like abandoned wrecks in front of the house. He pulled in to the driveway behind the '78 Buick that Gino was saving for the day it became a collectable. The back end of his Taurus stuck out in the street. He wouldn't be long.

"Eey bro, you slumming?" Lopez turned around to see one of his old running buddies. His name was Caesar, but everybody who knew him and some who didn't called him King. His arms rode the sides of his body, proof of his latest stint in Chino.

"Whassup, man?" They grabbed hands and hugged at the same time.

Caesar punched Lopez in the arm. "Look at you, damn. You all cut like you been locked up. Solid, homes. You either been locked up or you got a new peach you're trying to impress."

"Definitely the peach. But I can see you've been doing a little idle time." Lopez was referring to the serpent tattoo that covered the side of Caesar's bicep. "What'd you do this time?"

"Aw man, picked me up for some ill shit. Happenstance, you know what I'm saying? Two fucking ounces of hash. It wasn't even the good shit."

Lopez opened the small fence in front of his mother's yard. "Let that be a lesson to you, young man." His best imitation of their sixth-grade teacher, Mr. Perkins.

"The only thing that taught me was to step up the product line. Next time it'll be worth it." He walked off, his arms puffed out like a body builder who'd overdosed on steroids. Another tattoo of a sword climbed up his neck past the collar of his Hanes T-shirt.

"Keep it safe out there." He wasn't mocking this time. He meant it. He was tired of seeing these guys rounded up like bodies in Beirut.

The TV was loud and blaring. He knew who was sitting in the living room before he pulled the screen door open just by the sound of the TV. His three nephews sitting on the couch like propped-up puppets. Cartoons. He touched their heads, all three in one clean sweep. Not one of them flinched, or blinked an eye. Their round dark eyes glazed over with the reflection of Bugs Bunny dancing before them.

"Maria." He called out his sister's name while he moved past the stacks of laundry that had been folded but not put away like bread crumbs in the forest. "Maria."

"What, what is your problem?" She came out holding her newest addition to her family. The tiny head bobbed against her shoulder. He felt a sudden urge to touch the baby's downy head. He inhaled the baby's hair before taking it out of her hands.

"How's my favorite niece?"

"She's your only niece. What the hell were you yelling my name for?"

He looked up, remembering. "Why don't you turn that TV off and put those boys in some kind of after-school program. Just turn the TV off period. Make 'em play outside, kick some cans around. That's ridiculous. They look like junkies lying up there."

Maria rolled her eyes and stuck out her hand. "Are you going to pay for it? 'Cause if you are, I'll be happy to follow through."

Lopez sucked his teeth and held the baby closer in the crook of his neck.

"That's what I thought." She tossed the baby's spit-up towel toward him.

He snatched it with one hand from midair. "You got a husband, that ain't my job." He followed her to the tiny bedroom that she'd been sleeping in since she was the size of the baby he now held. The two twin beds were pushed together to make one large sleeping ground. He could tell by the placement of the pillows that she, the boys, and the baby were sleeping in it. "Where the hell is he, anyway?"

"He ain't here."

"I thought you guys were only here temporary until he got his first couple of checks?"

"Well, he got 'em. He just decided they'd be put to better use."

"Than finding a place for his babies to live? That's capital."

"Don't be coming in here with that shit, Angel. Everybody's not trying to sell their soul to the devil to make a little money. Andre works hard. He's trying to save up some money so we can have a nice place, not just another rat hole over there on L Street."

"That's not what I heard." Gino walked into the conversation holding a blunt cigar, probably the same one he'd been chewing since Lopez was here last. His left eye was still half-closed, the skin heavy like a butterfly cocoon. "Ciro said he's shacking up with his cousin, the one with the big bootie. What's her name?" he snapped his finger, still wrapped around his stogie. "Sheila. Remember her, man, big ass, tiny little waist."

"Get out of here, Gino. Worry about your own sorry self. Look at you, can't even wear your shirt right side out."

"Don't be mad at me 'cause your man's banging some other ho."

Maria threw one of the towels she was folding in his face, then lunged at him with her nails. "Shut up."

Lopez reached out with his free arm while the other held the baby at a distance against his chest. "You guys still fighting like kids; you both need to grow your asses up."

Maria's wild wavy hair had fallen over her eyes. She was still scratching at the air. She wasn't the petite little thing she'd been before motherhood. He had a hard time holding her back.

"You one-eyed dog." She flipped her middle finger up and turned to her laundry. Her shoulders bounced with each shuddering breath. She was crying.

"Go, man."

Gino popped his cigar between his yellowed teeth and left whence he came. "Ain't my fault." Gino had been different since he'd been shot. Slower, void of any real depth in thought. The bullet was still in the bone above his eye.

Lopez closed the door. "Why do you put up with him?"

"He's my brother, and yours, too."

"Not Gino. Andre. You let him do whatever he wants to you. You don't have no respect for yourself, your kids? This baby needs a home." Throughout all the commotion, the baby hadn't made a sound, only watched the side of his face with pure amazement. "You know what Gino said was true, don't you? Do you even care?"

She wiped at her eyes, then smothered her whole face with the freshly washed towel. "He's all I got," her voice muffled through the cotton and tears. "He's just frustrated right now. He got laid off again."

"So it's okay for him to crash at another woman's pad while he looks for another job? Is that the excuse?" He turned her around and looked closely into her face. Dark circles under her eyes, healed-over scars around her mouth and nose. "You let him hit on you, disrespect you. Until you start caring what happens to yourself and these kids, he's never going to treat you right. You have to respect yourself, Mari, it's that simple." He held her close, his niece in one arm and his sister in the other.

Maria sniffed in his T-shirt, content, but only for a moment. She went back to her laundry, silently pulling up one piece after the other, folding in continuous motion.

"I gotta go, Maria. You know you can call me, and I'll help, but only when you're ready to make some real changes." He set the baby down in the small foldout playpen. She lay quietly, staring up into nothing, not really focused on any particular thing. He could only guess what the baby was thinking. *Loco,* all of them.

He pulled out his wallet. "Here's the money for Mama's party, I almost forgot why I came in the first place." He pushed six twenties into her hand. "Use all of it, Maria."

Maria followed him to the front door. "Angel, thanks." She backed inside. He heard the TV go off. The stillness was foreign. Her boys didn't move, but he knew it would be a matter of time. After he drove away, he realized he hadn't seen the person he went to see in the first place, his mother. She was probably at church, where she prayed every day for the salvation of her soul, her children's souls. Pray for them to get some jobs, some common sense.

He looked at his watch. He was running much later than he thought. He'd have to do what he planned on doing once he was on shift. All the better. He wanted Andre to see him coming.

* * *

She wouldn't let herself be alone with him, not ever again. Even when he washed up on her doorstep like seaweed on the shore, entangling her feet, snagging between her toes. It seemed every step she took, he was there. Harmless, but in abundance.

She could still feel his hands on her, walking, talking, sitting, standing, it didn't matter. She couldn't wash away the touch, ignore the rush of heat when she thought of him. And yet, right behind every flashback, in subsequent order, came shame. Culpability raging like a twin sister.

The harder she tried to drive Angel out of her thoughts, the stronger he returned. He was real. He wasn't going away, and deep inside, she didn't want him to. He was her *angel.* Shadowing, always a few steps behind. It made her smile, the thought of having someone looking over her, watching attentively. But it was dangerous as well, knowing the way she felt, being too close.

The children were her only saving grace, a buffer zone. When they left for school, she left the house, too, untraceable. She spent afternoons with Dell's mother at the Sunburst Home, reading to her, talking out loud about things she knew she wouldn't respond to. Twice she'd met Elicia for tennis. Another day, Elicia didn't show up at all. After waiting for over an hour, Leah simply went to a movie, sat in the empty theater eating licorice and washing the goo off her teeth with Pepsi. Not really sure what she'd just seen when the credits started rolling up. It was just another deterrent. Anything to keep her out of the house. When it was time for the kids to come home in the late afternoon, Leah would return as well.

In a way, she felt like she was using Angel, taking advantage of his desire to be in the thick of things. He was the presence that they all missed so deeply from Dell. Or maybe what they'd needed all along and had never received. Attention, constant and intense.

The shifting images of their life as a family, so many of the pictures didn't include Dell. She wondered if the children felt it, too, Josh especially, feeling like he finally had someone who would spend time with him, someone who was in the present moment, listening to his words instead of fazing out to some faraway place he'd rather be. The playing field.

With Angel, there was no doubt where he wanted to be. She could tell being with the three of them made him feel like he was walking on clouds... which made it even harder to think about ending whatever this relationship had become. She knew it would have to end, eventually, not if, but when, Dell returned. She held on to what Elicia had said. Dell was probably in a rehabilitation center... would he give his real name? It was the only thing keeping her sane, the belief that he was healthy, being treated well, and on a journey home.

chapter 24

MOVING WITH THE SWIFTNESS OF A ROCKET. Lightning bolts of speed moving from base to base. No pain, no pain. He ran and continued to run.

But wait, he'd already crossed home plate, not again. He ran around the bases. The crowd became familiar. The same people, the boy wearing a blue-and-white-striped shirt with the red baseball cap, the woman holding the camera, smiling, cheering. He was passing the same people, over and over again. How many times had he run the bases? He only had one base hit, yet he was swirling from running in circles. He needed to sit down and rest, but he couldn't. The boy, the woman, the crowd still yelling. He was tired, but the crowd kept yelling to "Go!"

"I can't do it anymore, wait. I want to stop." Dell's breath became short. As hard as he tried, he couldn't stop running. The momentum seemed to increase and his legs pumped faster. As he rounded the bases at a ninety-degree angle, the dust kicked up from his speed making him gasp for air, for sight. "Please, let me stop."

With an abrupt thud to his entire body, as if the heavens above spit him out, he landed on the floor. He woke up sitting in the spot where he'd fallen earlier, the sparsely furnished office. His head was spinning with dizziness as if he'd been swung in circles. Always the dreams about baseball. He could feel himself playing the game like a pumped-up athlete. So real. But when he looked at the limp posture, the soft tone of his arms and legs, there could be no way. He was merely a man, nothing more.

He used the desk to pull himself up. The city lights twinkled in the distance outside the large sliding door. The house was dark, only the red illuminated numbers from the digital clock sitting on the desk. It was nearly midnight. Just like clockwork, he knew she would be arriving soon. Was it a coincidence that he slept away the hours while she was gone? He'd be a betting man and say that it was not.

chapter 25

PARKING WAS IMPOSSIBLE. Full signs were posted at every entrance. It was obvious Squire had chosen this place as payback for suggesting that they meet in a public area. She looked at the clock on her dash, fifteen minutes late. He deserved to wait. He'd called her constantly trying to set up a meeting. She'd said no until the fifth try. She didn't want to hear his apologies for saying the things he'd said about Dell. Insinuating that he was out on nothing more than a binge. Pure and simple. But it wasn't that simple. Not this time. Leah knew it. Regardless, it was her business, not his.

She and Squire had been more than friends at one time. A very long time ago, before she'd met Dell. She knew Squire still carried a torch for her and carried an equally heavy gavel for Dell. Squire's side of the story was that she'd dropped him like a sack of rotten potatoes the minute Dellonzo Fletcher entered the picture. Choosing Mr. Baseball Star, a man who could give her everything she wanted, over him, an aged film student who'd dropped out of corporate America to pursue his dream. But the real reason, he'd chided, was that Dell was Black and he was white. She'd chosen color over love, he'd told her. Sometimes she wondered if it was true.

The black sleek Jaguar in front of her pulled along slowly, searching for street parking as well. She watched it swoop into the last open space on the street. She'd have to park one street over and walk back.

As she turned off the ignition, she realized that by the time she came back to her car later in the evening, it would be completely dark. Even though she was a block over from the posh Melrose restaurant row, she was sitting in a bevy of beer cans, trash, cars from the seventies, and rundown apartment houses as far as the eye could see. She slipped her wedding ring off and let it slide down to the bottom of her purse, then pulled the shoulder strap around her for security before putting on her jacket. She dropped the keys into her pocket and strolled nonchalantly toward the bustle of cars and streetlights ahead.

Squire sat in the center of the restaurant with his glasses on the edge of his nose, reading from a stack of scripts. He took his work everywhere with him, bundled in a tattered portfolio that he'd been carrying since college. It was like carrying around an old friend since it was Leah who'd given it to him as a graduation present some fifteen years ago. She saw him peek up to see if she'd arrived.

"Leah, over here." He stood up, waving, tall enough to be seen above the crowd.

"I'm sorry I'm late. This place is a circus. Absolutely no parking available, not even valet." She took off her jacket, revealing her purse strapped against her sweater.

"You did say you wanted some place where I couldn't, or wouldn't, try to accost you."

"I never said that, and it certainly isn't what I meant." She plopped down in the thin iron chair, out of breath.

"Then why not just come to my office, as I suggested? You wouldn't have had to run here with your purse tucked under your shirt." He snickered, amused at her usual coolness now in disarray.

"Ha, ha. You're so funny."

"I'm sorry. I don't want to piss you off any more than you already are." Squire placed his pale hand over hers. He was taken aback when he noticed that the large pear-shaped stone that was always in place was no longer there. His large hand engulfed hers, but she quickly pulled it away.

Her eyes checked around for voyeurs. "Why am I here, Squire? Has something changed? You called like it was an emergency."

"I read your script. I mean really read it this time." His dark lashes lowered from the confession. "I was floored by it. It's incredible. The reason I needed to see you was to ask your forgiveness for not taking the time to read it earlier. More to the point, I'm glad you chose me to share it with. That means a lot to me, your trust. It's not like I'm the most influential person you know. You could've gone to anyone with this, it's good work."

"Squire, is this an attempt to appease me for the moment or did you really like it?" Her voice softened, at the possibility.

"It's a great idea, I want to talk to Ed Gravitz about taking it. He's had two previous flops, back to back, so he'll be less picky..."

"But I thought you said it was great." Her eyes searching his, she leaned in closer to hear him over the crowd.

"It is. But it's not in the mainstream of things, you know the formula. Right now everyone is looking for the next Seinfeld. This doesn't actually fit into that category, if you know what I mean."

"I thought you could take it to Samson and Weinburg first, and if they don't like it, then we can look at other options?"

His long fingers ran through his hair. "Look, you asked for my help. Going to those guys when I already know what they're going to say is not my idea of helping. Trust me, Gravitz will give it the respect it deserves. He's hungry."

The waiter was standing by their table for the fourth time, unable to get a word in on the first few tries. This time they ordered, a Caesar salad for her, and a cup of coffee for him. The studio types filled the small café tables with their heads pushed together. Kink's was a famous location for deals and scandals. Leah kept her eyes above and beyond his head, as if she could be in two places at one time.

"I've missed you the last few weeks." He tried to retain her attention.

"Kinda boring without me to kick around, huh?" She took a mouthful of her salad.

"It's the same old thing, but it was always less painful when you were around."

She put her fork down. "Don't start, Squire. I've got a lot on my plate right now. I can't come back. You not taking my script seriously wasn't the only reason I walked out of there. I needed this break."

"So it is just a break, i.e., not permanent?" He lifted his fingers to make quotations in the air.

"Honestly, right now, I don't know. I'm just trying to hold myself together. I feel like someone used Elmer's glue on me instead of the good stuff and I'm falling apart little by little."

"Is there something I can do? The kids have always liked me."

"I'm doing all right with the kids. It's mostly me, I'm forgetting where I put things, hearing things, I'm overall falling apart, and I don't know how to get it together. Losing Dell—"

"I know. I know. Your life, it's not over, Leah. There's still more pages to be filled in. And I'm not just talking about your career. I'm talking about the part of you that's going to need someone to lean on. I'm here for you. I care what happens. I never stopped. As many times as I tried, I never stopped."

Leah looked around to see if anyone had noticed the scene, his hand comforting, rubbing her shoulder, touching her face, wiping away the tear that hung on her cheek. She felt exposed. Not here. Not in public.

"You all right?"

"I'm fine, Squire. Really." She shrugged off his hand, leaving a cool spot where he'd last touched.

Frustration appeared in his cheeks, a bright shade of pink, the words came out in a raspy whisper. "Why can't you let me be your friend? Friends touch, Leah; it's okay. No one is going to call the *National Intruder*. There's no camera hidden in the flower centerpiece. We're two friends having dinner, stop being so paranoid."

He rose up and tossed the linen napkin to the table. "I'll call you when I have news of a meeting with Gravitz." He shoved the thick booklets into his bag, then walked off with the heaviness of his carryall slung over his shoulder.

Déjà vu struck her, watching him walk away in anger, his dark shoulder-length hair, now highlighted with gray, bouncing with each step. It was odd how much he'd stayed the same, slim muscular build, still able to make a pair of jeans seem effortlessly fashionable.

She pushed her salad away and surveyed the room.

No spectators. She was relieved, even though the feeling of constantly being watched permeated her skin. It was the same uncomfortable feeling she got whenever Squire tried to show affection in public. The same way she felt holding her mother's pale fleshy hand when they went to the grocery store, or into Belmont Elementary, with everyone staring at the Black child being escorted by a short stocky Chinese woman.

The sixties had produced a new generation of multicultural babies. Leah was one of those free-love offsprings. Her mother and father were no longer together. It would have made sense if the three of them were seen together as a family. She had her father's noble chin and nose, his high arched brows and thick unruly hair. From her mother, the eyes, soft and trusting. Through those eyes she watched as people stared at the odd couple, she and her mother. The questioning looks always made Leah uncomfortable, generating a dizzying sensation that sent her running to the nearest bathroom.

She remembered vividly an embarrassing episode. She was five years old, shopping with her mother in a Montgomery Ward department store. Everyone they passed seemed to be looking down at the wild-haired Leah, staring at her and her mother as if they were aliens from another planet. The tingling heat pushed through her bladder. She rushed off to relieve herself, unable to make it to the toilet seat in time. Leah stood crying for her mommy with warm soggy panties, when a polite saleswoman with orange hair and orange eyelashes asked the distraught child where her mommy was. "Out there, out there." Leah pointed toward the bathroom door. The saleswoman grabbed Leah's arm, "Come on, we'll find her." The tears trickled from embarrassment as Leah waddled in the direction she was led. "Ma'am, ma'am, your daughter has had an accident. I think she's a little too young to be going off alone in the first place." Before either Leah or the shocked Black woman could respond, the saleswoman had disappeared in another direction, mumbling something about, "these people and their children." The tears were now falling in misshapen lots, landing in puddles whichever direction her panicked face searched. All at once she was moving again, being pulled in another direction. "Excuse me, Miss, but this is not my child," the coffee-colored woman practically spat at the orange-haired lady. "You need to stop assuming." Once again Leah was standing in a puddle. She could feel the warm liquid as it rapidly streamed down her leg. The saleswoman squealed in disgust. She picked up the phone and started talking, "We have a lost child in ladies apparel," she turned her head to deflect her voice, "and she's pissed all over the floor. Get someone over here now."

Her mother had arrived at the scene at the exact moment the security officer had come to take her away. "Oh, baby," she whispered in Leah's hair. "I looked everywhere for you." The saleswoman stood speechless. What little compassion and sentiment the woman had for the poor lost child had completely drained from her face. Leah recognized the stare. Feeling shame and anger, she wanted to scream at her, you "stupid heifer," the same words Aunt Jackie had yelled that very morning at her mother. Screaming through the door when she had come to pick up Leah for her court-ordered visitation with her father, "You the one don't want him over here to pick up his own child. Now you got to deal with me." Aunt Jackie was her father's sister and had never liked her mother, simply because she wasn't Black. Her mother's face had been filled with fear. Backed up against the door, refusing to unlock the bolt latch. Her index finger gently placed to Leah's lips to keep her from making a sound. But before Leah could put the words together just right, in perfect order, to strike the same chord of fear in the orange-haired lady as Aunt Jackie had struck only that morning in her mother, they were off to the car and heading for home.

Leah met the cool air outside of the restaurant like an old friend she'd missed dearly. She walked briskly in the darkness, which was intensified by the light rain that had come and gone. She held her purse tight against her side. She didn't take a second breath until she was safely locked inside her car, seatbelt securely fastened. The street, as expected, had become a train of parked cars stacked neatly in a row. She barely had enough room to maneuver her car backward and forward to get out of the cramped space.

"You need some help getting out."

Her heart jumped near her throat. The small man spoke through the closed window causing a round circle of fog in front of his broken teeth. Using his hands as a guide, he motioned for her to go up, then stop, "turn your wheel, yeah, this way," he lifted his dirty palms up, his voice faint as she strained to hear him through the air-tight windows, "doing okay, forward now. You got it, keep going."

She pushed a five-dollar bill out the small opening of her window as a thank-you and sped out like a zoo animal that'd broken free. Before she could get good speed, blinking police lights appeared in her rearview mirror. She slowed down and moved slightly to the side, not sure if the blue-and-white flashing lights meant to pull over or get out of the way. The police car trailed her down the entire length of Melrose Avenue. She got the hint and pulled over. The bright police-car headlights stayed on the back of her head, illuminating the inside of her car while she struggled to get her purse, still strapped around her body and now bolted underneath her seatbelt.

"Having a problem, ma'am?"

Leah looked up to the familiar voice and even more familiar smile. "What are you doing stopping innocent citizens?" She let go of the stuck purse. She relaxed back in the seat. "I'm glad it was you . . . I think. What'd I do?"

"Not a thing."

"Something happened?" She bolted upward, her face square in the window.

"No, nothing like that. I just recognized your car while I was making my rounds. Where you been?" Angel leaned on the open window.

"I've been busy, sort of. Just trying to stay busy." Leah gripped the steering wheel tighter.

"No. I meant tonight." Angel kneeled to a comfortable squat next to the car door. The lights from the squad car behind them added a sheen to his healthy black hair and the silky straight lashes. "I was headed to take my break when I saw you. You look nice. Had a date?"

"Not really. Met with a friend for dinner, really my old boss, Squire," she added, not knowing why she felt the need to explain. "I really should get home." She started the car.

"Come share a cup of coffee with me. The place isn't too far from here. A quick sip and you can be on your way."

Leah looked at the illuminated time on her dashboard. "It's late, Angel. The kids—"

"They're fine. You don't believe me, call. Check for yourself." He snapped the small phone off his waist and held it up for her.

"You've been by the house?" she asked, her words slower than her racing mind.

"No. I called . . . looking for you. Kayla answered, said you were out on a date."

Leah let out a hopeless sigh. Her daughter had a way with words.

"Just a cup of coffee, please."

She started her car, giving in to his determination. "Okay, but I can't stay long."

"Follow me." He walked back to his car. He swung around and she pulled right behind him.

They parked in front of a small coffeehouse with a neon sign that sputtered and blinked "Open." Inside was darker than outside. He grabbed her hand and led her to the back of the building where the wall was shoddily laid brick. The seats and tables were empty. They passed the one person who seemed to be working there. Angel held up his hand with two fingers up. The man nodded in acknowledgment. Before they were completely seated, the coffees were put before them. Hot steam rose off the top. Leah wrapped her hands around the cup to stave off the sudden chill she was feeling.

"Guess you're a regular?"

"Gotta stay awake." He opened up two packets of sugar at the same time and poured them in together.

"So you were saying about your boss... dinner, was it?"

"Oh yeah. Squire... ex-boss. He and I are actually friends. I mean, we were friends before we were colleagues. I'm working on producing my own television show. He's going to help me."

Two more packets of sugar. Leah tried not to look.

"Would I be too personal if I asked what kind of friends?"

Leah put her coffee down before it met her lips. The look she gave shut down the conversation.

"I'm sorry. I didn't mean to offend. I'm sorry, it's just that I thought... you and I..."

The slim balding man appeared with more coffee in the glass pot. Leah put her hand over her cup and politely declined. She hadn't yet had the pleasure of tasting her coffee but noticed Angel's was nearly gone.

"Why haven't I had a chance to be alone with you?" He blinked a shy slowness. The lips she'd kissed so fully days ago were calling her attention with their perfect arch and curve. His bottom lip she recalled with more intimacy, the way she'd sucked it, pulled it away from the other.

The murmuring of the police radio gave her a reprieve. He silenced the noise with a roll of his finger. He reached out and touched her hand. She didn't resist.

"It's just not a good situation. It's wrong." She looked him directly in his eyes, ready to stand for what she believed, regardless of how sexy his smile or how strong his chin.

His fingers wrapped tightly around hers. He leaned into her face and waited while they breathed the same air. "What's wrong about caring for someone?"

"I still love him. What I feel for you is confusing, it's crazy. I don't know what I feel. The only thing I'm sure of is that I love my husband, and what I'm doing here with you is wrong."

"What are you doing here with me?" Angel touched her face, the smooth skin under her eye. "We're simply having a cup of coffee." He slid her cup closer toward her.

She grabbed one of the few sugar packets that hadn't yet been opened.

"I wouldn't ask you to do anything you didn't want to do, or feel anything that didn't come natural." He slid around in the booth until his shoulder and chest found their way against her arm, against the side of her breast. She wanted to scream. Was she the only one losing her mind, her body out of control?

"I have to go." Leah stood up, knocking the table and shaking his freshly filled cup. She grabbed a handful of napkins out of the dispenser and attempted to soak up the spill. He reached out and touched her hand. "I have to go." She left the soggy mess on the table and walked out.

Angel followed closely behind; he grabbed her arm and turned her around. He gripped her tightly around her waist and held her. She didn't pull away. Her hands went up and found their place on his shoulders. Her forehead leaned on his chin.

"This is wrong." She spoke quietly into his uniformed chest. "You can't imagine what a hole this puts in my soul. If I feel this way for you, it makes me a horrible person, someone even I wouldn't want to be around."

He tilted her chin up, leaning in enough to part her lips with his own. Her head swam. The sound of cars, one at a time in no usual hurry, the voice of a man telling someone to go pay for the gas. A truck, large diesel engine, passing through. The ding ding ding of someone's open car door. Closed now with footsteps on the graveled pavement. On the outside, all things were clear, but in her head she was confused, small and frightened. Where had she gone? This wasn't the Leah Willow who put herself through school by working two jobs instead of dancing naked like her college roommate. This wasn't the Leah who picked up the twenty-dollar bill by her foot and handed it to the old woman standing next to her even though she, herself, hadn't eaten anything but rice for three straight days. It couldn't possibly be her, the one who'd sacrificed an A grade in Reel Expression because she wouldn't have coffee with her professor. It's just coffee. Leah Willow Fletcher had backbone, structure, and beliefs that were good and valuable. This wasn't her.

She backed away. "This is wrong." She walked to the car with the ground unstable beneath her feet. She listened for him to follow but was grateful that he didn't. He remained in the spot that she'd left him standing in as she pulled off.

chapter 26

"Vulnerable woman in search of rescuer need help, need love." She wanted to strip it off, whatever it was, that the sign read on her forehead, stop the feeling-sorry-for-Leah pity party.

She drove home in silence, thoughts swimming through her head. Dell had always depended on her solely. He trusted her as his woman, whole and complete. He never feared his house would not be in order when he returned home from one of his many road trips.

Just as she depended on being Mrs. Dell "Roadrunner" Fletcher, no matter how much she pretended it wasn't who she really was or all that she was. She didn't have to make any real decisions. Every day lived by expectation. Now, without him to be her guide, she was falling on the job. Falling for a man, a younger man, the one who'd actually had a role in the disappearance of her husband. It didn't make any sense. None. No matter how she tried to logically see what was happening to her, it was incomprehensible.

She played out the scenario, the what if game. What if she let Angel Lopez into her life, her world, completely without restraint... who would be hurt? She set the list of players one by one in her head, each reacting as she introduced him. There would be Kayla and Josh—no, Mom, you can't love anyone but Daddy. Then there would be her friends, strike that, friend. She only had one and that was Elicia. Of course they'd already met, but what would she say if Leah made the declaration "This is my lover. I'm waiting patiently for Dell to find his way back to me; if he doesn't, it will not have been in vain"? Elicia would laugh, "Don't be ridiculous. He's not good enough for you." Stupid girl, silly girl.

She pulled up to her house and fumbled with the garage door opener. As the large white door folded upward, she crept inside, pressing lightly on the gas. Dell's Porsche sat, untouched, but this time there was no sigh of relief. Seeing that car sitting there was a chained lock on her heart and mind. She was married. End of discussion.

Leah stopped in front of Kayla's door and tapped lightly, "You still awake?"

The door popped open. "I'm up." Her wide eyes, streaked with redness. Leah stepped inside, thwarting Kayla's efforts to only open the door wide enough for vision. "Are you all right? Is everything okay?"

"Fine, why?"

"I thought I heard you..." Leah knew Kayla would never confess to the sobbing that was heard through the door. "Can I come in?" A room of a teenager for sure. Posters lined the wall, Back Street Boys, Tyrese and Janet Jackson. She took a seat on the midnight-blue comforter, the moon and stars seemed to be moving in waves in front of her. Leah focused on the poster of Dell; he was in his glory in that shot. Someone had caught him striding over home plate. His legs and arms were flexed in conqueror's position. His muscles taut and unbreakable. "We're all going to get through this, together." She turned to her daughter. "You're only hurting yourself when you shut everybody out. I know you're devastated by everything that's happened. We all are."

"No. I don't think we *all* are," she repeated Leah's words.

"What do you mean?"

"You don't seem very devastated to me, having dinner dates and hanging out with a man probably closer to my age than yours. Seems like you're doing all right to me."

She looked up to the ceiling. Not this conversation again. "I had a meeting with Squire, whom I think you know as a friend of this family, and as far as Angel goes, we are not hanging out. He's been there for me, you, Josh, all of us. You need to put whatever is stimulating that little imagination of yours to rest. Is this what has got you so out of it? It's me? I'm the problem here?"

"I didn't say you were a problem. I just said I don't think all of us are taking Dad's disappearance the same way. You're running around business as usual." She crossed her legs Indian style, her thin arms strapped across her chest to show she was not going to be convinced easily.

"Uh-uh, no, you must have me confused with someone else... after two weeks of being unable to get out of my bed, you're telling me I'm acting like business as usual. I've grieved. I'm finished. I'm not going to stop breathing, stop living, because your father isn't here. You, on the other hand, need to start dealing with it so you can stop lashing out at the world. If you don't stop treating everyone who comes within ten feet of you like gum on a shoe, you're going to look around one day and find you've got no one left to beat up on but yourself."

Kayla's eyes watered slowly.

Leah rubbed her cheek, sliding the tear away. "Kayla, I'd do anything to make you smile again. Give anything to make you feel better." She wrapped her arms around her daughter's slight shoulders. "You're still my baby, no matter how old you are, you'll always be my baby. You know what babies do when they're unhappy? They cry, no pretense. They scream and shout until the whole world knows, and when they're finished crying, they sleep in a peaceful slumber, forgetting about whatever pinched a nerve in the first place." She touched the braids hanging from the top of her daughter's head. "You have a right to cry, Kayla." She held her daughter's head cradled in her arms. The usual contract she and Kayla had between each other to keep their distance and tread lightly had been suspended. Leah relished the warmth even though she knew it was a temporary moment. Right now she could hold her daughter, enjoy the new scent of the young woman that had replaced the simple Ivory soap and tennis-shoe smell. It brought back memories of how she could make her daughter feel better with a simple hug after a bruised knee or tumble from one of the trees she liked to climb.

Leah came back to the embrace. She was still holding Kayla even though her daughter's arms had turned limp. *Don't stop hugging first.* She tried to live by that rule, made a concerted effort, but this time, she really wasn't through. She wanted to hold on, talk to her about life, boys, sex and drugs. Plug up all the holes she'd left in their relationship. She wanted to tell her daughter that sex didn't solve problems, didn't make things go away. Neither did drugs or alcohol. There was no escaping life, no temporary fixes. You had to take it straight on, eyes wide open.

They awkwardly disengaged themselves, leaving a large wavering void. Leah pushed Kayla's braids away from her face. "You're so beautiful, so smart. You've got so many great things waiting for you. So much to look forward to."

"Can't wait." Kayla said between a fresh burst of tears. "I can see it's going to be a blast."

Didn't she remember? It wasn't all bad. Didn't she remember riding her bike for the first time without training wheels, Leah waiting with open arms after Dell had just given her a firm push? They jumped up and down for their little girl's accomplishment. Didn't she remember the two-hand swing, Dell and Leah on opposite sides of her, letting her leap from one crack in the sidewalk to the next? What about the trip to Sea World, the entire day spent on top of her father's shoulders, pointing at Shamu?

Didn't she remember?

Leah touched Kayla's cheek, brushing away the tears. "Try to have sweet dreams, babygirl. Sometimes that's all anyone has. We were lucky to have had the real thing."

chapter 27

THE REST OF HIS FOUR-HOUR SHIFT may as well have been underwater. He couldn't function knowing Leah was pulling away from him, slowly in fragments. Like a carpenter, she was whittling away at her desires, her needs, small slivers at a time. *It's wrong.* She was the type who couldn't be wrong, therefore, Lopez would have to go.

He felt like a drowning man. He could see her face swirling at the top, through the whirlpool of water. Save me, Leah? His hand reaching out for her, but she wouldn't, because *it's wrong.* She had to see that he needed her, that this was more than a play for her affection, a game that he had to win. It was so much more.

Lopez moved in slow motion, hearing, thinking, and speaking all in a surreal state. When a call came in for a domestic altercation one block away from where he sat parked, he couldn't figure out how to get there for the life of him. Response time was the only real measure of merit in the quiet space of Northern Hollywood. After spinning in circles, he finally arrived a half hour later to find a housewife locked in the bathroom and the husband sitting down watching football. The TV was turned up loud and the house was sickeningly stuffy.

"It's Denver and St. Louis. All I wanted to do is watch the ga'damned game in peace." The red-faced man sat holding a warm can of beer. He pointed in the direction where he could find the missus.

Lopez knocked on the bathroom door. "Ma'am, this is Officer Lopez from the LAPD. Can you come out and talk to me for a minute?"

"Not until he's out of my house." Her voice muffled through the door. He could hear body-shifting stubbornness.

"I can't do anything until I see you, ma'am. Open the door so we can resolve this."

"I'm not coming out until he's gone!" she screamed.

Lopez wanted to be gone, too, sitting back in his car, in quietness, alone with his thoughts of Leah. This was all an annoyance.

He turned to the husband who was already back on the couch watching the large television screen. "Sir, I'm going to have to ask you to step outside, just for a minute, until I can get her statement. Hopefully you'll be back by halftime."

The husband acted like a scolded child, sucking his teeth, half finishing sentences. "She's craz... You'll see... I tried..."

"Okay, ma'am, he's gone. Now come out." Lopez wasn't in the mood to let this go on much longer. His tone let the woman know, time out. The door opened slowly, first only showing a red-veined eyeball, then wider to reveal a full head of dry wispy hair and tired slumped shoulders. Her face was clear and solemn. There were no apparent bruises.

"Tell me what happened."

Her lips started moving, her mouth tight with rage. Lopez heard an expletive after every other word, not bothering to interrupt and ask for only the facts. Pretty soon he heard nothing, only seeing her lips move. The wet lines squeezing back and forth like violin chords.

At the end of the evening, when he looked at his notepad to log in the names of the couple, their stories, respectively, and all other pertinent information, there was nothing there. Lopez flipped through, several pages, up and back. Nothing. Not one single word. He slammed his fist on the desk that was his for at least fifteen more minutes. He couldn't get Leah off his mind.

The afternoon they spent together wasn't supposed to scare her away.

If anything, it was supposed to make her want him more. What backfired? He replayed every moment of Leah wrapped in his arms. She was his, right there in the palm of his hand. He'd walked out that door confident, feeling his work was done... then her friend showed up.

Elicia Silvas. She'd probably laughed, embarrassing Leah. Compassion wasn't a pretty girl's strong suit. Most of the beautiful women he'd known took things for granted, assumed life was easy for everybody, decisions based on reward. *What can he do for you?* she'd probably asked. *You're better than that, Leah.*

Elicia Silvas—he scribbled her name on the notepad in front of him. He wrote it six different ways, big, little, exaggerated. He listed things he assumed about her, or, to be more direct, things he knew: a newswoman, Latina, smart, affluent, sexy, dangerous. Probably used men for gain and status, driving around in her shiny Benz—

It wasn't something that hit him right away, it sat on the tip of his brain like having all three letters except one, and Vanna White standing off to the side with her Mary Poppins smile. The smile that said I don't care if you guess it right or not, you're just another contestant, and I keep going and going like the Energizer bunny. The last letter popped into his brain, Vanna's smile didn't break stride. She simply moved over to the other side of the board as if to say, you guessed it, so what's next. "A dark Mercedes picked him up."

The homeless woman couldn't make out the color, only that it was dark. The small kind. *No conversating, he just got right in.*

He leaned back in his squeaky chair with his hands behind his head. He was going to win, no matter how he played it. Whether he guessed all the letters right, whether he filled in all the blanks, he was going to win.

chapter 28

TYPICAL WOMAN, FLOATING AROUND the grocery store aimlessly. Lopez had already been down this aisle twice following her around. Men came to the grocery store with lists, and that's it, no floating around, changing their mind, and second-guessing themselves.

He was tired and wanted to get it over with. He'd sat outside Elicia Silvas's house since five this morning, waiting for some sign of life. Way too early to be up when he was on the nightshift. It was ten now. He followed her to the masterfully displayed produce department. Whoever merchandised this store surely had a career in set design. The lighting gleamed on every pear, apple, and plum like it was about to be photographed for *Gourmet* magazine. He parked his cart a few yards from hers and reached past her.

"Hey, how's it going? Elicia, right?"

She blinked and tilted her head slightly to the side. "Officer Lopez?"

He didn't give her a chance to start interrogating. She was the suspect, not him.

He reached across her, "I saw you throw that bunch back in." He picked up the cast-away asparagus. "They're all like that, don't waste your time. The thing to do is take them home, snip off about a half inch on the bottom and set the stalks in water, let 'em soak, standing up, and it'll be like you picked them from the garden yourself. Fresh and crispy." Her eyes followed his muscular arm as he set the asparagus in her basket.

"Thanks for the tip. So you live out here?" Her tone was that of a snob, as if to say, what are you doing shopping in our neighborhood on a cop's salary?

"Actually, I'm running a couple of errands for Leah." He gestured to the nearly full grocery cart with colorful boxes and sucker packaging. "The stuff kids eat." He shrugged his shoulders.

Elicia smiled. "You're shopping for Leah?" She was trying to swallow the uncomfortable lump in her throat. "You've really stepped up to the plate, I see."

"Interesting choice of words." He kept his eyes on her. She wasn't so tall without her heels, five feet two or three. She looked tired. Lopez stuck out his hand. "Well, nice seeing you. Don't forget to soak your tips."

Lopez pushed off, then stopped and turned around, catching her still staring at him. "Hey, you know, I was thinking about doing some cooking, putting together something to liven that Fletcher crew up, they've been so down. You think you'd be interested in coming?"

"To Leah's house?"

"Yeah. Of course." He stood all confidence, his hands resting on his belted jeans waistline.

"You're cooking at Leah's house?" Elicia surveyed the possibility and all that it meant.

"A barbecue or something. You can bring a date, hang out. Is there a Mr. Silvas?" He gave her a one-sided smile.

Her eyes fell into a confused squint. "Thanks for the invite and, no, the only Mr. Silvas right now is my father."

"You mind giving me your number, I can give you a call, that way I won't have to go through Leah, who'll probably be a little strained and not want to partake in the festivities. I can already hear her telling me no. You understand probably more than anybody else what she's going through. Her husband disappearing in thin air. Not knowing where he is."

"Sure." Elicia dug in her purse and pulled out her wallet. She gave him a card.

Lopez looked at it and handed it right back. "You think you can write your home number on there?"

"Sure." She pulled out a pen and chicken-scratched, probably hoping he couldn't make out the numbers clearly.

"Okay, well, I'll let you know when." He held up the card and tapped it with a finger pop.

"You do that." This time she turned and walked away first. Lopez watched her go around the canned goods aisle once again. Good thing she was in her jogging shoes; she was probably going to be in this store all day, giving him plenty of time to accomplish his goal.

He ditched the cart near the bakery section and walked out of the store. He sat in his car for a second, dialing the number quickly. A machine picked up. "Sorry I missed your call, but please leave a message." Great. Nobody else home and little Ms. Muffet still here, shopping for curds and whey.

The five-minute drive led him back to the secluded hill of lush green trees and houses set high enough to reach the heavens. The same thought crossed his mind from earlier, when he'd sat out staring at the three-story glass house: How the hell did she afford this monstrosity on an anchorwoman's salary (late night at that)? He parked and took a few minutes to check out his surroundings. The neighbors were flanked behind walls of trees. A quiet, secluded area where people drove into their garages and shut out their neighbors and the rest of the world as soon as they were home.

He walked up the winding stairs. It looked like three glass cubes stacked on top of one another. The front door was made of solid wood, a rich golden-brown tone. He knocked and rang the door bell, but he already had his fingers on the special Allen wrench set in his jacket pocket, one he'd hoisted off a kid thief on a routine stop.

He knocked again for good measure. The thick shrubbery and tall trees protected him from being seen by a passerby. The air whistled in his ears, the same wind that shook the leaves behind him, making him turn around suddenly.

Lopez returned his focus to the door but now had a turbulent combination of unsteady nerves and fear. His hands vibrated, too shaky to get the miniature wrench in the keyhole. He pictured the man who everyone thought was the Roadrunner, shot, laid out with blood all over his face from breaking and entering. No doubt that man didn't know what hit him. The second he entered, the woman had probably come out blasting.

He stopped what he was doing and looked around again. Maybe he was jumping the gun. In Los Angeles a dark-colored Mercedes was like a blade of grass in a football field. He had no proof that it was Elicia's car that picked up Dell Fletcher that evening. He backed away cautiously, pushing the tool deep in his jacket pocket. He hated being scared, afraid of the unknown. Little pussy, faggot, wimp. He could hear all the names Gino called him when he didn't want to go along for the ride. Take your mama's tit out of your mouth, boy.

Moving swiftly down the stairs, skipping the last two altogether, he walked across the street to his car. When he was safely inside, he looked up at the large glass house. The glare of the sun bounced off the windows. He thought he saw a shadow move inside. Lopez put his sunglasses on to see if the picture became any clearer. He was losing it. His imagination was getting the best of him.

Why would Elicia have anything to do with Dell Fletcher? A dark Mercedes—that's it, that's all he had to go on? She was Leah's friend. Friends don't let friends drive *husbands.*

Instinct told him different, but logic prevailed. Why would Elicia keep coming around Leah if she'd already gotten what she was after? He looked up again, blinking under the blinding glare. No one knew where Dell Fletcher was. Maybe he was truly dead. If that was the case, Lopez was wasting time chasing ghosts.

The drive to his apartment seemed endless. He parked in the covered spot with the large white number eleven. Next to the same rusty red Datsun. The guy who lived next door was a bass player in a rock band and drove the raggedy piece of steel about once a month when he had a gig. Lopez pushed his Taurus door open, letting it fall into the already beat-up Datsun's siding. When he got out, the Taurus shifted and the door wouldn't budge, stuck like a dull knife in a thick watermelon rind. "Shit." Lopez tugged, then kicked the Datsun, then kicked at it again.

"Hey!" The voice got closer, "What the hell are you doing to my car?"

Lopez, too busy kicking decent-sized dents in the rusty red Datsun, didn't hear his neighbor shouting. He kicked it one last time as if that's all it needed. The door unhinged and fell closed. He turned around to see the spike hair and raised eyebrows.

"Have you lost your bloody mind?" The English accent, that was the other thing Lopez hated. The way he stayed on the phone all night, his voice not deterred by the drywall in between. Lopez took two steps toward the leather-clad lad before he bolted in the other direction. Lopez was grateful the guy ran. He didn't know what he was capable of right now.

Nothing was going right. He needed to try and get the sleep that he'd lost following Elicia around all morning. The cheap hollow door of his apartment felt heavy. The curtains and shades were closed, making the light on his answering machine illuminate and blink feverishly. He pushed the button and dropped into his sunken-in couch.

"Angel, something's happened to Andre. I need your help. You said you'd help if I called."

He scooted closer to the machine and leaned his chin on his balled fist.

"Nobody knows where he is." Her voice shook into the machine. "Is there something you can do? I need to know how to report someone missing, Angel... can you help me... can you help me find him?"

He leaned back on the couch. He closed his eyes, waiting for the exhaustion to settle in and take over. His sister's voice kept playing in his mind. She was hurting, scared, a nervous wreck. She'd get over it. One day she'd realize she was better off.

chapter 29

It had taken him a few days to figure out what was going on. The way he felt like he'd been hit over the head the minute she walked out the door. She was drugging him.

When she walked in, he was sitting in the farthest corner of the living room. Dell held up the small yellow prescription bottle in his hand. The moonlight shone on his hand like a spotlight. He shook the bottle of pills to get her attention.

"What are you doing sitting in the dark, sweetie?" She still hadn't noticed the bottle of pills in his hand. She turned up the dimmer in the hallway, emitting enough light to see her way to him. She dropped her purse and kicked off her shoes. Her scent already filled the room, or perhaps it'd never left.

He shook the bottle again. "These have my name on them. Guess that means their mine." He turned the bottle over. "Oxycontin. And these... Take one tablet twice a day. And this Valium, says, take two tablets. How many of these have you been slipping in my sleepy-time tea every day before you go off to work? You think I'm going to get away? Am I your prisoner here? Is there something I should know... besides what the hell is going on? You can at least tell me who I am! You can do that, right?" The thunderous rise in his voice sent her on her toes. She stood motionless, trying not to breathe.

"I tried to play your house game. I wanted to be whatever you pretended I was, but something's not right. I don't even remember you, do you realize that? Has it occurred to you that I've never called you by your name? I have no recollection of who you are, or why I'm even here. Did you know that? Of course you did." He held up the evidence again.

She still didn't move, a silhouette standing straight in her stocking feet.

"Answer me! Tell me what the hell is going on!"

She took a slow first step, then another and another before falling to her knees. She crawled the rest of the distance to where he sat. She reached out cautiously, afraid the frustration could lead to something else. He didn't flinch, or tense up. She rested her hands on his thighs and pushed herself between his legs.

With the closeness came her warmth. He wanted it to be good, whatever she had to say, he wanted it to be right because in all honesty, he had nowhere else to go.

"You called me," she said, close enough to feel her breath with her words. "Something happened to you, you were lost, scared, hurt, and out of all the people you knew, you called me. When I picked you up, you were bleeding, here," she brushed a finger across the bridge of his nose, "and here," smoothing her hand across his forehead. "You couldn't remember how it happened, if you'd been mugged or in an accident. You didn't know if you'd been drinking or taking drugs. You didn't remember anything.

"I report the news every night. Well, on that night, I reported you dead, then minutes later, it's retracted... your wallet was found on a man who'd been shot, but it wasn't you. Do you know how hard it was to read that story in front of millions of people without jumping up out of my seat and running out the door? I found out about all of this as each word pulled up on the teleprompter. I was dying to know myself, and I'm sitting there reporting this... my lover is dead, no wait a minute, that's a mistake, my lover's wallet was found on a dead man, but it wasn't him. I walked out of that studio numb with fear, then I hear your voice, and you're calling for me to help you. It was like a bad dream, a nightmare I couldn't wake up from. I came to you, not knowing if you were going to be shot, or stabbed, not knowing what kind of shape I was going to find you in. But there you were, standing in the rain, and all I thought was, thank God, he is standing on his own two feet."

She lay on his beating chest with her body still perched between his legs. "I brought you here and I took care of you. I wasn't lying when I said you may be in danger. The way I found you, I didn't know who or what had hurt you, and you couldn't remember either. Those pills I gave you were prescribed to you by your own doctor; I took them from your house. You were addicted to some heavy drugs at one time. I didn't want you to go into withdrawal, especially while your body was trying to heal from whatever blow you'd suffered."

He grabbed her by her shoulders and lifted her up to meet his gaze. "You knew I didn't remember anything, nothing, and you kept pretending like everything was all right? You couldn't tell me a simple truth. Why should I believe you now?" He shifted his body and managed to stand up, leaving her on the floor.

She stood up now, feeling foolish for groveling. "If it weren't for me, you probably would be dead."

"While you're feeling truthful, explain this." He held up his left hand. The ring was gone, but the lighter shade of skin where it had unmistakably been worn remained. "If you're my lover, who's my wife?"

The question shook her, a hard jolt, but she regained her balance. She stood up and walked around him. Standing in front of the framed window, city lights twinkling like a Christmas tree, varying colors—red, green, blue, and white—all in the distance. She pulled the clip out of her hair and let it fall. He took the spot next to her, on cue, as he'd done many times before. In fact, fragments of his past were filtering in, more and more on a daily basis. Pieces scattered from one time frame to the next.

Her head leaned on his shoulder. "You and I are lovers, but you're married to someone else. She doesn't have any idea you're here with me. She doesn't know about us at all. We're actually friends... she and I. It sounds ridiculous, but we are. I care for her." She laughed at herself again. "I met the two of you on the exact same day. I liked her, but I fell in love with you."

She was reliving that moment, the impressiveness, "You were Dell Fletcher, the Roadrunner."

"Wait, I'll show you." She left and came back carrying a shoebox-sized chest. A burnished weaved basket with a gold clasp for a lock. She flipped it open and pulled out neatly folded newspaper clippings, pressed flat. "These are all about you." She began handing the clippings to him one at a time, unfolding them carefully as if they were endangered species taken out of preservation.

"This is me." He digested the pictures, grainy color shots of a man sharp and muscular. Agile and fit. The dreams. Now he understood. They were flashbacks of his career. He looked at the dates, the pictures, the headlines and bylines. All the way back to 1990, more than ten years. "How long have we been . . . ," he cleared his throat, not quite sure how to say it, ". . . together?"

"We met during an interview last year."

He looked at the dates again, to make sure he wasn't mistaken. *But how long have you loved me?* He held his tongue and waited for her to finish.

"It was the worst time of your life; you'd just found out you couldn't play baseball anymore. You had an injury that left you in chronic pain. It was rumored that you tried to kill yourself."

"Did I?"

She turned to him and he knew the answer. "You were unhappy with your life. When I sat there talking to you in that interview, getting to know who you really were, I knew you were hurting. You tried to downplay it, like an athlete knows his time will come, like it's all part of the recipe, but I could see that you were lost."

Her hand stroked his cheek. "The first time we met alone, you told me that you loved your wife and nothing was going to change that. But the way you held me for hours afterward, after we'd made love, I knew there was something missing in your life. That's what made the second time you called so amazing. I was thrilled. I just assumed you'd be so overwrought with guilt, it would never happen again. But you called. You came to my home and nearly attacked me right in the doorway." She was tickled with the memory. Her smile was bright in the reflection of the glass door.

"An entire year and someone who's supposed to be my wife never found out? What kind of woman doesn't know?" He pushed the cut-out news articles back in the box and slammed it closed.

She winced, feeling the fissures in the dated newsprint he'd surely caused. "The two of you were already having problems. The love just wasn't there." She took her box and put it out of harm's way.

Dell felt a stab of memory. "Fighting?"

"Yes, arguing, fighting."

"Then why did I stay? Why didn't I leave and come to you?" Before she had a chance to answer, he figured it out for himself. "Children. How old?"

"Your son, Josh, is ten; your daughter, Kayla, is fifteen. They're the loves of your life. That's why you stayed, for them."

It hurt. Not remembering his own children, his own wife. It felt like his heart had been sliced out and left on someone's table. What was he to do now? Where did he belong?

He felt her hand move into his.

"Do they know I'm here, does anyone?"

"No one knows. I thought it was best to keep you here, safe, until we found out what really happened to you, till you regained your memory."

"Where does my family think I am?"

She hesitated, looking far off, ambling for an answer.

"What, they think I'm dead?" He searched her eyes.

"They don't know where you are or if you're ever coming back. The last they heard you were being arrested for hitting your wife."

"Wait, wait," he stepped back, refusing her hand. "I hit my wife?"

"The two of you had an argument. It turned ugly."

Dell walked back to the chair and plopped down. "I hit her?" He put his face in his folded hands. Then pulled them away to examine, to assess whether they could be the hands of an abuser. Someone who would take advantage of another's vulnerability. His wife.

"Let's go to bed, sweetheart. It's been a long day for both of us." She grabbed both of his shaking hands.

Dell stopped her. "I still don't know you. I don't remember you."

"My name is Elicia, and I love you. That's all that matters." She wrapped her arms around his neck and pressed her lips to his. He closed his eyes and kissed her back. He tried to remember what a man must feel in the other woman's arms. Ecstasy, intoxication, hope and betrayal. A high far greater and more lethal than any drug. He pulled back.

"I have a lot to think about." He pulled her arms from around his neck. "Do you mind if I look through the articles again?"

She picked up the precious box and walked it back to him. She kissed him on the chin before sweeping up the iron staircase. He waited until the light disappeared from the closed door of *their* bedroom before tearing into the box like a man dying of hunger.

• • •

Dell woke up with the frivolous saying on his lips, a cliché created for everyday life without meaning. For some reason the words were taunting him—time is of the essence.

Time waits for no man. He rolled over to see his mistress sleeping, her bare shoulder rising and falling with her breathing rhythm. She was real. The sheet draped over the curve of her body. He could see how a man could stray into the arms of a woman like her, especially an unhappy man in an unhappy marriage. The thought dawned on him, what did his wife look like? Was she as beautiful as his lover?

He ran his hand across Elicia's hair that covered the pillow. Was his wife Black or white, Asian or Latin? How had they met? He rose out of bed and slipped on the silk shirt and drawstring pants, now his current uniform.

He tiptoed out of the bedroom and into the spacious white living room. The morning sun lit up the entire house. A warmth that turned hot if he stood in one spot too long. What he was looking for sat on the glass coffee table. He walked over and picked up Elicia's purse and looked inside. Even a purse this small had to have... he pulled out her organizer. He flipped the address book portion to F's and looked up his own phone number and address. Fletcher, Dell & Leah. What kind of couple had they been? Did they invite friends over for Superbowl Sunday with beer and hot wings? Did they go on family vacations and eat out in restaurants where they served ice cream for dessert?

He dialed slowly, what would he say? Hi, I'm your husband, I wanted to know if I could come over and talk to you? I need to know what my life was like, what my home and children were like.

Someone answered on the first ring. He wasn't expecting it. It was the same voice he'd heard speaking into Elicia's answering machine, Leah. A sudden, gripping panic swirled around him. He hung up, his heart racing.

Time waits for no man.

She sounded soft and loving. He couldn't imagine her voice in anger, the two of them fighting, stepping on each other to be heard. The children standing in the foreground, feeling ripped down the middle. He remembered that feeling with his own parents, loving them both, but you had to choose, one side over the other. There was no way around the decision of which parent was in the right and which was in the wrong. Someone had to be at fault; if not, it fell on the child's shoulders. Dell remembered standing next to his father, leaning on him as if a hug would make the difference of being able to go to camp in the summer with his friends. "We can't afford camp, son. I don't have that kind of money right now."

"When do you ever?" was his mother's response, raging from what she'd overheard in the next room. She held the white paper with the large printed black words that gave the deadline to vacate the premises. "Right now means forever with you, and I'm sick of waiting."

He remembered slipping out of the house, sitting outside the door in the hallway with his hands over his ears. They fought because of him.

The sound of Elicia circling the bedroom above him returned him to the present. He slumped in the butterfly chair, letting his head hang over the back, looking at the ceiling that extended indefinitely, a white fusion of space. He wondered whose side his children were on, or did they blame themselves?

"How'd you sleep?" She kissed him on the top of his head.

"Excellent, considering all the information I had to absorb."

"I know, it's a lot." She sat across from him; it seemed like a great distance. She lay sideways, her white silk robe matching the couch. "Are any other things coming back to you?"

"Mostly what I see is me as a kid."

"You still don't know how this happened to you, if you were hit over the head or in some kind of accident? I mean, it would make sense that the guy who stole your wallet clobbered you. But you don't remember anything?"

Dell closed his eyes, shutting out the offensive brightness of the room. He tried for a minute to will it to him, something, anything. His eyes opened to her loveliness. She had slipped her robe to her shoulders and become the seductress, shining in the sunlight.

He knew what was next. Since he could get out of bed and walk straight she'd constantly tried to get his equipment to work, to get him back in the saddle, but with bitter results. He wondered if he'd forgotten how to be a man as well. As beautiful as she was, he'd been unable to fill her, unable to fulfill his lover's duty. He looked the other way to let her know nothing had changed.

chapter 30

LEAH HAD BEEN HIDING from Angel. What else could explain his sitting in the car on guard, waiting for her to arrive? She pulled in behind the tan

Ford Taurus and hurriedly got out and walked to the side of his door. The window was down and Angel was reclined all the way back, as far as his seat would allow.

She leaned in, "Napping outside of a woman's house? That's pretty serious." She tried to make light of the situation, but her heart was dancing outside her chest.

"I need to talk to you."

"What's going on?" Her first thought was of Dell. Had they found him... dead? She shut his car door and followed him to the porch, as if it were his house they were entering. She fumbled with her keys before getting the door unlocked. As soon as she pushed it open she felt his hands around her waist, propelling her inside. Her purse dropped to the floor with a thud, the keys quickly followed. She was pinned against the wall, his body up against hers. Heat smothered her. Fluttering waves passed through his mouth to hers. He stroked the sides of her face, pausing, then kissing again.

"I'm not going to wait anymore, Leah."

He turned her around, hugging her waist from behind. He walked her like a child to the base of the stairs, his hand pressed against the flatness of her stomach, sliding past her waistband. He whispered in her ear over and over, "I'm not going to wait anymore. Do you hear me?"

Closed eyes, but she could see everything he was doing to her. Sight in the form of touch, so vivid, so real, he put his hand down the front of her skirt, past her panties. His fingers searching gently. Her head flew back against his shoulder. Her knees couldn't hold up, his arm tightened around her waist, the other hand rubbing, dipping, tasting the slickness of her inside. Her moan waved and floated at the top of her throat, waited then trickled out like a baby's first stir.

"Tell me, tell me, I don't have to wait anymore. Say it." He turned her facing him once again. She was being backed to a seated position on the edge of the stair.

His hands slid up the sides of her thighs, past the smooth lining of her skirt. He pulled the black satin panty down over her knees, over her ankles, tossing them to the side. He touched the smoothest part of her skin, the inside. She could hear the slit on the back of her skirt tear when he pushed her legs to open farther.

"Don't." She heard the voice but her body was still complacent, still submitting. "I can't."

His fingers crawled to her lips to shhh her.

She felt his mouth, wet, starting above her knee and climbing toward the inside of her thigh. She wouldn't scream. She didn't dare, she wouldn't scream. He was thorough, leaving warm wet kisses on every inch of her skin. A chill rose through, from her toes to the last strand of her hair.

She cried out, almost with shame, for needing him, for begging with her lips, her words. Her skirt was moving farther up, she felt the cool air of her exposed center, the pressure from his hands pulling her hips toward him. The closer he got, the louder the words became in her head . . . this is wrong . . . I can't. "Angel, please."

She felt his face, thick and full between her legs.

"Angel, no. I can't." The voice was louder, real. She was back on earth, seeing the top of his head bent down between her open thighs, her knees pushed up. She shoved at him. "Stop, Angel, I can't." Her legs felt locked into place underneath his weight, but she managed to pull them together. Her hands, his hands, entangled like octopus tentacles. When he finally gave up, he looked like he'd been in a fight, red streaks across his forehead and nose where she'd clawed him away.

Now he was pulling her up to help her stand. He held her firmly. The stream of her tears rode down the crease of his chest. She wanted to be free of it, through with the wondering, the whys, the miscalculations. This wasn't supposed to be her life. She married the man she loved. Period. This wasn't supposed to be happening. She was supposed to be safe and secure, her heart and mind protected. Sheltered from the dangerous terrain of new lovers, new friendships. In sickness and in health.

She pushed him away.

His eyes were pleading, still.

She wanted to tell him she was sorry. Sorry for leading him on, sorry for making him feel dejected and unwanted. It's not you, Angel. "I can't" trailed out behind her thoughts. She bent over and picked up her panties, balling them in her hand. What would the children think? She pushed her skirt over her thighs, then bent over again to grab her shoes. She turned and took one heavy step at a time, heading for her bedroom.

"Leah." He was standing at the base of the stairs, resembling the man she was more familiar with. The straight shoulders, the orderly hair and clothes. He managed to turn back into himself as if nothing had happened out of the ordinary, while she on the other hand was drained and empty, a disheveled mess, inside and out.

She didn't answer when she heard him call her name, even with the wave at the end. She found her way to her bed and crawled under the cover. Let yourself out, she would have said if she'd had enough strength. Don't be a stranger, she would have said through clenched teeth. Come back anytime, she would have feigned. An even greater strength was necessary if she wanted to say the truth—I care for you, but I can't love you—I need you, but I can't have you.

She found her way to her bedroom, gently closing the door behind her. She crawled underneath the covers and closed her sad eyes and prayed for peace of mind.

Josh walked in the house first. Kayla was close behind. The open window over the kitchen sink caused the gauze curtain to lift lightly and fall with each shift in breeze. The house was quiet, but not empty. They knew that by the two cars parked out front, Mom's and Angel's. Awkward like twisted puzzle pieces, causing concern as to the status of things. He could tell Kayla felt the same way, both of them taking cautious steps through the house, assessing which cups were used, plates, forks, knifes. If the pillows were in their respective corners of the couch. If the rugs were straightened on the tiled floor. The things they normally took for granted were now important, things that told them their life would not change again. That things were in order.

Kayla called out, "Mom?"

Josh rolled his eyes. Thanks for the warning. Josh ran up the stairs and picked up where she left off, "Mom."

"Hey." Angel came from the back of the house, his finger to his lips. "She's sleeping." What was he doing coming from that direction? The room, more like the size of a closet, where their father's trophies and pictures were shelved. Books their father said he'd read, even though neither could recall him reading anything but the sports section.

"Let her rest." Angel dusted his hands on each other. "Come down." He waved for Josh, but he continued standing. He needed to see her, sleeping or not.

Kayla stood behind Angel like a ghost in the kitchen doorway, not wanting to be seen or part of the exchange. Josh looked to her, waited for her to distract and detain.

"Why is she sleeping? She all right?" Her words were forced, but it was all Josh needed. He finished the length of the stairs and stopped outside his mother's door. He listened before knocking.

He whispered, "Mom?" He knocked lightly. "You up?" He heard sheets rustling and felt an immediate relief. His hand was already twisting the knob. He bounced in and sat on the edge of her bed. "You all right?"

"I'm fine, babe. How was school?"

Josh waited for her to forget she'd even asked the question. He could see the slight glaze over her eyes. She was somewhere else. He touched her hand, played with her fingers. He never remembered his mother's fingernails without some type of color. He studied the length and shape of her natural nailbeds, up close and personal, leaning his face on his bent arm. Wait. Mom, where's your ring? He picked up her hand as if it were not attached to the rest of her, surveying, analyzing.

She felt the heat of his eyes and put her hand under the sheet.

"Is Kayla home?"

"Yeah, downstairs talking to Angel." He said the name and waited for her body to twitch or her eyes to blink too many times. He gauged her reaction like a lie detector, nothing.

She sat up. "Well, don't snack too heavily; I'm going to take you two out for dinner tonight."

"Where we going?"

She corrected him, "Where are we going? Wherever you want to go, how's that?" She put her nose to his and kissed him lightly on the lips.

He stood up and put his hands in his pockets. If she wasn't going to show him hers, he wasn't going to show her his. "I'll be downstairs."

"Okay. Tell Kayla, too."

Josh closed the door and headed down the stairs. He sulked into the seat at the table. A glass of milk was waiting with peanut-butter crackers on a plate. Kayla gave him a don't-look-at-me expression.

Her eyes darted to the fairy godfather out back standing on a ladder. Josh could see the lower half of his body, the top half too high for the window.

"What's he doing?"

"Says he's clearing out the rain gutters." Kayla stayed leaning against the refrigerator, out of earshot or vision. "You'd think he didn't know it doesn't rain in Southern California."

"Mom says not to eat too much because we're going out to dinner."

"We as in the three of us, or is Uncle Lopez trailing along?" Kayla picked up the plate of peanut-butter-slathered crackers and shoved them into the trash. "Guess he didn't check his handbook."

Josh was still appreciative of the effort. How would Angel know he was allergic to peanuts? He sipped the milk. "I don't know, she didn't say. She just said we."

She flattened herself against the pantry and scooted to the other side. "Well, if he's going, count me out." She grabbed a bag of Doritos out of the cabinet, then scurried off like a raccoon stealing from a picnic.

This was a hard one. Josh felt the dread of something bigger than all of them. His mother and Angel. He had short crisp images of them together, laughing, talking, talking too close. It wasn't real, or was it? How long had he seen it, but not really seen it? They acted like the kids at school when they were around each other, the kids who liked each other but didn't want anyone else to know. Talking in clusters, always making sure someone else was around so it wouldn't be obvious. How long? He closed his eyes. What was his father going to say when he got home? It was Josh's fault for letting his guard down. For being too comfortable. Enjoying... himself.

He'd have to put things right, fast. There would be trouble if his father came home to this. He looked to the man moving in short jerky movements outside the window. Rain gutters?

He watched Angel tackle one thing after the other. The hibiscus bush in the backyard that had turned into a monster, growing larger than anyone had anticipated. But still harmless. The sprinkler heads now had a foot of space around them, making their grass lawn look like a blind man's golf course. It was actually amusing, but something told Josh not to point and laugh. This work was important to someone. *Him.*

It was getting late and he began to wonder what was going on. Was his mother waiting for *him* to finish, and then they were going out to dinner? They. Was Angel waiting for his mother to get out of bed, and then he would stop working like a hound, digging up holes, searching for bones?

The doorbell rang, interrupting his analysis of the situation. He didn't wait for anyone, he pushed up on his tippy toes and saw Squire's back facing him through the round distorted eyehole. Who else could it be with the same brown tweed jacket and long hair? He unlocked the door and pulled it open.

His eyes rounded when he saw the pizza box Squire was holding.

"Hey, buddy, where's your mom?"

"Upstairs." Josh reached out and took the box.

"Well, I'm doing fine, thanks for asking."

Josh laughed, opening the box. "Hi, Squire."

"Hey, buddy." Squire closed the door and followed him to the kitchen. He went straight to the window, as if a sign were posted, "look here." He didn't ask. Didn't even cross his mind. Maybe Angel looked like he belonged. Josh slid the first piece to the farthest corner of his mouth. Hmmm. "We were supposed to be going out to eat, but my mom is still in the bed resting."

Squire leaned against the counter with his arms crossed, ankles crossed, "Do you mind going and telling her I'm here?"

Josh was up on his feet and moving without verbal confirmation. He was pretty curious himself as to why his mother hadn't come out of her room. She had been doing better, seemed like. This was two-weeks-ago behavior. He wondered what changed things, then he remembered the ring. Maybe something had happened, maybe she found out something about his dad. He knocked but didn't wait for an answer before going inside.

His mom was standing at her dresser mirror wearing a bright red sweater and dark blue jeans. She was putting on earrings. She turned around to face him. "Who was at the door?"

"Squire, he brought pizza. Are we still going to go out? Angel's still here," he added, almost as a warning.

She turned back around, closing her jewelry box. She picked up her lipstick, just as red as her sweater, and put it on, slowly tracing the full line of her lips. "Would you rather have pizza?"

"It's good, from Veranzzo's."

"He knows which is your favorite, doesn't he?"

"Yep." Josh hung on the door, determined not to go back downstairs without her.

He was relieved when she snapped the cap on the lipstick and closed the drawer where she kept her beauty arsenal. He followed her down the stairs, anticipating something, but not knowing what. He couldn't figure it out, why he was excited, expecting something to happen.

"To what do I owe the honor?" She walked to Squire and air-kissed him near his ear. He in turn kissed her solidly on her cheek.

"Wanted to share this news in person."

She stepped away. "Don't play with me, Squire Delvicio."

"Hey, I not only deliver the best pizza on the West Side, but I also deliver..." he reached into his pocket, "solid production offers." He pulled out a folded letter and shook it out like a paper sack. "Read that."

She took the paper with trembling hands, she read, she screamed. "Oh my God!"

"Well, I guess you could call me by my earned name."

She smiled harder, pushing him in the chest, still holding the letter, reading it again. "How'd you do it? I mean so fast, how'd you do it?"

"Miracles are my forte. *Oh my God,*" he mocked.

The excitement and noise brought Angel in slightly out of breath. "What's going on? I heard screaming." He searched Josh's face. Josh turned his eyes to the pizza, then the man who'd brought it and the good news.

"Angel, this is Squire." His mother instinctively stepped from the middle of the two men. They reached out and shook each other's hand, confused but obligated.

"Angel is a friend, he's been helping out around here." She realized how it sounded after noticing his usually shiny black hair, now patched with dust and ragweed. His T-shirt covered with his own handprints.

"Oh," Squire made the assumption. Gardener, handyman. "Nice meeting you."

An immediate fury rushed Angel's face. Josh knew it, wondered if anyone else saw it. He closed the pizza box, thinking if anything happened, at least he'd have something to eat.

"Nice meeting you, too." Angel's teeth almost didn't move when he spoke. "So what's all the excitement about?"

"My show, someone wants to produce it." She waved the letter like a flag.

Squire remained silent, observing.

Angel reached out with muddy fingers and read the letter for himself.

Squire observing.

"This is great, congratulations." He put his dusty face to Leah's cheek.

Squire observing, legs no longer crossed, arms no longer folded. He was gripping the edge of the counter for bona fide support.

"So how're we going to celebrate?" Josh broke through, still clutching the pizza box.

Silence. His mother was now put in a more awkward spot. He didn't mean to do that.

Squire still observing.

No one spoke. No one volunteered to do anything, leave, stay, go. Angel and Squire both looking at his mother. No, he didn't mean to do that.

"Angel, you want some pizza?" He pulled the cardboard top open. A peace offering.

"Uh, no thanks, I think I better be leaving. I'm on duty in about an hour and a half, and I got some cleaning up to do. This isn't my day job," he added, looking at Squire. "I'm a police officer." He rubbed his hands on the front of his chest and stuck his hand out again, trying to be the bigger man. "See you around, Squire."

"Yeah." Squire shook his hand with an ambitious grip.

Josh felt like yelling out, "CUT! That's a wrap. Ladies and gentlemen, you can all go home now."

chapter 31

ELICIA EXPLAINED TO HIM that it had only been a month since the first day of this nightmare. Dell felt like months had passed, spinning off of the calendar, shooting off in succession. Dog years would have been easier to comprehend. As it was, he felt like every day that he spent in this fog he was losing something much greater than days and nights, something more priceless than time.

It was Elicia's idea that they go out for some fresh air. They walked the edge of the Santa Monica shore. The sand was fine, almost dust under his feet. He took advantage of the crisp air and inhaled the early November breeze. Elicia walked leaning on his chest.

"Your heart is ticking like a bomb. Let's sit down over here."

He felt it, too, the quickening of his heart, the shortness of breath, but it was like a gift he didn't want to give back. The opportunity to walk, to move, to get out of that stagnant space was one he wanted to take full advantage of.

"Over here." They moved to the edge of the pier and sat with their legs hanging over the edge.

Dell closed his eyes, listening to the seagulls overhead, the movement of the water crashing underneath. A blinding flash moved underneath his lids. "One minute it's a whole heap of knowledge and the next good loving."

"What?" Elicia lifted her face to meet his. "What were you talking about?"

"I don't know. Just a flash."

"Maybe you were telling me how you couldn't live without me." She pushed her head close to his, then turned his face to kiss her.

He felt it again. He opened his eyes. "I know who she is. I remember Leah."

It came back to him, the first time he saw Leah Willow. She was walking on campus. Her hair trailed behind her, bouncing with her every step. That was the first thing he'd noticed about her, her shoulder-length hair. It was a strange burgundy color, almost like raspberry-flavored sorbet. He hadn't wanted to stare. He was with someone else at the time, Glory somebody. They were drinking coffee sitting outside in the plastic chairs. He remembered how hurt Glory was when Dell couldn't take his eyes off the raspberry-haired girl with the half-moon eyes.

"I'm over here," she said while socking him in the arm. "You need to get over it and quick. She's only into white guys."

All the more of a challenge, he'd thought. Yet it turned out to be no competition at all. Leah had fallen straight into his arms, and all he had to do was ask. In the beginning, Dell felt like a rat in an experiment. He thought she only wanted to be with him to squelch an old curiosity that had never been satisfied. Her eagerness almost frightened him. He began to question what she really saw in him.

"You're beautiful," was her response. "I know that I'm going to spend the rest of my life loving you, I only wish you hadn't taken so long to find me." She rolled over and went to sleep in his arms. He stopped asking. He wanted to protect her, provide for her, give anything in the world he could, from that day on. He remembered the day they found out she was pregnant with their daughter.

Dell was twenty-one, lying beside the woman he loved. Their heads facing each other, sharing one pillow. "All I've ever wanted was to have a family of my own. I wanted to prove that it wasn't so hard, that a real man could take care of his family."

The two of them rolled around in the bed tangled in sheets, half wrestling, half making love.

"Is that all you want me for, to hatch out a few baby chicks so you can prove your manhood?"

"Maybe. Too late now, little girl, 'cause you're having my baby." Dell pressed his face into hers, almost cutting off her oxygen.

She kissed him back, struggling to get on top. She pushed his hands back near his ears. "All I've ever wanted was to have a family to prove I could keep it together. So you know the only way you're getting away from me is by stretcher, 'cause you won't be walking."

For hours they played tit for tat in between the love play. She should have been studying for finals, and he should have been at a practice game, but they couldn't contain their wonderment when they'd received the results of Leah's pregnancy test earlier that day.

She still had one year left to finish school, and he had no definite prospects for his baseball career, a few minor league teams interested, but no one making any promises. They were both ecstatic to learn they were going to be parents. Unlike the others who found themselves in the same boat at the University Health Center, lapsing into fits of tears or silent devastation, Leah boastfully signed the acknowledgment form of her test results with her left hand sprawled across the page. She wanted the student nurse to see her ring, to know she was engaged. This wasn't a one-night stand or the result of too much alcohol at a frat party. She was part of a family that was about to take shape.

Dell stood outside the hardly private curtain while the nurse gave the mandatory options package describing the safety of an abortion, and the unique joy of creating a life for an adoption. Leah took the blue folder and whispered a no, thank-you to the nurse, who offered a shoulder to cry on—momentarily, of course, there were other students waiting. Leah stepped from behind the curtain and squealed while jumping into Dell's waiting arms. The nurse stood dumbfounded, watching as the young Black couple swirled in a full circle, kissing each other as if they had won the lottery.

They couldn't wait to get to their little love nest where they celebrated with nonstop love-making. He wrestled her back down underneath him. He licked her warm belly, stopping to suck in spots and leaving raised red marks. He worked his mouth down and in between her legs, still sucking, marking his territory. "I want to get married now, this summer," he said while crawling his way back to her face. "Let's do it after finals, the day after." His square jaw tightened with determination. "I don't want to wait." He followed up with nuzzling kisses between her neck and shoulder. "Tell me you want me, baby, forever, like I want you."

"I want you." Her face tilted up with determination. "I can't live without you."

"All right then, let's do this." His hand stroked her hair, then moved down the side of her face.

They were a family, and nothing could ever change that.

"Dell, we're here."

He awoke to Elicia shaking him gently on the shoulder. The beautiful image of Leah faded like a floating cloud. He was now sitting in the darkness of Elicia's garage. They were both still buckled into the seatbelts of her car. The garage was warm and stuffy, but neither one of them moved, just sat, staring at the unnamed boxes stacked rail high, the chest that was big enough to store a body. Skis, boots, and poles hanging against the wall.

"I don't know anything about you, do you realize that?" He turned to her. "That doesn't bother you?"

"Does it bother you?" Elicia reached out for his hand. He balled his fist.

"Very much so. This whole thing bothers me. Not knowing my own mind bothers me very much."

"It's coming back, right? Little bits at a time. That's good. You need to take it slow. I want you to stay with me, you don't have to rush."

"Why do you keep saying that? I don't have to rush. Why? Nothing to rush to? My kids hate me, my marriage is over... so nothing to work myself up over?"

Her mouth hung in an angle, "Your kids don't hate you."

"But my marriage is over? You left that part out."

She twisted her body slightly to get his full attention. "I didn't want to tell you because I thought it would just make you rush over there, this territorial thing you men have, but yes, there's no need to rush back because—"

He felt the fist in his stomach before she said it. The air leaving his body.

"She's with someone, a man who makes her happy."

He thought of the possibility that Elicia was lying. She'd lied before, even if it was by omission.

"Who is he?" His mouth was dry, cakey with fear.

"You might know him if you saw him."

"How long? I mean, before... were they together before all this happened?"

"I don't know. She loves him, though. I know that much."

"Who is he?"

"His name probably wouldn't mean anything to you right now, but you'll know him when you see him, I'm sure of that. He's been her saving grace while you've been gone. She says he makes her feel alive again."

"Well, of course. The way you tell it, why shouldn't she be? An ex-athlete who tried to off himself, strung out on painkillers, running around slapping her; well, damn right she's seeing someone." He got out and slammed the car door. Elicia stayed behind; he looked back at her and figured she was next. She'd be the next person to throw in the towel.

chapter 32

LOPEZ WASN'T THE SUPERSTITIOUS TYPE. He didn't walk around ladders or skip over cracks, but this morning when he'd elbowed the mirror in the bathroom, trying to get the seal off a bottle of Excedrin, he felt like he was in store for seven years, maybe more, of bad luck.

He picked up all the glass and swept the smaller pieces into the dustpan. It was bad enough he had to deal with the invisible Dell Fletcher, but now there was another threat, Squire, the friend of the family. He wanted to shove those glasses up his long nose. Who the hell did he think he was, looking down on him? He felt it, first the question marks, then the "not a chance" assumption. He felt like backing his car into the grill of his Mercedes. Another dark-colored Mercedes. Maybe Squire had picked up Dell Fletcher from that lonely street corner and killed him, got rid of the competition.

He couldn't sleep all night worrying about Squire Delvicio. He'd driven by Leah's house and watched the car still parked there until way past midnight. Even after his shift, he'd sat outside, waiting for him to leave. He finally had to check in, post his reports. There was a possibility that Squire had spent the entire night there. His head was pounding, a splitting headache that wouldn't go away. He knew it wouldn't stop hurting until he got to the bottom of this.

Leah wasn't answering her phone as usual. He had no choice but to make a personal wakeup call; Winding Wind Road would be his first stop.

Lopez pulled into the curved driveway behind a souped-up VW that was headed out into the street. He didn't have to guess that it was Kayla and her boyfriend. The foolish mistakes girls make and continue to make all their lives. Where did she think that little geek could take her in this world? Absolutely nowhere, no farther than around the block as he'd probably done today. His foot pressed hard on the gas pedal. The surge of rage fueling his foot sent his patrol car slamming into the petite frame of the flawlessly painted chariot of sin. Both their heads jerked back. The VW pulled over. He could see the driver checking his passenger before turning to get out of the car. *Yeah, come to me you little piss ant.* Lopez got out of the car and stood, leaning against his hood.

The piss ant was marching toward him, screaming, or more to the point, whining. "What the hell are you doing? You're going to pay for that. Look what you did to my car."

Kayla got out and trailed behind Virgil. "Angel, what'd you do?" Lopez kept his dark Ray·Bans covering his eyes. She was better off not seeing his eyes. It would scare her.

"It's a little early to be out of school, isn't it?" he asked, ignoring the large gash where his car had penetrated the chrome bumper of the VW.

"Why did you run into us? Oh my God, look at his car."

He peered around their bodies, as if to really assess the damage. "Did I do that?" An innocent upside-down smile appeared on his face.

"What the hell do you mean, did you do it? You know damn well you did it," Virgil yelled.

"Accidents happen. As for you," he turned to Kayla, "I believe you're supposed to be in school." He looked at his watch. "Am I mistaken?"

"No, you're not mistaken. I needed to come home and change my clothes. Virgil said he would bring me. What's wrong with that?"

"Not a thing. He's a regular Boy Scout. Is your mother in there?"

"No." Kayla answered before she thought about the repercussions. She'd already been warned, at least it felt like a warning, a threat.

Lopez looked at the boy with a new repulsion.

"You don't know me. You don't know shit about me. Kayla is my girl. I wouldn't disrespect her like that."

"Yeah, I know. I'm real grateful."

"What the hell you got to be grateful about? You ain't her daddy. You ain't shit."

Kayla grabbed the arm that was pointing into Lopez's face. "Stop it, Virgil. Stop screaming."

"Why is he acting like he got some damn rights? Why is he trippin'?"

"He's like our... he is our..." She didn't know how to explain. He was important, but she didn't know how it had come to be. She sucked on the inside of her cheek, biting down too hard. She let out an exasperating squeal. "Just forget it. Let's go."

"Nah, fuck that. He's paying for my car."

"You want to keep your voice down. This is a private neighborhood. I don't want to have to arrest you for disturbing the peace."

"This is my neighborhood." Virgil slapped his chest with both hands.

"You mean a tough guy like you lives up here in this big beautiful hood? Well, excuse me. I assumed you were from the lower east side, but I see you're just another white boy who's been hanging out in front of MTV raps too long."

A sound escaped Kayla like she'd been socked in the gut.

"Fuck you, you don't know me," Virgil said, brushing the insult off his chest.

Lopez pulled his sunglasses off. The piss ant's ranting had sprayed on his dark lenses. He pulled up a part of the kid's T-shirt and began wiping them off.

"Let go of my shit." The swing toward Lopez's face was exactly what he'd been hoping for. He dodged the strike and twisted Virgil's bony arm around until it was pinned against his back.

"Get in my car, Kayla."

She stood paralyzed by the events that were taking place right before her. "Let him go, Angel. Please, he's my friend."

"Your friend needs to learn some manners. Disrespecting an officer is not showing good manners. I'll drive you back to school as soon as we finish having our conversation." He motioned his head toward the cruiser. "Go have a seat, everything will be fine." She stood still. "If you don't get in the car, Kayla, our friend here might lose his arm."

She hesitantly stepped in the direction of the waiting cruiser.

"As for you, the next time I see you anywhere near her, I'll rip these scarecrow arms off your body and you'll be playing basketball with your head and shoulders. Do I make myself clear?"

"Get off me. Let me go."

The grip tightened. Lopez pushed up until he could feel the resistance of his arm pulling away from his shoulder.

"Oh God... let me go." The moan of pain sputtering from the little piss ant stretched past the neighboring trees. The wail sent Kayla running back toward the scene.

"Let him go, Angel," she screamed in his ear. "Let him go." She dug her nails into his arm.

He let the boy go and watched him fall to the ground. Kayla scrunched down next to him, still screaming. Lopez leaned down to pull her up.

She slapped at his hand. "Leave us alone. You're crazy."

"Kayla, get into the car."

"No!"

"I'm not going to ask you again. You either get in, or get dragged in."

She twisted her mouth and narrowed her eyes in threatening slits. She growled before stomping off in the direction of the cruiser. He followed closely behind, opening the back door for her. He helped her along when she stopped to look back.

"I can't believe you did this, I can't." She gave her twisted-up boyfriend one last look as he sat in the middle of the street on the hot pavement.

Lopez got in and eyeballed her in the rearview mirror. "You know what I can't believe? I can't believe you'd let some little pecker get the best of you. You're still a child, and he's nothing but a child. Two children trying to rub sticky bottoms. It's sickening." He turned the car around and began the drive back to the school.

"I told you we weren't doing anything. I had to come home and change my clothes. What business is it of yours?" she finally squealed out. "You're not my father, you're nobody!"

Angel took advantage of the stoplight and turned his body around to face her. "So you're trying to tell me he didn't try anything... nothing?"

She rolled her eyes and shifted her head around on her neck like a chicken. Indignant.

He shook his head in disgust. "I don't have to be your father to care what happens to you. Next time you have a problem, call me." He held the small black plastic pager so she could see it. "This is for you and your family, so I'll always be there for you. I know you have the number, I made sure. I gave your mom cards with all the information you need to find me for anything, no matter how big or small." He watched her squirm uncomfortably in the back seat. "Kayla." She ignored him. "Kayla."

"What?"

"Next time, call."

"All right!" She tried to let herself out of the car when they arrived at the high school but found no latches to pull. "Can I go now?" She fumbled with the handle.

He stepped out and opened the backseat door for her. A few students started whistling and chortling. Being escorted to campus by a cop always brought excitement. Someone was being busted.

"Thanks a lot. You've really topped off a stupendous day." Her almond-shaped eyes fought back tears of embarrassment. She swung her body, causing her thick ponytail of braids to lasso around, barely grazing his face.

"You're welcome, anytime." He gave her a military salute and waited patiently leaning against his car until she was planted firmly on the campus grounds.

Where was a daddy when you needed him?

It was a full-time job and it was getting better all the time.

It seemed oddly self-prophetic that he was now in Dell Fletcher's shoes, so to speak. Lopez felt he was worthy of the job. It was bestowed on him as a blessing, a secret fate that he deserved. If he could only stop asking himself "why." He pondered the thought that maybe it wasn't just his gift, that possibly he was the gift to Josh, Kayla, and, of course, Leah. Dell was never home, anyway, not really. And when he was, he wasn't. That's what Josh said, "He seemed to never really be here even when he was." Then there was Kayla, a classic case of father-gone syndrome, looking for attention in every boy's eyes she came in contact with. So now, Lopez was filling the space that had been left empty and abandoned. He'd filled the boots quite nicely and he would not be removed. Not by anyone.

chapter 33

KAYLA WALKED THROUGH the front door and headed straight for the stairs. She could hear Josh and Angel in the kitchen while she took light steps, trying not to shift her bookbag, avoiding the nylon sound brushing against her back. She heard glimpses of Josh's conversation with the crazy man. They were like old chums sitting over a cup of tea. She locked her door and put the chair up against it. She looked out the window of her bedroom, nervous. Her mother would be pulling up at any minute like clockwork. Kayla planned to tell her everything.

Virgil may have been hurt badly. He hadn't come back to school. The worst part was feeling responsible.

She called from the pay phone in the cafeteria, but his mother said he was lying down, didn't want to be disturbed. She knew that trick well. He just didn't want to talk to her. She was the girl with the lunatic watchdog in her yard. Barking and growling at everyone who passed by. Why go with the threat of being bitten?

She picked up the phone and dialed again anyway. His mother answered on the first ring. She held it for a minute, reconsidering. "May I speak to Virgil?" It was as polite as she could possibly be. *Please.*

"Who's calling?"

"Kayla," she said with defeat, as if his mother didn't know. Any other time she would have tried to start an inane conversation ... how's school this year, how's your mother, how's your ... dad?

"He's still sleeping," Virgil's mother said. Kayla could just picture her with her overly madeup face, long spider eyelashes, and opalescent pink lipstick. Her bleach blonde hair in need of a trim. Virgil's mother was constantly being mistaken for the thigh master lady, the one who refused to age. But it wasn't her, she just liked to pretend she was.

"Well, can you tell me if he's all right, I mean..." She swallowed hard. A lump was interfering with her sentence. "I think he got hurt earlier today."

There was silence, then movement.

"Hello."

"Virgil." She took her fingers out of her mouth. "Are you all right?"

"I'm fine."

"I'm so sorry." Kayla breathed out in relief.

"I'm fine, all right. You don't need to call anymore."

She chose the collar of her shirt to gnaw on. The wet fabric a crumpled ball when she went to speak. "Virgil, please don't act this way. It's not my fault this guy is a lunatic. He's my mother's creation, not mine. You can't blame me."

More silence. The phone moved around a bit. She was afraid he was going to hang up on her.

"I know it's not your fault, I just don't think it's a good idea for us to hang out."

She put the shirt collar back in her mouth. Virgil was the only real friend she had. Regardless of how bad she treated him, he was still her best friend. When they were little, he used to pull her around in his red wagon. She had weighed more than he did, but he still pulled. It hadn't mattered that he was white and she Black. She didn't know that it presented a problem until she started high school. The sometimes dirty looks that she'd get from the small crowd of Black girls that gathered in the lunch area and never left room for her to sit. She didn't need them anyway, she had Virgil. But now she couldn't believe he was turning his back on her.

"I'll see you at school...but..."

"But nothing. You're a coward. Don't put yourself out!" She slammed the phone down in his ear.

Angel the fiend needed to be removed, destroyed. She felt her nails biting into his eyelids, scratching. She felt her knee raising to meet his groin with one harsh thrust. If he ever came near her again, she'd pull his hair and scratch his eyes out.

Leah saw the police car and slowed down. The same hollow feeling spread throughout her body. She thought about how she'd spent the day sitting with Kay, Dell's mother. Kay had always treated Leah like her very own daughter, more so than her own mother did. Mothering wasn't supposed to end because a young woman turned into an adult, had her own children, her own family. It changed, but it wasn't supposed to end. Leah and Kay at times forgot that they were in-laws instead of the real thing. Leah's own mother had made it clear she didn't approve of her marriage to Dell. She was pregnant at the time, four months. Her mother refused to come to their justice-of-the-peace wedding. She eventually came around, but not before explaining her fear... a Black man will use you, her mother had whispered during their good-bye hug. "If you allow yourself to be used, it doesn't matter who it is." Leah had responded face on, closing the door quietly while staring at her mother's concerned eyes. It took another year after that for them to be on speaking terms, but their relationship remained strained. Too many I-told-you-so's looming in their conversations.

The half-smile always appeared when Kay looked up and saw Leah entering her small room in the Sunburst Home. The stroke had left one side of her face numb and slack. But it didn't stop her from smiling. Her head was raised on a starch white pillow, the sheet and blanket neatly folded across her chest. Leah picked up the book that she had been reading to her over the last few days. "Now where did we leave off?" She opened it and flipped to the bent corner. She knew Kay wouldn't answer her question. Talking was one of the motor skills that had been impaired. But communication was so much more than words.

"Here we are." Leah took a deep breath before she started reading. *"Her grandmother told her, 'if a man is going to lick your pot, he'd better do it right and thorough, clean and good, so there were no scraps or crumbs to attract a stray dog—'cause stray dogs know where to look for what was left behind and forgotten. Stray dogs knew how to get to the bottom of a pot, polish it clean with its tongue so you'd know undeniably that he'd been there.'"*

Leah looked toward the door, then to Kay, feeling slightly embarrassed by what she'd just read out loud. A rush of heat in her cheeks. She turned back to the book after seeing the half-smile on Kay's face, then steadied the book in her nimble fingers.

"So that would make it rightly true that she'd done nothing wrong. Lucas Breadlow coming her way had nothing to do with what she'd done or didn't do. Everything to do with what her husband had not. He left the pot out . . . forgotten and overlooked . . ."

Leah stopped again to look at Kay. Her eyes stared straight up at the ceiling. Leah's voice went lower, deeper into the tone that this woman, the one that suddenly looked like herself, might have used, *"Lucas Breadlow was her stray dog. He'd appeared on her doorstep, overalls strapped around his bare chest, arms gleaming from the sweat of his work. He'd sniffed his way right to her doorstep, asking for a glass of water, even though what he'd really come for were the scraps. The pieces of her womanhood that had gone untouched and unsatisfied. The crumbs of her importance and self-liking. The bits of her heart that were left to fester under the harsh sunlight. The scent of her need, loud and strong, had brought that man to her door. And she'd let him in. Without a second thought she opened the screen, pushed wide enough for him to fit through. He smelled like the brine used to clean off the metal plates. She gave him the water, she watched him drink it down in two hefty swallows. He turned to her. When she reached for the empty glass he took her hand and kissed it sweetly. 'I'm married,' she told him while he tasted the tips of her fingers. He pulled her close and whispered into her face, 'Indeed you are.'"* Leah closed the book. She rose up and kissed Kay on her forehead. "I have to go. We'll finish this tomorrow."

When she left Kay's side she took the book with her. She was determined to find out what became of them, Lucas Breadlow and the woman, *I'm a married woman . . . indeed you are.* She thought about those words. They turned in her head like rocks in a dryer, thumping loud with each tumble. Was that what made her desirable, the fact that she was a married woman?

Annoyed now, as she sat in the driveway, unable to pull in, his car constantly in the way. She got out and slammed her door in frustration. She listened to her high heels clack against the pebbled concrete driveway. Her heels were being ruined, scratching against the jagged pavement. If she'd taken a moment to really assess, she'd know that not being able to park in the garage wasn't the true issue. A symptom, maybe, but not the problem. The truth was, she was growing more irritated by the day. Angel's being here made her feel all the more foul. She'd made the decision to never be alone with him, to keep her distance, but he was like water, seeping underneath cracks, spilling over walls. Still too close.

"Hey, I'm home." She called out to the air to get a roundup. She closed the door and waited for the reply.

"We're in here, Mom," Josh called from the kitchen.

She knew the "we" was he and Angel. Josh had reached the point of actually expecting him to be waiting here after school.

"Okay, sweetie." Leah went up the stairs hurriedly before Angel could make a polite exit from Josh and start her way. She heard the loud belting of Christina Aguilera coming from Kayla's room. She knocked loud to overcompensate for the lyrics, "what a girl wants, what a girl needs . . ."

The door opened just when she was on her way to giving up and retreating to her own bedroom. "Kayla." Her face was in an unusual downcast, not her usual pouting, but a true sadness. "What happened?"

"Mom, come in here."

She was being dragged inside, her arm tightly gripped. That alone was enough to send her into alert mode. Her daughter inviting, no, begging, for her to come in. "What happened?" Leah automatically grabbed her, holding her shaking body. Rhythmic gasps, more tears. "Kayla, tell me, right now, what happened."

Her heart was sick from what she'd just been told. Heat and fire burning in her eyes, ready to lash out, Leah tried to calm down before she hit the arched kitchen entry. Angel was sitting at the table with Josh, relaxed, feet splayed in front of him as if he belonged nowhere else.

"Angel, can I talk to you for a minute?" She turned around and headed for the front door. He'd know to follow. She couldn't do this in front of Josh. Angel had become his friend, his hero, not the best replacement for the void in his life, but a close runnerup.

She counted, she prayed, she paced in a circle while he took his time coming, proof that he knew what this was about. He stepped out the front door, the picture of civility, the black uniform smooth over his firm chest and wide shoulders, his clean-cut appearance, all a lie. She wanted to slap him. One step closer.

"Leave and don't come back."

"What?" He leaned in as if he didn't understand, couldn't quite make out her words.

"You..." Leah swallowed the cloud swelling under her tongue. She would not cry. She was angry, she would not cry. "You bastard!"

He caught her hand in midswing. He held it. "What's going on?" She swung with the loose arm. He grabbed that one as well. "Wait a minute..."

"You tried to kiss her." She said it fast before another rumbling cloud came. His insistence of ignorance only infuriated her more. "Kayla. You tried to kiss her!"

He let go of her arms, letting them fall. He backed away. "I what?" He tried to get direct eye contact, "Leah, you believe that?"

"Just go. Something happened, I don't know what. What I do know is that she's scared to death of you." Her heart was racing, her mouth and tongue coated with the metallic taste of loathing.

"Leah, let me explain."

The wave of repulsion, an undeniable nausea crept over her. "I can't do this right now. I have a daughter up there who's shaking out of her skin." She held her stomach, the sinking feeling was real. "She's my first concern. I don't have time for you to clear your conscience." She left him standing in a pool of quicksand, sinking deeper into his shame as she walked away.

Josh heard their conversation, every word. He wasn't a baby, it's not like he was going to stay put in his highchair playing with blocks while the adults went outside for a secret conversation. He heard everything that was said. He was up the stairs and knocking on Kayla's door before he realized his body had moved. The music was loud, too loud to hear him yelling her name. He shook the doorknob and banged hard. If his father were here—

He hit the door again; the music shut off, then the door opened. His mind was spiraling—if his father were here, he'd go down and beat the crap out of Angel, he'd use his fist, a bat, anything.

He saw her tired eyes. His mouth wouldn't speak. Kayla hugged him and for the first time in years, he hugged her back.

"Is it true?"

"Don't worry about it, Josh. There's nothing you can do. Mom's going to handle him. He's done, finito."

Before he knew it, an emptiness had fallen on their embrace. She left him standing while she hurried to the window. "We don't have to worry about him anymore."

Josh was still confused, still lost in his own imagination. Had Angel come up here when he wasn't looking? Thrown his sister on the bed and tried to tear off her clothes like he'd seen in *The Player's Club,* a movie

Elliot's dad had left in the VCR. It was vivid, he could see it happening right before him. Angel. Kayla. He shook his head, no. It was still too hard to believe, even if he could see it, imagine it to life.

None of this was happening. "What'd he do to you?"

She kept her face in the window, one knee propped up on the bed for better balance. She couldn't hear him.

The number 64 on the hood of the police car rolling down the driveway brought a bright smile to Kayla's face. Good-bye, she thought to herself.

"Kayla."

She turned around, replacing her smile with something more in line with the misery she should've been feeling. Her mother's arms were extended. Another hug; she didn't know if she was going to be able to stomach the sympathy.

"Josh, come here." Her mother lifted her arm to hold both of them at the same time. "You guys know you can come to me with anything. I'm so sorry if I wasn't there for you. I've been so busy walking around in my problems that I ignored you guys. I love you both so much." She squeezed them together.

Kayla and her mother were the same height; when did that happen? She let her head hang over the edge of her mother's shoulder while she stared up at the poster of her father. Handsome, so strong. She wished this nightmare could end. She closed her eyes and felt Josh hiccup and sputter.

"Josh, no, don't cry." Kayla didn't want to fathom the possibility that he was crying over Angel being gone.

"I should have protected you. It's all my fault. I wanted him to stay around." He muttered over gulps of air. "I didn't know he was gonna—"

"You are not responsible for another person's actions." Their mother bent over to eye Josh directly. Her concentrated stare made him cry even more. She held him. "It's not your fault."

Absolutely not. Mom's the one who wanted him around. That's what she wanted to tell him. Don't you dare feel guilty, sad, or lost. We've just won the war. Kayla rubbed his shoulders, trying to soothe and calm him down.

Her mother initiated another group hug. For a minute, Kayla pondered the thought of confessing, if for no other reason than to cease and desist with the lovefest. Once again, she caught the eyes of her father, the steel determination, the will power and the strength. Angel was no replacement and never would be.

That too could've been her problem; that's the only way she could see her father, nothing less. Her hero, the man tall as a mountain who would let her swing on his steady flexed arm. The horseyback rides that carried her from room to room and deposited her safely under the blankets. The wonderment on his face when she could read through an entire book without pictures. The mornings she and her father would wake up before her mother and Josh, who was still a curlytoed baby, and sneak off to the swap meet to look through the junk being sold for one dollar. It wasn't the salvage shopping that excited her; it was the trip to Tommy's Burger Stand afterward. He'd park his car and they'd keep the radio on and listen to the Temptations sing on his tape player. He said they were oldies but goodies, some even older than him. His favorite was *Smiling Faces;* the music would make his head bop while he patted the top of his thigh. *Beware of the pat on the back... it just might hold ya back.* Kayla knew that song, every word, especially the chorus. She kept the tape in her antiquated Walkman. Someone might think she was batty if they knew what she listened to when she was doing her laps before cheerleading practice.

The other part, the bad part, she wanted to stay neatly blocked off. When she was too big to be picked up, too old to be tucked into bed, too mature to want to hang out at the swap meet and stop for greasy burgers and root-beer floats. Too tall to swing on his arm. She buried it in a square box that she didn't dare open, not even for a peek. She preferred to keep things as they were. But every now and then, something would slip out of the box, through no fault of her own. The realization that her father had not hugged her since she was ten, maybe nine. That his wonderment with her ability to read and write had died right along with checking if she'd lost any new teeth while he was gone on the road.

Kayla pulled out of the entwined group and sat on the edge of her bed. "I think I want to lie down for a while, Mom." She was genuinely exhausted. There was no faking this one. She stuffed the pillow under her head, closing her eyes. She felt a kiss on her forehead, a smoothing hand against her hair. A hollow feeling swelled through her stomach, dark and cold. With all that she'd accomplished, getting rid of Angel, she still felt empty and dissatisfied. For some reason, it still wasn't enough. When would it ever be?

She drifted into a peaceful sleep where she was light and warm. She was happy in this dream, full of love. The open field, the green grass, it must've been a park of some kind. Sloping slightly into the calm thin stream of water. Her father stood on the other side, smiling. He was proud of her, he loved her for all that she was. Tell me again, Daddy. "Smart, creative, pretty as sunshine." She wanted to get to him, she stepped into the stream. Tell me again, I can't hear you. Her heart started pattering, the water was cold. The stream was widening. He started walking away, into the trees set back behind him. Both feet, she was standing while the stream turned colder, the water rose higher. Around her knees, then to her thighs. When she tried to go to him, the water pulled at her in the opposite direction. She fought to get across, she screamed his name, and he simply kept walking. She was drowning, screaming for help.

"Kayla." There was an arm trying to save her.

She woke up still feeling the water in her nose and lungs, realizing that she was drowning in her own salty tears.

Her mother held her, squeezed her while she let it all out. Kayla felt her mother hold her even tighter when she let the truth fall from her lips. Angel hadn't touched her, she'd made it up.

"Tell Josh I'm sorry for lying, okay?" she whispered before falling back to sleep.

• • •

The steering wheel couldn't take one more blow. He'd slapped, shook, pulled. A rage covered his face like a steaming towel. It didn't make any sense. She knew how he felt about her, about Josh. How could she believe that? Why would he destroy everything, all for nothing? The arrows were pointing to "any excuse would do." She wanted him gone. There was no way she could believe that about him. If she thought an ounce of it was true, she would have called the police or, worse, pulled out his gun and shot him right between the eyes.

He wasn't some savage pervert who would feel up a child. A sicko. He'd stick a gun in his own mouth before he stooped that low. Leah knew it, as well. She took the easy way out. Simple as that, she saw an opportunity and she took it.

Lopez knew what this was about. Squire Delvicio. 8859 Rossmore Street. Dark-blue Mercedes, license number 2234V1. Birthdate April 12, 1960. He hit the steering wheel again. He'd memorized it the night he'd first met him. The way the two of them stood there, as if he were the outsider. The information popped up on his computer screen: He had no record, not so much as a parking ticket. Mr. Perfect. "A production deal," he mocked in Leah's voice, "for me?" There wasn't much he could do on any level, wasn't much he could give. What did he have to offer? Himself, and that was plenty . . . until Squire showed up.

Leah was embarrassed. Lopez could see it all over her face, her movement. He'd thought she was deeper than that, grounded and real. But even she had her weakness. Respect, which had little to do with money and power. Leah needed to be revered. How could she be dignified with the patrol officer slash handyman? The light of judgment had shone on her, dead in the face, and she couldn't take it.

He hit the steering wheel again. He thought she was stronger than the influence that her snobby friends would have over her. "This is my friend, Squire." He rolled her words over and over in his head. First Elicia, now Squire. Any excuse would do. She thought she was too damned good for him. He hadn't expected this turn of events. Plans change. It was necessary to deal with the bumps in the road. Sometimes, they were too big to simply go over. Sometimes they had to be removed.

chapter 34

WAKING UP TO KISSES on his neck and chest, he opened his eyes truly expecting to see Leah. So many dreams (or were they memories?) one after the other, it felt like a constant video running through his head. He sat up in bed, grateful that it had been a true sleep, not drug-induced, not hallucinations. Real memories of his wife, his family.

Elicia leaned over and kissed him again, this time deeply in his mouth. Dell knew she was waiting for him to feel it, to regain what he felt for her at one time. She wanted him to make love to her. He had no excuse now, not really. His body didn't ache like it did when he'd first come under her care. No more strained muscles and bruised knots. Fully healed from whatever put him in this strange predicament.

She pushed herself on top of him. He rolled her to the other side of the bed, not missing a kiss. He felt the emotion stirring. His body was responding to her touch. He pressed her lips harder into hers, causing the pressure from his teeth to cut into the tender skin of her underlip, then pulled away. He held her face so she would listen. "I can't stay here."

"Dell."

"No, listen. I appreciate all you've done, I can't begin to thank you." He couldn't look when he said it, "... but I know I'm supposed to be home with my family. I know what you've told me, but I have to see for myself. There's something there, unfinished. I know it. I can feel it." He stood up, finding the robe on the edge of the bed. He slipped it on. She stood up next to him and tied it for him.

"What are you going to tell her? Where have you been all this time? You have to realize that what the two of you had is over, Dell. She's going to find out about us the minute you step back into her life."

She stood in front of him, her sultry lashes low, then looked up to let him know she wasn't through. "I assume the first order of business would be honesty, telling her where you've been. With who."

"What is there to tell? I don't remember anything about *us*. You keep saying that we had a relationship. I don't remember, so for me there's nothing to tell."

"But there's something to tell now." She reached out and grabbed his hand, placing it on her face. He couldn't be honest and tell her that he felt nothing when he looked into her soft brown eyes, saw nothing. She was beautiful, obviously successful and intelligent. She was a catch for any man, but not for him. The void was large between them. Growing larger by the day, as much as he'd tried.

"I have to see my kids," he almost whined. "At least, I have to go there and see my kids. They need to know I'm here. That I didn't fall off the face of the earth. This isn't about you and me, or even Leah."

She walked around him in a circle, something she did a lot, he noticed, when she was contemplating. As if his life were in her hands. As if her decision were all that mattered. He felt her hand on his shoulder.

Elicia pulled her silk top over her head. Her tangerine-colored bra pushed up the natural swell of her breasts. She fingered the edges of the lace against her chest. "Try to remember." She pushed her breasts together, then slid her hands down the sides of her waist. She began opening the zipper on her own jeans; they fell to her feet. She kicked them to the side. "I can make you remember me, loving me." The tangerine panties matched the bra. Delicate flowered lace etched her pubic line. Bright orange against her butter-rum skin, a perfect combination.

She pulled his face into her chest. The perfume filled his senses. Elicia's scent, she smelled good. The firmness of her chest, his face between her breasts, his hands on her waist. She knew she had something to work with, at least a small ember. She kissed the top of his head, lingering in his full head of hair. Her fingers massaging the skin underneath, pushing his head down farther into the fullness of her chest.

He lifted his head to meet her eyes. There wasn't a lot he could say that would change her mind. She was determined. He stepped back, turning away from her tempting body.

"Dell, please."

He walked away, meandering into a guest room down the hall from the one they'd shared, and locked the door behind him. He crawled into the bed, shivering underneath the comforter. God, did she spray her scent everywhere? He threw the pillow against the wall and curled himself in a ball.

Was he friend or foe? The words "you'll know him when you see him" pushed past his throat. But would he? His memory was coming back in such small pieces. Tiny crumbs of a much bigger pie. Elicia wouldn't tell him who the other man in Leah's life was, not even a hint. She wanted him to be tormented by the thought, and he was. The first name that came to mind was Gervis, his agent and, when-things-were-going-great, friend. Gervis always had a smile and kiss for Leah when he came in contact, whether it'd been two days or two months since he'd last seen her. His shiny bald head always found its way into her hand. Then came Squire. Oh Squire. The man who should have been king. Leah didn't waste time clearing the air on that one; he had to deal with the "he'll always be my friend" speech. She wouldn't tolerate Dell trying to remove him from her life. He was invited over on holidays, barbecues, and kids' birthdays. He laughed and drank up their liquor and made sure Dell knew what a lucky man he was. When Leah came into the room, his eyes became floating marbles. He definitely still loved her, no doubt about that.

His mind swam with possibilities, at least the ones he could remember.

What about the people he forgot? A studly-do-right who was a part of Leah's past that he couldn't recall.

It didn't matter. He'd see for himself.

Dell checked the time again on the dashboard of Elicia's car. Once she'd fallen asleep, he got up and took her car keys. He'd have it back to her by noon. Probably before she awakened if all went well. He was anxious. He sat outside the house and waited. His throat was dry, his lips were beginning to crack. It had been a long night, and it was going to be an even longer day. As the sun ascended a chill crept over him. The day was rising.

The house looked serene. Nothing out of the ordinary. He noticed that the magnolia trees were beginning to bloom again as they had done just six months before. Had they forgotten, too? The honeysuckle was growing wild and trailing on the sidewalk.

A paper boy came riding up the street on his bicycle, armed with a white helmet and chin guard, pads on his knees and elbows. He must've had a few accidents in the past. As he approached, Dell scooted down in his seat for no real reason. When he went by, he sat back up. He heard sprinklers kick on, he checked the clock again on the dash. Six. That was late enough. Someone had to be up getting ready for school.

He got out of the car and trotted across the street. The gate squeaked when he barely touched it. He looked up and saw another entry that had no gate. He walked around and took nervous steps to the front door. The fear swept over him, kicking his heartbeat off rhythm. He pushed the doorbell and stood back.

For a minute he thought about running, darting around to the other side so when she looked out the window, he'd be gone. For a minute. Honey, I'm home. He took a deep breath and stood firm.

What's the worse that could happen?

Another man could answer his door.

He tried to breathe right, in-out, in-out.

The doorknob twisted then stopped, then twisted again and pulled open. It was Leah. Her soft voice cried out, strange, not how he'd heard on the phone, not how he remembered. Her mouth was moving, emitting a sound that didn't sound human.

The door was pushed to its widest. Leah ran out and jumped into Dell's arms. Her feet off the ground. He held her, spinning in a full circle. He could hear her now, understand what she was saying.

"JesusGodthankyou, JesusGodthankyou . . ."

He couldn't let go. He wasn't ever going to let go. She was happy to see him. It was nothing like Elicia had said, "You two fought all the time. She's in another relationship." He spun her around again, then put her down.

"Leah." he held her face in his hands and kissed her eyes, tasting her tears.

"I was so scared."

He held her tighter. "Where're the kids?"

She led him inside. "They're going to scream. Oh, my God. Dell, I prayed for you to come home. I'd never prayed before, Dell. Not like this . . . and then you're standing on this doorstep." She fell back into his chest. "Just like that, you're home."

He gently enfolded Leah in his arms, then suddenly lifted her away from him. Elicia's scent. He didn't want Leah to smell her, to inhale his betrayal. She looked up at him, her moist, low eyes.

"Where were you, Dell? I was so scared."

He let his hand slide across her cheek, tracing the fullness of her heart-shaped face; she looked different with short hair, softer, younger, like when they'd married. Avoiding her question, sidestepping it like it was a cobra ready to strike, he went around her and straight up the stairs. He turned left when he reached the top. Three steps, the door on the right. He tapped, double-tapped, single, double-tap. The door swung open. Josh jumped into his arms. He held the boy's head to his. "Look at you. Look at you."

Josh's tears were more than he could take. How was he going to break

Leah's heart without ripping everyone else's out, too? *Are you going to tell her about us?*

"Dad, where were you?"

Dell held him tight, his heart racing. He had to answer the question...it would come like forty days and forty nights of rain, nonstop, he'd have to answer the question.

He felt a tap on his back. "Daddy." When he turned around, Kayla was standing before him, but it felt like she was far away, a space between them, large and frightening, as if she were standing on the other side of a raging waterfall.

He had to reach out to pull her in. This hug lasted a lifetime, where had the time gone, what's twenty years between friends, ten between fathers and sons, five between a father and his daughter? He pressed his cheek into hers. He swayed her side to side while something poured out of her. A release flooding out and through to him. "Don't cry, baby. I'm home, now." He rocked her like she was only months old, when her entire body fit into the curve of his arm. "I'm home now, I'm never leaving you again."

chapter 35

HE'D TOSSED AND TURNED all night before finally giving up; rising out of the darkness of his bedroom at four in the morning, he paced around the house nude. He thought about calling Tanya but remembered the last phone conversation they'd had. She'd told him to go to hell. She wasn't going to be used while he obsessed over another woman. Like he'd known all along, he and Tanya were too much the same, she knew his thoughts, his actions. She could tell when his mind was inside of another woman even though it was she who sat on top of him. Tanya read his newfound need to simply hold her as a clear notification that it was someone else he envisioned in his arms. She didn't like that cuddly crap. She wanted to be sucked, penetrated, and fucked. A constant reply.

He opened the refrigerator door and pulled out a half-empty can of flat Coca-Cola. The sweet syrupy liquid felt good going down his throat. He put it back and grabbed the only other thing that was in his refrigerator, the white tulips still in their plastic wrap. He put them back gently, the smooth heads of the flowers heavy with all the responsibility beauty carried.

Lopez had bought them for Leah with a card, a long letter enclosed explaining the truth, denying Kayla's lies. He'd planned on leaving the tulips and card on her porch. But after the message she'd left, it didn't seem appropriate. He walked over and pushed the play button on his answering machine. He wanted to hear her voice again, even if she was saying what he didn't want to hear.

"Kayla cleared things up. I . . . we wanted to apologize for everything, she for lying and me for not hearing you out. But I still think it'd be a good idea if you didn't come around . . . at least for a while." Her voice drifted off, then came back with the final blow. "Please don't come around, Angel. I hope you understand."

He understood quite well.

More than anything, he wanted Leah to know that he understood what was going on. That she didn't have to feel ashamed of what she felt for him. He only needed a little more time. He knew Leah's type; she didn't play when it came to commitment. If he could make her feel it, know what she felt for him was real, not a rebound or feelings based on vulnerability. Make her know she had nothing to be ashamed of.

He pushed play again, deciphering her words. Looking for a hint of reconsideration. What kept popping in his head was Squire Delvicio.

Lopez kept thinking of the man's disapproving stare, his bewilderment and shock when he'd leaned over and kissed Leah on the cheek. It boiled down to that one moment when Leah felt it, too, the feeling of disgrace.

But it was Squire who'd made her feel that way, not him. It was his fault. And like all persons scorned, Lopez needed someone else to blame.

Lopez sat outside of the tall lean building, wondering why someone would want to live in anything higher than ten stories in earthquake country. The apartment building was old, bricks and mortar, but here in Beverly Hills he knew the rent was more than he made in a month. He watched a few people come in and out and thought about just sliding through the entrance and making life simple on himself. But security cameras were a real threat. His face would be caught on tape. Time of death coinciding with the time a Latino man, moderate build, walked in without a key or ringing the buzzer.

He'd seen people suspected and arrested with even less than that.

No, he'd wait for him. He knew what kind of car he drove, he knew what the bump in the road looked like, smelled like. How could he forget his smugness. Come on out, little chicky chicky. "This is my friend Squire."

chapter 36

DELL WOKE UP SOAKING WET, the rim of his T-shirt heavy around his neck. Leah and the kids were gone. He'd fallen asleep on the couch. He was still worried that Elicia would do something stupid. He'd called her and told her where she could pick up her car. He couldn't drive it back over. He simply waited until the celebratory mood dissipated. Their reunion made Josh miss the school bus and Kayla miss a ride with a friend. As soon as Leah pulled off with the kids, he drove the car two blocks over and parked it. He trotted back to the house and called Elicia. She nearly spat in his ear. He would see, she warned, the honeymoon wouldn't last long. "Have you met him yet?"

He knew who she was talking about, but he played dumb.

"He's not the type that's going to go away easily."

Dell hung up and sat on the couch like a man waiting for the lever of his execution to be flipped. He would die if he'd lost what he'd just rediscovered. This time he knew he would.

It wasn't like before, when it didn't matter. When nothing mattered. He remembered the first day when it seemed like his life had gone up in flames, at least the first flick of the match. Forty thousand and counting. The California Angels had never seen attendance of that magnitude. The people were packed into the seats with their perspiring skin gleaming against the sinfully hot July sun. It was worth it for them; many had not seen a live professional baseball game in their lifetime, or if they had, so many years had passed in between that it made it null and void.

The one thing they all had in common was their love for the "Roadrunner." It wasn't about the game of hitting the ball and running, the basic game of touch and go. The skills didn't matter, the stats, the score, they were all inconsequential. The crowd was there out of sheer admiration for the athlete who had revitalized a city, an entire state of millions, and had given them all something to cheer for. The nation knew his name, like a proud papa for his child, "that's my boy." Everyone laid claim to the Roadrunner. His life was theirs. He was everyone's boy. His triumphs were theirs. Each person felt a responsibility for him, a gladness, proud to be a part of something special.

Underneath his feet, he felt the tingling. The faint tickling started every time he was at bat, telling him it was time to run. He needed to run. Unlike most of his peers, he cared less about the hit, how far it went, how it registered in the log, base hit, homer. It was all about how far he could get. Shorter base hits brought more joy to him than a home run. There was no need to sprint for a home run. Anticlimactic. The power of the drawing sensation started in his feet and flexed through the raw muscle of his calves. In half-stance he was ready. He could feel the pressure of the quiet like a sack of concrete weighing on his shoulders. The field of silence was busted wide open with the crack of the bat to the speeding ball.

He sent the ball sailing into left field and shot out like a rocket. Rounding second base, a pain shot through his body like a bullet, brief and intense. For the first time, he was glad he had time to stop and assess. Stop and assess. Like a computer scanning for viruses or dilapidated files, his brain sent inspectors from his head to his toes. What is it? What was that? He shook it off, focusing back on the game.

Delahambro was up at bat. He'd send the Roadrunner home. He was the planned follow-up, a young Puerto Rican rookie scouted and recruited for a lousy $100,000 a year. It translated to a million where he came from.

Send me home, baby. Send me home.

Dell bounced, stretching his feet for the takeoff. Shit. The pain was a sword in his inner right thigh. He'd had muscles tighten up before, gripping spasms visibly the size of a football. This was different. This pain was deeper, somewhere untouchable deep through his groin. He squeezed his eyes shut momentarily. Focus. Let's go baby, send me home.

With the connecting sound of the bat to the flesh of the ball, Dell shot forward. He lunged, stopping in midstep. The fall landed him face first in the pebbled dirt. His first instinct was to get back up. He could make it. He could outrun anything these fools had to serve. With his body pressed in the ground, he rose up and was a cannonball once again.

The masked Napoleon stood over him with his arms outstretched. "You're out!"

Dell couldn't believe it. Six hands were reaching out for him to give him a boost up, but he was still unable to fathom what just happened. Even after the dust cleared, he wasn't sure what they were trying to tell him. He was out. Wait a minute, let's replay that scene. He blinked the sun out of his eye and grabbed a gloved hand.

"It's all right, man. Don't let it get you down." Thorsen slapped him on the butt. The guys all gave him inadequate high fives as he took his seat in the dugout.

"Can't win 'em all," Cedric Nunez chuckled through the wad of tobacco stuck in the corner of his cheek.

The Roadrunner could and had for some time won them all. Now he had to sit and listen to a jealous outdated loser tell him what his capabilities were. "Screw you, man."

"Hey man, I'm just trying to tell you, you can't stay on top forever. Everybody has a down day. Even the almighty Roadrunner."

Dell could feel the heat rising in his cheeks. He watched Nunez thrust the wad to the other side of his grinning face.

"Just let it go and accept it. Don't beat yourself up, you know what I'm saying." Nunez turned his attention back to the game, sending a brown package of spittle to the outside of the fenced-in dugout. Nunez never saw it coming. The slamming fist into his jaw sent the wad down his throat.

It took four guys to pull Dell off. He couldn't separate himself from the rage. It had devoured every rational thought. He couldn't see who he was reaching after. It didn't matter. The face sitting on the other side of the barricade of bodies belonged to insecurity and fear. It had no name. He charged again. The weight of the lockdown increased when more uniforms surrounded him. He felt a hand reach across his face, strong-arming him to stop moving and look straight ahead.

"Get a hold of yourself, Fletcher. Right here, right now." The manager of the team, Seldon Russo, spoke too close, sending a moist spray in his face. Russo's face was pitted deep burgandy, a stark contrast to his colorless crystal-ball eyes. His grip tightened, pulling Dell's face in closer to his.

Dell had no choice, every fiber of his limbs was held tight by the others. Unmovable. The team had attached themselves, drowning him in their musty, tobacco-filled air. The suffocating heat took over his face, neck, and down to his chest, choking him. "All right," he managed to whisper. "Let me go."

"Not until you calm down. Are you going to get it together, or do you want to start tasting the dirt on this concrete?"

Dell shook his head, no, like a wayward child. "I got it. I'm good, let me go."

The team leader gave an okay nod, and the hands and arms fell off of him like the tentacles of an octopus liberating its victim. The crowd pulled away, revealing the red-faced Nunez standing on the wood bleachers, still not comfortable with the release of his torturer. He swallowed hard before taking a hesitant step down to greet the Roadrunner's extended hand.

"I'm sorry, man." Dell pulled him into his grasp. "I lost it, man. No excuse."

Nunez gave him a conciliatory hug but remained silent, afraid his words, any words, could unleash the madness.

"All right guys, break it up. We got a game to win." Seldon Russo slapped his crew on the back one at a time as he sent them back on the field. It must've been the pressure, Russo whispered into his second-in-command's ear. "The weight of 200 million could crush any man."

That day was the beginning of the pain.

The doctor's words came out effortlessly, as if he'd said them five times a day, routinely breaking the news that he had a torn ACL. It was a bad tear but he still had a 50-50 chance of playing again.

As dull and lifeless as the words were, it was still as if they'd been flung at him like bricks. Dell's heart pumped fast, in his ears was a light buzz that became louder until he could no longer hear. He watched the doctor's thin lips moving. "I'm only thirty-five, I just signed a new contract to play five more years," Dell heard himself say. "Please," as if the doctor had the power to change time and space.

* * *

A force greater than himself led Lopez to Leah's door. He wouldn't tell her how he'd waited for Squire Delvicio, thinking of a thousand different ways to hurt him, how to inflict half the embarrassment and insult that he'd caused him. How sitting there for hours outside of that apartment building, his thoughts turned to melted wax, losing shape with the intensity of the heat his anger expelled. How eventually it came to him that if Leah was going to love him, it had to be against all odds and suppressors. The Squires and Elicias, the naysayers of the world, were never going to go away. Around every corner there'd be one more, and then another and another. If she was going to be with him, he couldn't be on constant guard, constantly challenging everyone who didn't agree.

He pressed on the bell and knocked all in the same second. He didn't know what he was going to say, not prepared for anything. He'd left the flowers at the apartment. The card, too. He looked at his watch and knocked again. Nothing, not a sound. The kids were in school, but Leah, where was she? He went around the side of the house. The gate was locked. His adrenaline was rising to a new level. He had to get it together, back it down a few notches. Jumping fences would scare the eyes out of her sockets. He went back around to the front door. The possibility that she was home and not answering the door grew large and painful in his gut. He knew she wanted to be with him, he felt it in her kiss, in her breath.

He knocked again, feeling a surge of power, a new strength and hope.

When the door swung open, he nearly lost his balance. He gasped, not out loud. His throat was trying to close up on him. Wait a minute. Think. The blood was racing through his heart, pumping, overflowing, in survival-of-the-fittest mode. Wait a minute. Lopez geared up for the hands that would reach out to shake him for redemption, the punch, the slap, the yelling... you son of a bitch. But only one word fell like a pebble, insignificant, void of feeling.

"Yes?"

Yes? That's it. Lopez's mouth was stuck between open and closed.

Dell Fletcher asked again. "Yes?"

Lopez was speechless, trying to keep his expression from wandering into confusion. But his mind was racing. He observed the healed-over gash on the bridge of Dell Fletcher's nose. The blank stare in his eyes. His expression was weightless, as if Lopez was just another officer standing at his door. "I'm sorry to disturb you. Someone reported some suspicious activity in this area. Have you seen or heard anything unusual?" The words came out trite, without conviction.

"Not a thing."

His throat seized with the realization that the Roadrunner didn't remember him. He couldn't say one more word. He felt the needles pressing into his hands, the tingling rush. The need to squeeze something. He could do it. No, his car was parked right out front. He wouldn't get away with it.

"Okay, well, is there anything else?"

Lopez looked into the blank eyes, the dark skin taut. Healthy, well fed, well taken care of. Would Leah believe he just decided to disappear again? Walked off and left, this time for good? "Would you mind if I check out back?"

There was a hesitancy, he was thinking... was he remembering?

Lopez stayed put, his feet feeling like bricks. He didn't know what to do. This wasn't the reunion he pictured. His fingers tensed around the snap of his gun holster.

"It's that way." Dell Fletcher ushered him on like he was a deaf mute. Lopez watched the firm arm stick out threw the half open door, pointing past his face. He flashed to five different ways to break that arm. How he could leave him snapped like a pretzel.

"Around back, that's where you want to check?" Again, the patronizing tone.

"Yeah, be right there." Lopez turned and started walking. Between the tall eucalyptus trees that shrouded the side of the house, he stopped and grabbed his knees, hunched over. He needed a minute to think, gain his resolve. He couldn't take another step. The breath left his body. What was going to happen when Dell Fletcher regained his memory? He stood up and paced in a shaky circle. This man had the power to ruin his life. He'd go straight to his sergeant, recount the story, different from the one he'd given. This new story, the true story, would be enough to make him lose his job, his career. Enough to make him lose any chance he had with Leah. His turn with Leah.

He started walking again toward the gate. It was wide open. That meant the back door was probably unlocked. He could do it. Broad daylight. Dry leaves crunched underneath his feet. A car passed. A siren in the distance. Just like Andre, he could make him go away. Andre deserved everything he got. He'd beat on Maria, neglected his children, and brought drugs into his sister's home and life. When Lopez pulled him over, his eyes looked like white saucers, a haze of loathing, a hate of himself and anything good. He was high, drunk, and spaced out. He asked him for his license and registration, then listened to the obscenities drool from his thick tongue. Lopez responded with a fist across his face. Andre didn't know what hit him and never would.

Dell Fletcher was just as guilty as Andre. *He'd hit Leah,* swatted at her like she was a fly, only to silence her to his satisfaction. That was a crime, a moral sin.

But his car was out front. Someone would see him.

He stopped in his tracks and did an about-face.

Coward, pussy, wimp, the voices of Gino and Jose shouting in his head. He trotted back to his patrol car and started it up. The bumper scraped the bottom of the driveway when he raced out. He needed to talk to Leah first. He'd let her decide Dell Fletcher's fate.

There was only one way in and one way out. He figured she'd have to come his way eventually. He sat in his car, watching every dull-faced socialite drive by. Kids with too much of their parents' money driving sport utility vehicles that cost more than his yearly salary. He pointed the radar gun at them just to fuck with them. He had to look busy. But he was waiting.

And not a moment too soon. Leah's car was facing him at the stop sign. He got out and flagged her down. She slowed, rolling down her window.

"Angel." Her eyes blinked slowly.

"I need to talk to you." Lopez didn't tell her that she didn't have a choice in the matter. "Please."

She moved her car off to the side of the road. She unlocked the doors when she saw him moving to her passenger side.

He got in and noticed her face. "If you honestly don't want to see me, I'll get out of the car right now."

She put her head in her hands, sealing herself off from him.

"I miss you." He said it quietly, "Do you miss me, at all?"

She nodded her head up and down. Her eyes rose slowly, "But it doesn't matter now. Dell is back."

He tried to act surprised, deflated, running a hand through his thick dark curls. He turned to look out the window. He rested his forehead on his fist. "I guess you're real happy about that." His eyes misted, he pushed his thumb and forefinger to plug up the emotion. "When?"

"Today."

"Where was he?"

"He was…" She twisted the wedding ring around on her finger. "I'm not sure."

"He just dropped out of the sky and landed on your doorstep? That's it?" He faced her. "No explanation, nothing?"

"I told you about his addiction to the prescription drugs, the alcohol; well, he's better. You can see it in his eyes. I'm sure he was in a rehab center. He's different."

"Different? As in he doesn't plan on hitting you again anytime soon?"

"Don't do that."

"Don't do what, Leah? Tell you something that's going to bust up your fantasy?" The muscle of his jawbone twitched and tightened. "Did you let him..." His tone weighed down by the intensity of his fear. "Did you make love to him?"

"Angel. I have to go." She turned the ignition. She punched the gas pedal, the engine revved, but the car stayed put.

He slammed his fist into the car door, then pushed it open.

She jumped.

"Wait, no. I'm sorry. I didn't mean to scare you. Leah, come on." He pulled the door closed. "You know you can talk to me, I'm not going to judge you. If you feel like it's right, it's right. Enough said. I don't want this conversation to end like this. I'm your friend, Leah." He leaned closer to her. His voice in a cooled softness, "Know that you can call me, for anything. Whatever you need, I'll be there."

She put the car in drive.

"You know that, right? I'd do anything for you and Josh, even Kayla. I know why she was mad enough to lie. That's water under the bridge. Don't shut me out. Please, not like this."

"I have to go, Angel."

He leaned in closer. "Please... Leah." He said it slow. Her name on his lips a love potion, he'd seen it transform her before. He said it again, leaning, waiting for it to take effect.

She looked, checked her rearview mirror, then the sideview mirrors, before meeting his kiss halfway.

Her lips tasted like cinnamon, hot but sweet. His head swam.

"I have to go." She bit her bottom lip, then wiped the wetness from her mouth.

He got out and closed the car door. She sped away, leaving him standing on the side of the curb like it was trash day.

"I love you." He mouthed the words, just in case she looked back. Just in case it mattered.

"Baby?" Leah walked through the house. Her heart was still racing from the mixed emotions that she carried. *Lucas Breadlow.* No. Angel Lopez.

Dell was back, and that was the end of it. *Then why'd you kiss him?* She searched the entire downstairs, opening and closing doors. "Dell."

She'd finished the book. Lucas Breadlow had come to an untimely death at the hands of the woman's husband. *A stray dog sometimes has to be shot, put down to end his suffering and others.*

What if he found out? She stepped past the stair where Angel had pushed up her skirt, felt the intensity beating between her legs. Did she leave something behind, something that told Dell what had happened?

She headed to the second floor. The flush sound of ringing in her ears. She was telling herself to stop overreacting. He's here. Don't panic. She opened her bedroom door. The room was completely still, except for the sheer, pale lavender curtains blowing softly. The soft floral bedspread and pillows intact. The ringing in her ears reached a high irritating pitch. She backed away and started toward Josh's room. "Dell?" She opened the door to find him lying facedown on the unmade bed, in a solid sleep. His legs and feet hung over the sides. *Not again.* She rushed near his side, pushing an organized set of Hot Wheels out of the way to kneel next to him. She watched his eyes flutter and shift. She studied the smoothness of his dark brown skin, the shiny bridge of his nose. The curve of his lips. She couldn't remember the last time Dell looked so healthy. His face full, no longer sunk around his eyes. He was better. Just like she'd told Angel. It wasn't a silly fantasy, a wish in the dark. He was different. She stroked the unkempt hairline. He twitched.

His eyes opened. "Hey, you."

"Hey."

He sat up. "I felt like Goldilocks and the Three Bears. This bed seemed to be just right."

She nudged him. "Then you didn't try out the biggest bed of all."

"Oh, but I did; it just seemed too big without you."

"Come on." She led him down the long hallway to their room. They stopped every few feet and kissed. No fears or hidden secrets behind the closed doors. Dell seemed content in his own space with room to spare for her. His palms surrounded the bone of her hips, then trailed down the curve of her thighs. He lifted her up, carrying her the rest of the way. Once again there was the newness, something different about the way he held her, caressed her. Maybe it was the appreciation of having what he'd missed.

She wanted to float away, make the last year of their lives disappear, but then how would they have come to this point? She understood that tiny steps made a mile, gracious words, one at a time, told a story. All the pain and unhappiness, the turmoil and heartache, enabled them to start again, better than before. He carried her to the bed and put her down gently. His wide dark chest moved over her face, then slid down; they were face to face. "I love you," his body pressing down on hers.

The weight and shift of his movement were familiar and welcomed with open arms. This was her husband, the man she was given permission to love. She felt safe in his arms. No rush of shame or incomprehensible factors. It had always been like that with Dell. From the first time they'd kissed. She welcomed it, welcomed him. This was where her heart and mind belonged, safe.

The thought of Leah with someone besides him pulsed through his brain. At this very moment while he stroked her bare shoulder, he wanted to ask her what it was like, if she still enjoyed his touch. The questions were endless, but he knew nothing could make it go away but time. It would all pass. The man, whoever he was, would have to go away quietly. Regardless of what Elicia had said. This was no contest. The way Leah's body fell into rhythm with his told him all he needed to know.

Elicia had lied... there'd been no fighting, no physical altercations. There was no way she could have been telling the truth. He was beginning to question the relationship that she claimed they had as well... *over a year*. But then again, he couldn't deny the fact that his mind was ink-blotted. Spaces filled with black holes of nothingness. Basic things like not knowing which door led to his own bedroom. Or now looking across the room and wondering which drawer held a clean pair of boxers...or briefs.

He closed his eyes and laid his head on the pillow. His face directly in the back of Leah's head. He put his fingers through the short edge of hairs along her neck. It didn't matter which drawer was his, or where he kept his toothbrush, on the right side or left, he knew where he belonged. He kissed the back of her neck. She pushed her bare bottom into the concave of his abdomen, stirring his desire once again. He wrapped his arm around her waist and pulled her tight, curving their bodies into a slender S.

What he had right here and now was all that mattered. Not another man or, in his case, another woman. They had each other. He had his family. All that mattered was that it felt right and he belonged right here.

"What can I do for you, officer?"

Lopez saw Elicia Silvas come in by taxi, sitting in the backseat like a runaway bride. She was distressed, in a hurry. Now, she was leaving in a cooler state of mind, aloof and full of herself, back in control behind the wheel of her Mercedes. He pulled her over as soon as she drove past him. Her eyes were bloodshot, her hair in a ragged ponytail.

"Are you doing all right?" he asked, leaning on his firm arms.

"Don't tell me you stopped me for my health, or yours. Did I run a red light, drive too fast, too slow?" Her fingers strummed the steering wheel. She'd been crying.

Someone was in a worse mood than himself. Not possible. He took a deep breath, determined not to let her attitude push him over the edge. Women were always the worst drivers to pull over, feeling invincible, constantly daring him to say the wrong thing so they'd have a reason for their war cry. Verbal assault, discrimination, disrespect.

"Actually, I was a little concerned. You don't seem your usual charming self."

"Well, I guess you haven't heard the news or you wouldn't be your usual charming self, either."

"What news is that?" He gripped the edge of her open window.

"Dell is back in the love shack. You didn't know?"

"Now why would that kind of news disturb me? A better question is, why does it disturb you?"

She flipped up her middle finger and then punched the gas pedal. He hadn't realized the car was still running. He jumped out of her way. The Mercedes spun the corner nearly on two wheels. He stood with his hands on his hips, still watching the street where she'd disappeared.

Say no more. He didn't consider himself a genius, not by any means, but he certainly could do simple arithmetic. Elicia and Dell. One plus one equaled two. That no good piece of nothing. It was Dell's shadow that he saw in the window. The *Silvas Rehabilitation Center*, second floor. Dell Fletcher had left Leah fraught with worry. Devastated. All the while shacking up with the other woman. He didn't even have the decency to be on the other side of town. He'd been only a few blocks away... all this time. Elicia had put the color back in his skin, the weight on his body, the gleam in his eye. That was the best kind of medicine, good lovin'.

Elicia and Dell sitting in a tree... K-I-S-S-I-N-G. He hummed the song while he drove. He parked on the hill where Elicia lived, turning his wheels into the slant of the curb. The street was quiet, silent except for the occasional chirp of a bird, a soft breeze moving through the leaves of the overgrown trees. He called dispatch. He was on break, a coffee break. He hoped she had some, black and strong. It was going to be a long morning.

He pushed the doorbell and waited. He heard movement, then noticed the shift in shadows that cast on the concrete porch. The door swung open. "You must not like your job, 'cause I'm thinking stalker, harassment."

"Just start from the beginning, 'cause when I blow his game, I want the facts straight." He shoved past her and into the modern glass temple. The brightness flowing in from the uncovered windows accentuated the white, pure white, off white, gray white. The walls, the floors, even the furniture, white. Underfoot was a gleaming pool of clear shiny squares of tile. His reflection was oblong and out of shape. "Coffee, yes, please, thanks for offering," he mimicked.

She rolled her eyes at his antics but didn't protest. Lopez followed her to a spaceship-looking kitchen with steel cabinets and appliances. He took note of the Sub-Zero refrigerator and added another eight thousand to the tally. He wanted to ask her who was her daddy, 'cause talking heads didn't make that much. Oh, wait a minute. This was probably one of the perks of the job. He'd bet Dell Fletcher had a hand in this setup. He took the cup of coffee she poured and sipped it black. "Sugar." He put it back down on the counter.

She grudgingly walked to the cabinet and pulled out a bag of C&H and plunked it down. "Help yourself."

"I need a spoon."

"You're so macho, I thought you could just stick your whole hand in the bag and scoop it up."

"Spoon," Lopez demanded.

She took one out of the drawer and hummed it at him. It whizzed by, just missing the side of his face.

"We must've known each other in another life." His grin was full, deep lines encased his perfect smile. He was happy to feel at home, in his element. "Don't forget the sugar," he said to seal the irritation.

Elicia picked up the heavy pink-and-white bag and lunged it at him. He ducked, watching a dust cloud of sugar float overhead. The bag landed centimeters away from his hard toe shoe, letting him know it could have been his head.

"Why are you here? It's over, Leah wants Dell, you lose!"

He stood up with white granules in his hair and eyelashes. He looked like he'd been dunked headfirst in a pile of cocaine. "Why are you taking it out on me? You're the one who couldn't keep him, even without a memory. But I wouldn't concede so easily. The games aren't over yet. Leah doesn't know about you two, does she?"

"There's nothing to know. He stayed here while he was getting himself together. Simple. I didn't tell her because he needed the time, the space. I was doing them both a favor. I planned on telling her everything."

"Right, that's your story and you're sticking to it." He laughed, still brushing his uniform off. The thought that she could have an arsenal of silverware waiting to throw crossed his mind. He straightened up and eased on the humor. "He must've hurt you."

Elicia walked around the counter not doing justice to the baggy sweatshirt and sagging drawstring pants. Exhausted and defeated. Sleep had evaded her last night. She pulled out the broom and started cleaning the mess she had made. She scooted the pile of sugar to an open mouth that automatically sucked in the debris.

"You love him?"

She leaned on the broom, "You're not going to wring a bunch of information out of me, then run out of here to win your princess. Whatever you want to do, you're on your own."

"You didn't answer my question."

She gripped the broom tighter, he was prepared to duck again. A few strands of highlighted hair had escaped from her ponytail. She let out a depleted sigh, blowing the strands away from her face. "I could ask you the same thing... do you love her?"

Lopez put the cup of coffee down. It tasted bad anyway. Watered down and bland. He walked around the center divider and took the broom out of Elicia's hand. "Most definitely. I do. And the more I know about Dell Fletcher, the more I'm sure he doesn't deserve her. Or for that matter, you." He turned and headed for the front door, then stopped. "What'd you ever see in him? A liar, a cheat, unless the two of you are cut from the same card. Yeah, that must be it. Two liars. Thumbs up, we've got a love connection." His arms were bent on the sides, his thumbs perched in the air.

"Get the hell out of my house!" Elicia was already eyeballing loose objects around her, something to throw, swing.

He waved his hand in a halt signal. "I'm going-going-gone." He let himself out and trotted down the stairs, the weight of his belt and police paraphernalia bouncing with his steps. He was grateful for the fresh breeze, free of the clogged air of despair Elicia was breathing. She needed to be proactive; *don't be part of the problem, be the solution.* The cadets had to memorize that in the behavioral science class.

Lopez wouldn't give up; he couldn't even if he wanted to. He couldn't remember wanting anything or anyone as badly as he wanted Leah. A bout of sheer determination surged through his mind. He didn't need Elicia's corroboration. He'd win without her.

chapter 37

THE SKY WAS A BRIGHT infinite blue. The mountains that were usually hooded with a cast of smog could be seen from her biology class window, large pillars with drippings of snow like frosting on a ginger Bundt cake. Kayla wasn't listening to her teacher, although she knew what the topic of conversation was. Making sure she was well versed on the subject of splitting pollen from a red flower and mixing it with a white to create a pink one before she zoned out. There'd be no need to return to the monotone of Mr. Anderson until she heard the clanging bell to alert her that the period was over. Then she planned to rush out to catch Virgil going to his locker. She had good news to share. He'd been avoiding her, using the outside walkways to get to his classes.

For now, she was free to think about her dad all she wanted. He was home. Kayla could be her loving, exciting self. The shame cloud was broken into a million tiny pieces and sprinkled through the air to convene over the head of another unsuspecting victim. Free at last, free at last, thank God Almighty, free at last.

"Miss Fletcher, is there anything you want to share with us?" The intonation hadn't changed, as if he were still talking about Mendel's theory of hybridization. "Kayla." The two hands met in a loud clap missing the nose on her face.

"Huh?" She awakened to the reality of Mr. Anderson standing in front of her desk.

"The class and I are dying to know what's keeping you so amused."

Kayla looked around to see thirty bored faces. Of course they are. Anything but listening to Mr. Anderson, who spoke like there was beef jerky stuck between his teeth.

"Nothing... I'm sorry." Studious replaced happy. She picked up the pen and positioned herself to take notes.

The class let out a unified sigh of disappointment, hoping for more. Kayla had never let them down before, offering up a smug one-liner or quip that would turn into a full-blown confrontation that would suck up the rest of class time, alleviating the eternal boredom.

Mr. Anderson moved back to the front of the class. "As I was saying..."

No problem. She could wait ten more minutes. It would be worth it to tell Virgil that the psycho watchdog was out of their lives and her dad was back. Joy would be evident in her smile, the shine of her eyes. Virgil would see her face and know that she was safe to be near. They could be friends again, the way they'd been before she'd messed everything up. She was no longer contaminated with the Lopez Plague. No longer ready to scratch out anyone's eyes who came within reaching distance.

Instead of looking out at the mountains and clear blue sky, she concentrated on the shiny spot on Mr. Anderson's forehead. The rest of his face was dry from too many tanning-bed sessions. His lips moved slowly. Kayla still couldn't hear him. Her eyes looped up toward the metal-rimmed clock above his head. Five more minutes, the seconds ticked methodically by, from one black mark to the next. She could hear the movement, tick... tick... tick. Nine minutes, eight, seven, six...

She was up out of her seat before the bell decided to coincide with her decision that class was over. She watched Mr. Anderson's lips mime, "Sit down, Miss Fletcher." The bell rang just as he was ready to chastise her. Books slipped out of her grip and to the floor; now she'd miss him. She stuffed them into her backpack like a girl on a mission and ran to catch Virgil.

The hall was already full of bodies, people pushing past one another like blood moving along artery walls and veins, pushing water and minerals through, expulsing waste and picking up oxygen. She was one of the foreign particles that couldn't get through. A freshman, drowned out by sophomores, juniors, and seniors. She was invisible. "Have you seen Virgil?" She'd reached out and grabbed Tyrel's arm like a lifeline as she stood in front of Virgil's locker.

"Nah, what you need him for when you can have me?" He smiled with incredibly white teeth, accentuated by incredibly dark raisin-black skin. Beautiful, like her father, after a full season in the sun-drenched baseball stadiums.

Somehow they'd switched, and Tyrel was now holding her by the arm. This wasn't what she wanted to greet Virgil with. She shook him off, but he held on. The crowd was thinning as people found their way to class. She peeled his fingers off one at a time, "If you see him, tell him I'm looking for him."

He flagged her off as if to say she was dismissed. Disrespected. He murmured, "A white boy..." Whatever he had to say, she wasn't hearing it. She turned to run to her next class. She ran straight into the center of Virgil's narrow chest with the silk-screened eleven, stretching the length of his torso. He grabbed her shoulders to stop her from bouncing backward.

She hugged him, even though it was against the bylaws, no frontal contact, no kissing, no hugging. Rules were made to be broken. She kissed him on his fresh lips. "My dad is back."

Virgil was still wobbly from the shock of her attention. "That's great, Kayla." He looked down on her, his eyes not understanding the gravity of what she'd just told him.

"That idiot is gone, too. The one who hurt you."

"All right, that's cool. I gotta get to my class, Kayla." He danced her around to be on the opposite side. He let a half smile pull on his right cheek. "I gotta go."

Kayla watched him walk away. Her blood was trying to soar, trying to fuel the beast that dwelled dormant. The thumping of her heart, rattling her entire body. She felt like she was teetering back and forth. She tried to get a couple of clear breaths to bring down the pressure. The thumping. Her head hurt. The halls were now completely abandoned except for her standing in a puddle of mortification.

"Do you have a hall pass?"

She turned around to address the nasal voice. It was the raccoon monster. Janeen, the girl who wore her eyeliner so dark and heavy, by fifth period she looked like she was wearing Zorro's mask. Kayla stopped herself from screaming in the girl's face, one, because she was nearly six feet tall and, two, because she held her little detention tablet that could have Kayla sitting with a bunch of losers after school, breathing their foul air, and watching them pick eczema scabs.

"I'm late. I couldn't get my locker open."

"Well, I have to write you a citation. You can explain that to Ms. Adams." Janeen's gum popped, then a fresh bubble bloomed between her lips.

Before Kayla could get a cleansing breath, her hand shoved into the raccoon monster's face, making a loud popping sound. She smacked her and would have no proof or recollection, but the gum stuck to her palm.

"You . . ." Arms started flailing, grunts echoed through the halls. The two of them struggling like they were on a time limit to beat each other senseless.

They fought hard and diligently, swinging, pulling, scratching. Kayla felt blows to her face and around her ear, which infuriated her even more. She didn't know where the strength came from, but she threw the girl on the ground and jumped on her like a wild monkey, pelting the girl's face until she was lifted up by the waist.

Her legs were still kicking in the air while the security guard swung her around, away from poor raccoon eyes. "Let me go!" She still had more to give. She tried to claw at the face of the tall Black man who had her cinched too tight.

"Calm down, and I'll let you go."

"Get your hands off me!" Kayla never liked Joe, the school security guard, always watching her, staring, especially the days when she wore her cheerleader uniform. That lurid look he'd give while leaning against the doorway of the cafeteria, twirling the toothpick in his mouth. His fat belly hung inches over his beltline as if the stomach belonged to someone else, the rest of his body lean and gangly. Now that fat belly was pushing against her back. She wiggled harder to get away, digging her nails into the hand that gripped her waist.

"Oh, I see right now where you're going."

The words didn't register with Kayla. Was that supposed to be a threat? Was she supposed to be scared? She reached back as far as she could and dug her nails behind his ear. His wail brought her immediate satisfaction.

"Damn it." He let go of her, nearly dropping her on her butt. He reached for his belt and snapped off his walkie-talkie. "I need police assistance."

Kayla couldn't believe what she was hearing. She stumbled, still off balance from the swinging he'd given her. Her heart did double flips... worse than the anger she'd felt before. Now it was fear. Wide outstretched fear that enveloped her face, ran down the center of her back, and bolted to the muscles in her thighs. She ran. She pushed herself, with what energy she had left. Sprinting through the hall, her Sketchers landing loud and heavy with each step. She could hear him right behind her, cussing, out of breath, his footsteps landing in between hers. Air filled her ears. She faintly heard him yelling for her to stop. Faintly heard classroom doors banging open with the crowded heads of her fellow students. Kayla never considered herself popular. With the sensation of everyone knowing you came the wretched twin of everyone judging you as well. Now here she was a glowing light, a burst of flame running through the hallways with a raving maniac chasing her as if she'd robbed a bank or stuck up the cafeteria line.

Grinding it out until she was through the parking lot and down the sloped pathway to Lankersheim Drive, she looked back and saw no one. Her heartbeat was rapid and erratic. Is this what a heart attack feels like? she had to wonder. The sharp beating pain seemed to connect her head to her heart. A surge of liquid revved up her stomach, causing her to lurch forward. She wiped the remaining fluid off the sides of her mouth, suddenly feeling a whole lot better. She could at least stand straight up now. She paced a little. If someone didn't know, driving by, she'd look like she was practicing a cheer, forward and back, to the side she bobbed, then started walking.

Home was a good five-mile jaunt, but she had no choice. Kayla wasn't about to be placed in the hands of the lunacy squad, the LAPD, one and the same, who'd taken part in her mother's drama, seizing her father and taking him away. The very group that unleashed crazies like Angel Lopez on the innocent.

A panic claimed her as the sound of a car approached her. In the same instant, it whizzed by, leaving a gust of dusty Southern California wind in her face. She kept walking, a marcher who wouldn't let the heat, the dry air, or the fact that she felt like falling down in a ball and crying her eyes out distract her. She blamed everyone for this moment in her life. Her mother, Virgil, Lopez, her face went into a natural snarl, the thought of him. She even blamed... her dad. When she got home, she would tell him so, tell them all. She marched.

Another car was coming her way. *Keep going.* She didn't dare turn around. In fact, she looked to her farthest right, hoping she could pass for just another Black girl walking through the middle of one of the richest neighborhoods in the country. A little tidbit Dr. McGowan, the school principal, dropped on the students during an assembly to make them feel guilty, "... help those less fortunate. Realize that you are lucky, there are many children that go hungry every day, that don't carry cell phones and drive nice cars and wear designer clothing. Always be compassionate, respect others for who they are inside, not what they appear to be from the outside." Dr. McGowan, a fair-skinned Black woman with heavy blonde streaks in her hair, talked like that in public. But behind closed doors she sucked her teeth and rolled her crystal-green eyes: "Being on my honor roll does not give you license to run around back-talking the teachers at this school. You're acting just like they expect you to, uppity with attitude. Being a young Black woman does not mean your head's gotta roll." She'd mimic the move of Kayla's just a little too well. That's where she should have gone, straight into Dr. McGowan's office. She would have put Joe in his place, she would have told him, "... no student of mine is going to be sitting in some jail cell."

The car stopped, she kept marching, feeling the ground move from underneath her. Meaningless steps, one after the other, as if she'd landed on an escalator walking backward.

Look. Stop being a baby, and look. She eased her neck up to the sky and turned far enough to see out of the corner of her eye. A flower delivery van. She breathed, she thought, for the first time. All she needed to do was keep walking.

Lopez circled Winding Wind Road again. The Fletcher house was unchanged. He didn't know what he expected, some kind of sign, a crooked shade, a scarlet letter in the window, anything to represent the bedlam Dell Fletcher's return had brought.

The afternoon was approaching, almost time for Josh and Kayla to come home. He didn't want to be in the area when they arrived. They wouldn't know how to play along. To keep a secret. Dell Fletcher didn't know who he was, and he wanted to keep it that way.

Here he'd been agonizing over Squire Delvicio, wasting an entire morning like a man sitting on the edge of the waterfront with a pole but no bait when all along his catch was on the other side of the river. This was the much bigger fish. Dell Fletcher had to be handled appropriately. The last thing he wanted was a martyr, his memory set in stone as the loving husband and father who'd just turned his life around, only to die suddenly.

It had to be as rich and scandalous as two adulterous lovers found dead in a bed of their own lies. Sensational enough for Leah to want to remove Dell Fletcher from her vocabulary. Shame and embarrassment to the point that the mere mention of his name would crawl up the smoothness of her skin, making the hairs stand up.

Radio dispatch was requesting a car for immediate assistance. Lopez didn't want to leave his post, but this would be the third or fourth call he'd ignored. Sergeant Chambers was already watching him, scrutinizing his motivation for switching shifts. "One would think you're trying to hold down two jobs, Lopez. If that's your angle, I suggest you reconsider your priorities." Those words were meant as a warning. Pulling double shifts led one to believe you were strapped for cash... which led one to believe if there were a stack of hundreds sitting on a dealer's table at a drug bust, you were most likely going to cop a few off the top. Simple debit and credit. That was one of the processes of elimination for the academy... a credit report. Bad debt equaled bad risk. Weeding out dirty cops was hard enough without planting them there. He couldn't explain to the sergeant that, yes, he did have a second job, but it was one that he loved. Truth be told, the cop thing was slowly becoming *the second job* before the setback caused by Kayla incriminating his good name. Taking care of Josh, loving Leah, that was his primary concern. To serve and protect.

He hated to leave, but then again, what good was he doing, circling, taking the chance of being seen... of being remembered?

"214 responding," he depressed the button.

"Assault at Hollywood Hills High School, need assistance apprehending Black female student, white top, blue jean skirt, believed to be unarmed heading south on Lankersheim."

"Got it." His response didn't follow protocol, his annoyance evident. He'd regret that later. He drove past the Fletcher house, *his house,* slowly. *Don't worry, Leah, I'll never be too far away.*

* * *

The noon sun was bright inside their bedroom, bringing along an uncomfortable dry heat, causing Leah to wake. She lifted Dell's arm from around her waist and slid from underneath. Anxiety filled her chest. An unidentifiable fear. She rose and walked to the bathroom feeling the liquid ebb its way down her inner thigh. A reminder that she should be happy. Her husband was back, safe and sound. Her family neat and intact. But still there was the awakening, the way she felt rushed, an incomprehensible restlessness.

She swept her robe around her body and walked past Dell, softly, trying not to disturb him. His bare chest rose and fell in slumber. She pulled the door, releasing the knob into its casing to avoid the shutting sound. Once free, she hurried down the carpeted stairs, holding onto the iron banister. What was she looking for? From room to room, she floundered, pacing, looking out the windows, opening closet doors, and cabinets, checking locks on the entrances. *Lucas Breadlow had returned, unannounced, determined to claim what he considered his.*

She picked up the phone and dialed Elicia's number. She had a way of seeing things more clearly, matter-of-factly. The type of friend every woman depended on to shake them back into reality.

Her voice was slow and unexpectedly groggy. "Hello."

"It's Leah." She'd never heard Elicia without a breath of control. "Are you all right?"

"I'm fine. Just sleeping."

Leah let out a sigh of relief, she was free to talk about herself, about Dell. "He's back." She said it, then waited.

The response was slow in coming, almost practiced. "That's great. How is he?"

"Miraculous. Like a completely different man. I mean, Elicia, you wouldn't believe it. It's night and day compared to the last time I saw him. It's like he went through this transformation, like some light went off in his head and he realizes how much he loves me, the kids, that now we actually matter." Leah used the collar of her robe to swipe at the incessant stream of tears. "He's sleeping right now, completely content. And I still don't know exactly what he's been through, what brought about the change. We haven't done much talking, too busy making up for lost time. But still, there's something." Leah wiped at her eyes. "Something I can't put my finger on. I'm scared, like it's not real, like it's all going to go away. Surreal, as if at any moment, it's all going to snap back to the way it was. The alcohol, the medication, the mood swings. I'm in a perpetual stage of waiting. It's driving me crazy."

"That would be expected, Leah." The deadpan of her voice shifted. "Why can't you just love him and expect good things? Has it ever occurred to you that you get exactly what you ask for? If you look for something hard enough, you're going to find it."

Leah looked around the room; it was true, she had so much to be grateful for. So much to be thankful about. The Shaker table against the back side of the sofa held an array of framed photographs of all of them—Kayla, Josh, Dell, and her together. Warm smiles and loving eyes.

"Give him a chance."

"I want to."

"How could you even second-guess yourself? Maybe it's not what you want. Have you asked yourself... do I love him, do I want it to work out? Leah, maybe you're thinking about someone else. Maybe it's Angel you want to be with. Have you thought about that? Reconciling with Dell, is that what you really want?"

The questions were fast and furious, rolling through her brain like a shake of the dice. The answers changed with every turn. She loved Dell, of course. Did she want to go through all of this again? His rise, his fall, hitting the ground so hard everyone's world caved in with it. She swallowed the last answer...*yes.* She clutched her chest, scratching her own skin with the fabric as she grabbed, *yes,* she wanted Dell. She'd prayed for him to come back and he did.

Leah felt a rush of air move past her. She looked up and greeted Dell's eyes. He ran a hand across her shoulder.

"I have to go, Elicia. I'll call you later. Dell's up and about."

"Tell him I said, hello, and welcome home." The deadpan voice returned with a hint of amusement.

"I will."

Elicia's name struck him hard in the chest. A flicker of rage, but more so, fear.

"She said to tell you hello. I thought she'd be a little more excited and want to know the details, but she seemed content that you were back home safe and sound." Leah watched him circle the couch. He came and sat next to her. "I guess that really is all that matters."

"Baby, there's something I need to tell you."

Her eyes wouldn't follow him. She didn't want to hear this, not now. She played in the palms of her hands, tracing her own lifelines. "We need to go see your mother."

Dell held the foreboding truth in his pocket, "My mother?"

"Yeah, sweetie, she's been just as worried about you as the rest of us. Even though she can't speak, I can tell. Whenever I visited, I purposely didn't take the kids, afraid they'd mention something to send her in a downward spiral. But she knew something was going on."

He had so many questions but didn't want to alarm her. "How is she?" A safe one to ask.

"She's doing well. She'll be even better when she sees you." Leah stood up. "I'm going to get a quick shower in, before Josh and Kayla get home. You should probably come with me." She held out her hands to help him up. They were unsteady, slightly shaking, her small hands so fragile in his.

He rose up and held her. "Leah, do you realize I couldn't live without you. You're my life." He put his nose on the top of her head. She had a subliminal scent, quiet like simple soap and lavender. He couldn't remember Elicia's. Only its numbing of his senses, leaving him smothered, unable to think.

"I love you, too." Leah kissed the underside of his chin. "Shower?"

"I'll be up in a minute."

As soon as he heard her footsteps fade to silence he picked up the phone. He pressed the redial button and held it tightly to his ear. He moved to the far corner of the room. He felt like the Pink Panther, sliding behind the leaves and standing between a potted palm tree and a standing mirror. The voice breathed out a reticent "hello," as if she knew he was the next call.

"I'm going to tell her." He whispered with his hand cupped over the receiver.

Sarcasm filled her words. "Good. I think it's best for everyone, especially her. She's torn between two lovers, you might say. If you tell her, you'll give her the strength she needs to make a decision between the two of you. Maybe just what she needs to follow her heart."

"Elicia, I know you're hurting. I'm sorry about that, but your mind games are going to destroy everybody. She trusts you. She trusts me. I just want to tell her the truth." A sudden pain shot through his thigh.

"Are you all right?" Her voice took a sympathetic tone.

He was hunched over for a second, "Shit." He cringed; this time the pain felt like it went straight to his bone.

Elicia was still talking "... you're right. I am hurting, but I still love you. I'm not trying to cause any trouble. I care for you, Leah, and the kids. I don't want to lose that. If you tell her, everybody loses. That's all I'm trying to make you understand. There is another man in her life who she's not sure about. He's the officer who arrested you. Has that come back to you yet? Do you remember? Telling her about us will only drive her straight into his arms. Don't you get that?"

"Dell?"

He stood straight up to move back in his corner. There were images that he could see, the rain, driving without visibility, talking to someone, a man's voice, but it always ended there. His hand instinctively reached for his head. *The accident* a year ago . . . the night he drove off the freeway and dived into the Los Angeles ravine, nose first, came into full view. Knowing that he was headed for a tranquility, dispensed into serene darkness. The numb state of his body, weightless, flying through air. The impact of the car when it hit the concrete slab, the sound of glass breaking all around him. Waking up in the hospital with Leah sitting next to him. He was confused as to which came first. Both accidents happened in the rain, both times it was dark. But someone else was there, driving.

"I'll let you know when and how, but I'm going to tell her." He put the phone down. When he looked up, a fully showered and dressed Leah was standing in the doorway of her office. How long had she been standing there?

"I was wondering if that came from the mugger." She walked over and touched the healed scar.

"What mugger?" It came out too fast. He didn't want her to know that his recollection of events had become a blurry screen of snow. Then Elicia's story came back to him, the dead man who'd been found with his wallet. "Oh, yeah, that guy." He sat down, sinking into the overstuffed sofa. He was suddenly exhausted, a hollow ticking echoing in his ears.

"Honey, I think we may have overdone it this morning. You don't look good." She went out, then came back with a tall glass of water.

His hand trembled when he took it, spilling a little on his knee. "Leah, I have to tell you something. I don't remember anything that happened on the day I left here." He took another swallow. "Honestly, things are swimming in my head in tiny pieces. I guess the guy who mugged me stole my wallet by knocking me over the head, but I can't remember a thing about it."

"That's normal. I would think a trauma like that could make you black out." She smoothed a finger across his forehead. "Do you remember the accident you had over a year ago? A car accident; you had a broken collar bone and fractured wrists. A concussion, the doctor explained, was life-threatening. Fluid had to be drained from the stem of your brain. The doctor cautioned that another blunt force could cause irreparable neurological damage. I'm surprised you even know who I am from the look of this scar above your head." She kissed him there, smiling.

"But there are things I've forgotten, or that are coming back to me slowly, things I'm not sure of." He wanted to say it, get it over with.

"What kind of life we had together, whether we were happy together or sad. What kind of husband and father I was. Call it selective memory. Call it a blessing or a curse, but the only thing I remember was the day I fell in love with you, the first time I saw you. I can see it vivid, like it was yesterday, the way your hair hung on your shoulders, walking around with this majestic air about you, as if you were destined for something great to happen and waiting for it at any moment. I remember introducing myself to you and then wishing like mad you'd fall crazy in love with me."

Her eyes watered. She blinked, letting the small trickle find its way to her cheek.

"I remember trying to hurt myself, Leah. Feeling like I didn't have anything to live for. I couldn't see you then, the kids. Like I said, call it anything you want, divine intervention, a miracle. All I know is that I've been given a second chance, with you, with Kayla and Josh. That's what it has to be. Not knowing how I came to this point doesn't bother me one bit, I'm just grateful that I'm here, with you, with the kids."

She leaned over and hugged him. Let me finish, he started to say, so when you hear that I was brought back to life through the heart and soul of another woman, know that it doesn't mean anything. It doesn't matter. This second chance is all that matters. Dell squeezed Leah, not wanting to let go. If he told her, she would surely pull back. Maybe run into the arms of the other man, wherever he was, whatever he was. Waiting.

He couldn't tell her. He'd rather put his energy into making sure she never found out. The phone ringing made Leah pull away. She grabbed the receiver, putting an end to his contemplation.

Leah sat back down on the couch. Her anxiety was real. She listened cautiously for the worst of the news. "The police, why in the world would you call the police?"

Dell came and sat by her side. He watched her face roll into a panic.

"Well, where is she now?"

Leah hung up the phone and stood up. "Kayla had a fight at school. When the security guard tried to break it up, she attacked him, then ran off. They don't know where she is. They called the police on her like she's some deviant. Can you believe that?"

A constant, never-ending wind was blowing through Dell's mind. The surety that his actions had caused Kayla's behavior. How was he ever going to set things right?

"They think she's already been picked up by the police. They don't know because she ran off the campus; they don't have any responsibility for her once she leaves the campus."

"I'll throw on some shoes, we'll go down to the station and see if she's there."

"But wouldn't they call us?" Leah was chewing on the inside of her cheek. "She's a minor, they would call if she was there." She picked up the phone and started dialing.

"Who're you calling?"

"I have a friend." She mouthed the words, then turned away from him. Dell followed her to the stacked books and potted palm that he was hiding behind only minutes ago. Leah held the phone tight and close to her face. "Angel, this is Leah, I need your help. Something's happened to Kayla, she may have been arrested, I don't know where she is." She burst into tears. "Please call me back as soon you get this message."

Dell tried to squelch the uprising jealously in his throat. Ironic, she chose that corner of the room like a vortex of deceit, *calling all liars and cheaters.* He backed away, his eyes still on Leah's face, tormented, worried. It took him a minute to turn off the fury, her *friend* wasn't the issue. His missing daughter was. "You wait here for *your friend* to call back. I'm going to the station." He walked out, for a second not knowing which direction would take him out of his own home. The hall broke off in three directions, wide like a T-square. Moving to the greatest source of light, he walked not feeling his steps underneath him, floating past the silent walls. *Her friend,* that's who she called to come to her rescue. Dell wasn't man enough. Dell was lost. He made it to the large entryway and pulled the front door open. A blaze of heated sunshine washed over him; he stopped, looking down at his bare feet. He was turning into the invisible man... little pieces of him disappearing.

He heard her voice from behind, "Dell, you need shoes."

"I know that." His angry tone took her by surprise. He tried to supplement with an apology. "I don't understand what's happening here."

Leah's softness reached around him, closing the door. She hugged him while he stood lifeless, watching the reflection of the two of them in the hall mirror. Her face sideways, her eyes closed pressed on his chest. *Her friend* was all he envisioned, her holding on for dear life.

"Kayla's been acting out ever since you left, maybe even before that," her voice moved through his chest. "But I hadn't noticed it like now. She's angry, beyond the general teenage craziness. It's worse than just wanting to be left alone and needing independence. I'm not surprised, not really. I think I'm the one who should go find her. It seems like I'm the one she's mad at. She blamed me for you being gone. You stay here and wait for Josh."

He watched her leave, drive out of the curved entrance. His mind was still on the name that she called out for rescue over the phone, *Angel.* Logically, he should have been concerned about the whereabouts of his daughter. But his thoughts kept drifting to the friend. *He was the arresting officer,* Elicia had said. The man that Leah had come to depend on. Angel.

The phone rang as he walked back into the house. He picked it up, "Yeah."

"Hello." There was a pause. "This is Officer Angel Lopez. May I speak with Leah?"

"She's not here." Dell renegotiated with himself. "She's heading to the police station looking for Kayla."

"I've got Kayla, right here. She's fine." The phone moved, Dell could hear the changing of the hands.

"Daddy."

"Kayla, what's going on?" Dell held his chest, sitting down, then standing up.

"It's not my fault, daddy. This stupid girl at school was bothering me..."

"Where are you? Put..." he couldn't even mouth the name, "...the officer back on the phone."

A changing of the hands. "Yes?"

The smugness, the tone was familiar. Dell gripped the phone tighter, "Where are you taking her?"

"We're on our way to your house, sir. ETA five minutes." The phone went dead.

Dell hurried around the house, putting himself together like it was a first date. He wanted to meet this guy on firm equal ground. The pants were loose, sagging a bit, the shirt he let hang over to hide it. What was he doing?

The doorbell rang. He hightailed it down the stairs. He pulled the door open. Kayla rushed into his arms. He held her, then looked past her to the figure still standing on the porch. He could only make out the silhouette, square broad shoulders but still slim. His hands rested on his waist while he stood straight and tall.

"Sweetie, go on in. Do me a favor and call your mom on her cell phone. Tell her you're home." Dell stepped outside and pulled the door closed behind him. Angel Lopez stepped closer into the gray shade of the porch, eliminating the glare and giving Dell a better view of his face. It was the same guy who'd been there earlier. The very same one, pretending he'd had a call about a disturbance. It all fit perfectly now. Mystery solved.

"I guess we need to talk." Angel's arms fell to his side, but not completely, more like a John Wayne dueling stance.

Dell could still feel Kayla hovering around the other side of the door. He pushed it open slightly and spoke through the crack. "Go now, Kayla." He heard the footsteps scurry off.

The two men walked to the farthest edge of the cobblestoned pathway. Tension bounced off both pairs of shoulders. Both wondered what the other had to say.

Angel stopped and faced Dell, "She's fine, just a little shaken up. I was supposed to take her to the department. Certainly glad it was me on the call, rather than someone else."

Dell was already onto the relevant subject, "Are you seeing my wife?"

"Excuse me?" A smugness that he wasn't trying to hide rose on his face.

"Don't play with me. You were here this morning. What happened? I surprised you, caught you off guard? That little disturbance story was a cover. You weren't expecting to see me." Dell's heart was racing, pumping blood to the swell of his fists. "I understand that you and I have met before." The statement unnerved his enemy but only briefly. "I don't have it in full capacity, but I'm getting the picture. You thought you'd step in while I was in a fog. Well, guess what, I'm back. That's it... I'm back. Whatever you had, or thought you had, is over. There's no need for you to come by here for your little disturbance checks or anything else. Do you get me?"

The calm before the storm. Angel Lopez looked him directly in the eye. "I get you, perfectly clear. Now you get me... I know about your rehabilitation facilities, the pretty nurse named Elicia. What do you think Leah's going to say when she finds out?" His eyes went into confident squints. "She won't hear it from me. The messenger always gets the raw end of the deal. No, I'll just wait for the shit to hit the fan. I'm a patient guy. You'll do it to yourself. I won't have to lift a finger or utter a word." He turned and started to walk away.

Dell reached out, unable to control his rage, grabbing the starched collar, twisting him down into a headlock, tripping on his side to the coarse ground. Dell's knee pushed sharp into Angel's back. "Stay the hell away from my wife, my family." He squeezed harder.

Angel's eyes were watering from the grip Dell had around his neck, but he gritted the words out, "Assaulting an officer could take you out of the picture, behind those steel bars. Time for Leah to think."

He let him go suddenly and stood up. "You come near my family again and it'll take more than a badge to protect you." He watched the untouchable officer walk to his patrol car with an added swagger. The weight of hatred was heavy like a foot on Dell's head. He wanted to throw his whole body into him, force him to the ground, and feel his face underneath his pounding fists.

When Angel Lopez got into his patrol car, he took his time driving away. They stared each other down with equal intensity, equal loathing.

Josh jumped off the bus excited. He saw Angel waving at him from the patrol car as he passed. Normally, Angel would have stopped and given him a ride back to the house, let him flick on all the buttons in the dash, pretend like he was calling into the dispatch on the radio. And then he remembered... his dad was home. His feet pumped with the heavy bookbag flouncing on his back. His friends chased fast behind as usual, thinking that it was a race. He ran across the street, leaping the distance of the entry stairs, up the cobbled path and into the house. He threw his backpack on the floor of the foyer and took two controlled steps. He listened before he called out, "Dad."

There was no answer. He walked up the stairs. He heard voices, murmuring, then identifiable. Kayla, singing like one of the Temptations. She was telling their father about Angel, how much time he'd spent over here, alone with Josh and Kayla. The basketball game. Josh, partaking in the festivities, the sessions of playing catch, the horseyback rides, *nooooo, not that.*

"Dad." Josh swung the door open before Kayla could go on. His dad was standing up, pacing, while Kayla sat on the edge of her bed like a stenographer, recounting his and his mother's disloyalties. "Hi," Josh breathed out in a gasp.

They both looked at him. Josh was expecting evil eyes but was pulled into a thick embrace by his father. "Hey, big man."

"Hey." He held on tight. He had to know he'd never do anything against him. He had to know no one missed him more than he did. Except, maybe Mom… "Where's Mom?"

"She'll be home soon. Come here, I want to talk to you."

Josh sat next to Kayla on her bed. His father took his pacing back to where he started.

"I know that you had a relationship, a friendship with this guy, Angel, but things have happened, son, and I don't want you talking to him. If you see him, head in the other direction. I don't care if he's a policeman. All policemen aren't good people; most are, but not this one. He's dangerous, and I don't feel comfortable with him having access to either one of you. Do you understand?"

Josh understood, perfectly. He looked over at Kayla and wondered if she'd lied again. The story about Angel trying to kiss her. He'd fallen for that one, too; so had Mom. But it wasn't true.

"From now on, I'll take both of you to school, and pick you up."

Kayla was now trying to slow the roller coaster after it was at full speed. "Dad, that's not necessary. You don't have to watch guard over me; maybe Josh, but not me. The only reason I got into the car with him this time is because I knew the school had called the police, and I figured I had a better chance of talking him into taking me home than to jail. Believe me, I know he's crazy."

Josh's twisted mouth fell open, "What happened? What are you talking about?"

"I got in a fight at school today, and those idiots called the police like I was some kind of thug." She finished putting the last coat of polish on her toenail. She capped the bottle, then pulled her toes as close to her face as possible to blow.

He looked at his dad, *and this is the person you're using as a credible source.* His sister was crazy. He didn't want to admit it before—no one likes to admit there's a crazed person in the family—but here she was... sitting next to him in the flesh.

"Dad, I'm not afraid of Angel. He's never done anything to me." Josh stood up nearly to his dad's chest. Before, it seemed his father was taller. Just as his father was about to lay the final gavel down on his decision, Josh heard his mother call out. Finally, someone for his side. He rushed to the door and called out with more conviction than was necessary. "We're in Kayla's room, Mom."

"I have to talk to your mother, alone. We'll finish this later." His father left the room.

Josh didn't waste a minute turning to Kayla. "Why are you telling Dad all of this... you're hurting his feelings... saying that me and Mom wanted Angel here all the time. Why did you say that? What's wrong with you?"

"It's true. If it wasn't for you and Mom, that crackpot wouldn't have been around here ruining my life."

Josh stood up, "You're the one who lied on Angel. You're the one ruining lives."

"You want to be with him so bad, go get him." She got up and shoved Josh hard on the shoulder. She opened her bedroom door and gave him one hard push, "Be my guest."

"Anything's better than being around you." The door slammed in his face.

* * *

Leah looked at Dell, they each knew what the other was thinking... my, how they sounded familiar. Clones. Breathing talking replicas. They sounded like an old married couple. And why shouldn't they, they'd learned from the best, the art of war. Love and hate. The thin line. Leah put her keys and purse down. "I guess things are back to normal around here."

"No, they're not." Dell was fuming, "I had a run-in with your boyfriend."

"I don't have a boyfriend." She stood almost paralyzed.

"Well, what would you call him?" His voice rose.

"Dell, this isn't a good time. We should be dealing with Kayla. I just got an earful from her principal. She's—"

"...going to be fine... were you two together? Are you still seeing him?"

Leah felt light-headed. Dell was facing her, standing on the very step where Angel had slid his hands past her skirt. Moved past the line she'd so neatly drawn. She stepped toward him to whisper, "I'm not seeing him, we weren't together, not like you think." She forced her feet to move, she started walking, knowing that Dell would follow. She didn't want her children hearing whatever words she could come up with; no matter the excuse, it would be a lie. Saying that she never meant any harm, only invited him in for Josh to have someone to lean on, kept him around to help her deal with the loss, never felt anything beyond friendship, it would be a lie.

They were now in the quiet of her office. She closed the door. "I started depending on him, sort of, but we were never 'a couple.'" She clutched herself. "We spent a lot of time together, but not alone, I mean he spent time here with all of us. Not just me." Leah knew she sounded ridiculous. Dell knew her, knew that she didn't play games. She was either in or out, a black or white kind of girl. She always chose. Or maybe Dell had forgotten that about her, too. This image of him wasn't real, more like a puppet, saying what he thought he was supposed to say. Feeling what he was supposed to feel. Jealousy. Territorial. She was beginning to get angry but didn't understand why. Wasn't it she who'd kissed another man, touched him, held him? There was no justification, but she couldn't stop the anger from rising.

"Since when did you start caring?" She blurted it out, hard as a slap to his face. "Am I supposed to believe that all of a sudden I'm all that matters, me and the kids. Since when am I the center of your life? You've never cared, why now?"

A shift in his posture, as if he could feel the blow to his stomach. His chest caved in, his shoulders visibly slumped. "How can you say that I didn't care? I may not remember every little detail of our life together, but I know how I felt, how I feel. Leah, was I that bad, was I that much of a rotten person that you would fall into the first open arms held your way?"

She wanted to scream, YES. Yes, you were. But she knew there was more to it than that. Angel Lopez had been more than open arms. He was attention and love. The love she wasn't getting from Dell. So many years had passed and she'd ignored it, buried the part of her that wanted to cry out. It was hard standing straight all the time, carrying the weight of this marriage all alone on her shoulders. YES, she wanted to scream, I wanted to be the weak one for a change, see how it felt to not care about anyone else's feelings but my own, to be selfish, to think about what Leah wants, what Leah needs.

The back of the couch was her crutch. She straightened her arms to lean on it. "I wasn't out to hurt you, Dell. For once, it wasn't about you at all."

"Promise me you won't see him again? There's something about this *guy* that's not right. Just promise."

Leah moved an imaginary hair behind her ear. "Fine," she agreed. She needed the boundary, the expectation. She was grateful for it. "I won't see him." She closed her eyes seeing a phrase from the Lucas Breadlow story, *the problem with stray dogs is that they have no conscience, only instinct and hunger.*

chapter 38

THE STREET WAS ALREADY FILLED with cars, nowhere for him to park. His sister, Maria, had decided the party should go on, even though she was broken up about the sudden disappearance of her husband, Andre. A banner hung outside the little green house, swaying "Feliz Aniversario 50th." Maria probably got it at half price and didn't care that it was a sign celebrating someone's fiftieth anniversary instead of birthday. Not to mention, their mother was turning fifty-seven today.

He rode around the block, turning down the narrow streets, not really concentrating on his goal of finding a parking space. His thoughts were of Dell Fletcher and Leah, complicated, fully wrapped with beginnings and endings. One action is followed by another with even greater force. Therefore, he played his scenarios out to the bitter end. Anything he did in retaliation would come back to him, twofold, finding him on the outs. Leah finding him at fault.

The brake lights of a car parked on the right side of the street blinked off and on. Lopez slowed down and waited. He leaned his head back against the firm headrest, trying to squeeze out the vision of Leah with Dell Fletcher. Lopez had to reprimand himself for thinking of Leah in that way. Dell Fletcher's naked body smothering her bare frame. The thoughts slipped into his mind, raw and uncensored. No matter how often he shook them away, they'd come back, strong in virtual reality.

"Hey," a knock on his window startled him. Lopez looked up to see the twitchy kid next to his car door. "How much you need?"

He'd forgotten that he was sitting in the heart of Crackland. He sat up and considered his options, snatching the kid's head through his window and slapping some sense into him, or shooing him away.

The rocket sound of gunfire sent the boy running. Lopez put his car in reverse and punched on the gas. He pulled back far enough to be out of the line of action. The car that he'd been waiting to leave for the parking spot was now twisted at an odd angle.

Lopez got out, carrying his off-duty revolver, and crouched down near the bank of cars. He crept to the Buick that stuck half in and out of the street. Peering inside, he wasn't surprised to find the driver slouched over with a red hole in the center of his head. Beside him on the passenger's side was a black leather bag. Lopez guessed money, but then again, whoever shot the guy would have guessed that, too. He opened the door and stuck his hand in the car, pulling the bag out. He looked around to the dark houses where he assumed everyone was underneath a table or bed, shying away from stray gunfire.

White clear bags, four of them individually wrapped like neat little sandwiches. He pulled the bag with him while he backed away from the car. The quietness of the street wouldn't last long. Someone would eventually look out their window, come out their front door to see who'd been gunned down this time. He ran with the bag under his arm.

He would have rather had money, but then it hit him. Crack, cocaine, either one—if Dell Fletcher was found with drugs, Leah would think he was the lowest of the low. "He's changed, he's different," Lopez mocked while driving cautiously through his old neighborhood. If he got pulled over, he'd flash his badge, tell them he was visiting his mother. Didn't hear or see a thing.

He wasn't going to stay long, double-parking in front of his mother's house, then grabbing the bag, he looked nervously out both sides of the window before getting out of the car. He carried the bag into the house. The music was loud, his mother's favorite, Jon Secada, who she swore must've been his father reincarnate. "He looks exactly like your father when he was younger. Your father could sing, too, you know." He slipped past the press of bodies in the narrow hallway. He worked his way around hands reaching up to greet him with a friendly tap on the face. Aunts and uncles he hadn't seen in years. Once inside his mother's bedroom and shutting the door behind him, he looked around, seeing the bronze cross that hung over her bed, the neatly placed crotchet pillows on the matching bedspread, the table set of miniatures on the nightstand. Nothing had changed, everything in its place. The same place as when he was a child. His mother would notice anything that didn't belong. Down on his knees he looked underneath the edge of the hanging bedspread. He could see clear to the other side, not even hindered by an old sock or a forgotten tin with hidden candy. It wouldn't be safe here.

In the hallway he slid past his Uncle Cornelius, a tight-eyed Panamanian with dark purple lips and a wide pear body. He was coming out of the bathroom. "Don't go in there," he instructed Angel, pointing to the bathroom.

"Thanks for the warning." Angel slipped into the second closed door. His brother Gino's room, the one all of his brothers had shared. It dripped of filth and grime. Posters on the wall from the 1970s and 1980s. Michael Jackson when he still had his nose, Luke's girls with their asses out... oh me so horny, me love you long time. Lopez loved that song. He'd played it so much the cassette ripped to shreds.

The closet was the perfect hiding place. He had to push the heavy wood doors that were off their track. Shoving until he could see into the dark pit. Clothing he and his brothers shared, old leather jackets, sweaters, and jeans. He threw the bag inside behind the extinct clothes. He'd come back and get it when he was in uniform. Right now he was just another brown face in danger of being exterminated.

"Happy birthday, Mama." He walked up and kissed her on her full smooth cheek. Just as he thought, she smelled of carne asada. Doing the cooking for her own party. He gave her the card he was holding. "Mama, do something for yourself. For you, please."

She held it to her heart, "*Mijo,* you're my gift. Knowing that I have a son who has done everything right. That's my gift. Thank you."

Lopez looked around over the dark shiny heads, surfing for Maria. The room was filled to the brim with cousins and relatives. He wanted to see Maria and then he was out of there. He had planning to tend to.

"There you are."

Maria sat on the edge of the shredded couch. Her eyes were squiggly red lines. "Angel, my angel, where for art thou?"

He kneeled next to her. "Hey."

"Hey . . . yourself."

Lopez stuck his nose in the plastic Dixie cup she was holding. He took it out of her hand and poured it into the plant sitting on the side table.

She laughed a strangled sound. "That's plastic." She pointed to the plant he'd poured on.

"Maria, I wanted to give you this." He pulled out a small wad of money. He took her hand and placed it in her palm.

"Get a place of your own, move out of this neighborhood. Get a job. Remember I said I would help you?"

Her face crumpled. A small hint of a smile. "You were supposed to find Andre. That's how I needed your help. I don't want this." She let it fall to the floor. He picked it back up.

The room was closing in on him. Music too loud. The wailing voice coming through the one speaker in the corner of the living room . . . *su corazon.* Lopez stood up, unsteady. There wasn't enough oxygen for all of these people. They'd come to eat and drink, but no one brought gifts. He saw his mother laughing, her tight small teeth gleaming with happiness. She didn't care about money or gifts, just the heart of a person, the soul. Like Leah, pure and loving.

He went to the bedroom where Maria's children slept soundly through all the chatter and music outside the thin walls. He put the money under the pillow where she'd find it once she was sober. So close, he couldn't resist kissing each one of his nephews on their cheeks, three in a row, then the baby in the playpen that doubled as a crib. Lopez reached in and stroked her rising and falling back with each small breath she took. So peaceful. Andre didn't know what he had, just like Dell. No appreciation for these precious gifts. Lopez couldn't wait to have children of his own. Leah was young, thirty-four or thirty-five; they could at least have one more. He wouldn't take anything for granted, not one day of his child's life would be wasted.

"Good night, precious babies," he whispered before shutting the bedroom door.

At three in the morning, he couldn't sleep. Dell rose and stared at the shadows of darkness in his bedroom. He was paranoid. He knew the way he felt and how it was affecting everyone else, like they were under house arrest. Martial law. No one left without him knowing exactly where. No one opened the door without his supervision. They didn't understand what he'd seen in that man's eyes, in his face. The power of determination. Angel Lopez said he would wait patiently for the self-inflicted damage, but Dell had a feeling he was up to no good. Exactly what, he had no idea. The only thing Dell was sure of was that he would not be caught off guard. Expecting things to die down after enough time had passed. No. If he lived to be a hundred years old, he would know that face, and always be looking over his shoulder.

Leah slept peacefully beside him. She'd kept her promise. She hadn't seen Angel Lopez, or talked to him. Dell had kept his own promise to himself. He hadn't talked to Elicia. He could feel her willing him to call, needing him to say something. But he couldn't. Whatever they had was over. He owed Leah for unknowingly keeping her side of the bargain.

Over the last few days, more of the pieces of his memory puzzle were coming together. Leah had made him an appointment with a specialist, even though he assured her things were coming along smoothly. It helped going through their family albums, seeing Kayla as a baby, Josh, too. Their smiles so bright and happy.

Regardless of how hard he searched the pictures, he couldn't find a definitive point where the happiness had ended, when it'd been replaced with heartache. A point when he would stop being grateful for the life and family he had. He had to assume that he'd suffered from shortsightedness, seeing only what was in front of him. Baseball. Believing in his career more than a devout religion. What more could he have needed? But when it was taken away, he was left empty, partly because he hadn't left room for anything else.

"What are you doing up?" The shuffle of her slippers across the kitchen floor echoed into the height of the ceiling.

"Couldn't sleep. You want to share some tea?"

She sat down across from him in the window seat. Neither one of them had bothered turning on the lights in the kitchen. The moonlight hung outside the paned window, illuminating his face.

"Are you nervous about getting the MRI results?"

"Nothing he can tell me is going to change how I feel. Absolutely nothing."

She reached across the table and took his hand. "I know everything is going to come out fine." She was smiling, but the pain was evident in her eyes. It was she who'd sat vigilant beside his hospital bed last year when he'd had the accident. She who'd listened to the doctor's warning that if he ever had another head injury, it could be life-threatening.

"Thank you for sticking by me, Leah. I've still been thinking about the conversation we had yesterday."

She let go of his hand, sitting up straight.

"I'm not going to bring that part up." Dell didn't want to scare her away, put her on the defensive. "I'm talking about us. You asked me why now . . . all of a sudden, I want to be the loving husband and father. I have no answer for that. Being out of my mind is the only excuse I have, I plead insanity. But now I'm sane. I see what I have here, what I could've almost lost." He took hold of the hand that almost got away. "I'm sorry, Leah, about the past. I can't change it, but I can promise that the future is going to be a different story entirely. I love you."

She climbed on his lap. She kissed his mouth and looked him directly in the eye. "Don't ever leave me again, Dell." He understood what she was saying more than the words she'd chosen to say it. *This is your last chance, Dell. Next time I won't wait.*

• • •

Waiting was the hardest part. He wouldn't be the officer who pulled Dell Fletcher over and discovered the bag of drugs in his possession. That would be a bit obvious. He called in an anonymous tip and gave it the proper amount of time to filter from desk to desk, waiting for someone to act on it. This was the good stuff; Dell Fletcher was going to end up under the jail. He'd planted the bag in his trunk under the spare tire. He can see it now, Leah's shock and embarrassment. The news crews filing in around the house. The moment when she picked up the phone looking for him to make it better, his shoulder to cry on.

But the hardest part was the wait.

"I told you."

"You told me what?" Leah held Dell's hand in the elevator. They'd just left the doctor's office and were heading to the car.

"I told you I was in good shape."

She leaned on his shoulder. "Yes, you told me, but I'm still glad we have proof. He said there's no reason why your memory shouldn't be in full swing."

The elevator stopped before they were at their destination. The doors rolled open. Dell leaned over and pushed the button to close it.

"Hey, some little old lady may have been trying to get to the door and you just closed it on her."

"Well, she should've hobbled faster." He leaned back into Leah's awaiting kiss. She slid her arms around his waist and up near his shoulder blades.

When the elevator stopped on the parking garage, the doors pulled open.

"Sweetie, I forgot my magazine. I left it in the doctor's office." Leah stood in the elevator with her hand on the open button. "I'm going to run and get it."

"A magazine, Leah? C'mon, we can pick up another one anywhere."

Leah nodded her head back and forth, "Not this one, it was a back issue that I ordered. It'll take me two minutes. Swing around to the front of the building and I'll meet you there."

"Don't be long."

The elevator doors closed.

Leah rode back up to the sixth floor. She opened the doctor's office door and saw the receptionist reading her magazine. She hated to be rude, but she'd ordered the magazine just to read the article about a man who'd suffered from loss of memory, living an entirely different life with another family before realizing he'd had another wife right around the corner.

"I left that." Leah pointed to the magazine being gripped by the plump fingers of the receptionist.

"I was going to call you and let you know." She handed it through the glass partition.

"If there's something good in there that caught your eye, I can wait while you make a copy of it."

"Really, you don't mind? It won't take me but a second." A pregnant belly extending beyond her stood up first. She used the arms of the chair to make it completely to her feet. "I was reading about the stimulation of the baby's brain while it's still in utero. All these years in a doctor's office and I never thought about reading the *American Medical Journal.* They got some good stuff in here."

Leah tapped her nails on the counter wondering where the young woman had to go to make a couple of copies. The phones went unanswered, patients came in, and Leah directed them to the sign-in sheet, explaining that the receptionist stepped out for a minute. She should have known a minute would turn into ten at the pace she was moving around, carrying the extra person in her belly.

"Here you go."

Leah didn't make any more pleasantries. She grabbed the magazine and trotted out the door. She reached the front double doors in a huff and was shocked that Dell was nowhere to be seen. The Cedar Senai hospital was the length of a solid block, but there was no misunderstanding as to which was the front of the building. The big concrete engraved sign. The hooded entryway. Leah walked to the other end, just in case.

He wasn't there. She went back inside the office building and listened to her heels cross the hard shiny acrylic floor. The elevator kept backing away from her, farther out of reach. She reached out, still not feeling the call button. A terrible fear quaked through her body all the way to her fingertips. She pushed hard, the downward arrow. She squeezed inside the opening elevator doors, then pummeled the number four button.

It seemed an eternity, one floor at a time.

The elevator stopped. The doors slowly opened, unfolding what had to be a nightmare. Absurd and remarkably real, but still a dream; possibly she'd gotten off on the wrong floor, exiting to a movie shoot.

Flashing hoods of police cars, guns pointed all in one direction. Her eyes followed the mark where the guns were pointed. Her heart froze. Dell! Her husband standing with his hands folded behind his head. "Dell!"

At first Dell thought they were talking to someone else. The words, "Freeze, police, get down on the ground" coming from all directions. He could see their lips moving in unison, five or six guys pointing guns toward him, wearing black jackets and jeans. Rogue, not the patrol types. They kept inching closer, yelling louder, get down on the ground.

As soon as he lay down he felt the bulk of bodies leaning on him, grabbing his wrists, twisting them upward to put on the handcuffs. He didn't bother to ask, to say it out loud, "What the hell is this about?" because he knew. There was no doubt that this was the work of Officer Angel Lopez. He went along quietly, determined not to get bruised and battered in the process.

They stood him up on his feet and escorted him to the back of a waiting police car. He watched as they opened up the front of his Porsche and reached in for the evidence. Funny how they knew exactly where to look. Dell put his head down. Even knowing it wasn't his, he felt a wave of blame. That somehow he'd brought this all upon himself.

"Dell!" The high-pitch wail of pain sailed over the confident and proud chatter of the police officers. "Oh, my God, Dell."

He saw her take a step before she was intercepted. A dark-haired officer held her back.

"Get your hands off of her. Let her go!" It was the first time Dell had resisted, jerking his shoulders in an effort to be heard. A solid forearm pinned his head against the side of the door, he was being shoved into the back of the waiting car. Nothing could have broken him down further. Seeing Leah in this much pain, the baseline, the narrow edge that surely would send her over for good. What if she believed what they were about to tell her? What if she bought it, the setup?

The car door slammed shut.

He watched as Leah called out his name, watched her small frame twist and writhe out of the officer's grasp as she broke free to chase after the moving police car.

• • •

Leah stuck the money in the taxi driver's hand. Ethiopian by the sound of his name, he inadvertently squeezed her hand when he took the money. Probably feeling sorry for her. When he picked her up, her eyes were already black mascara-rimmed. Red veins popping through the whites. The face of a woman who'd been scorned, stood up, or worse, dumped. But her situation was far worse. Far more dramatic.

The driver rolled away slowly, quietly, respecting the calm of the damned. Leah opened the front door and instantly released the second wave of shock and tears. Drugs. Dell. It wasn't possible. Or was it? What did she really know about his disappearance? His return? Where had he been the entire time? She never had the answers to those questions. Merely assumptions on her part. A hospital, getting well, recuperating. She didn't know where. Had no proof but no reason to believe otherwise, until now. Could her husband, the man she'd loved all these years, have changed his drug of choice to cocaine? Trading in the numbness for euphoria?

Leah ran to the phone when she heard it ringing. It had to be Dell. She wanted to hear him say it wasn't true. "Yes."

"How're you holding up. I can't believe this is happening." Elicia's voice sounded alien and unfamiliar, only because it wasn't the voice she'd wanted to hear.

"I can't believe it, either. He said he changed, I believed him."

"Oh sweetie, don't cry. Do you want me to come over and sit with you?"

"I'm waiting to hear from Dell. The kids will be home soon. I need to be able to tell them something, give them some kind of explanation." Leah's only concern now was for Josh and Kayla. They'd already endured enough foolishness. This was unspeakable.

"Let me take them. I'll pick them up from school and take them to a movie. They won't know till you're ready for them to know."

Leah broke down again, wiping the slowly falling tears. "Thank you. Elicia, you're saving my life right now." She hung up the phone, feeling like she at least had room to work, a minute to breathe and start from the beginning.

The vision of it all tore through her. Dell's face. Questioning and confused, but it wasn't the face of a guilty man. Holding the phone tight against her breast, she closed her eyes. More pictures appeared behind her closed lids. Dell turning toward her after she called his name. Remorse, yes, but that was only after seeing her. He'd done nothing wrong. She knew it. But she knew someone had. The only someone who hated Dell right now, all because of her.

She'd caused all of this to happen. "Angel," she whispered his name, opening her eyes as if he'd touched her. She dialed his home number frantically, then the pager. A slight chill ran down her back. What would she say? She hadn't spoken to him since the day Dell returned. Leah felt a small part of Angel die inside, the day she'd told him Dell was back. He'd asked if she'd made love to Dell. Those words scared her. She could hear his heart beating while he sat next to her in the car. That was a true sign that she'd been playing with fire.

The phone rang a few minutes later. Dell? Angel? She took a long cleansing breath before answering.

"Leah." His voice, her name, the wave on the end.

She steadied herself. "What have you done?"

"What are you talking about?"

Leah didn't want to have to say the words. Accusations were ugly things. There was always the chance that she was wrong. And an accusation never went away, lingering like a dull toothache. "Dell's been arrested," she said with a calm reserve. "Do you know anything about it?"

"Only what I've seen on the news this morning. I'm sorry to hear about it."

"Dell didn't do coke, Angel. Someone put it there. Someone who hates him or hates me. I was with him, they could've just as easily arrested me. They still might." Leah sensed that he was listening closely, that she could elevate him to a higher playing field, one of compassion. "Can you even imagine what that would do to Josh to see us both in jail? Josh misses you, by the way. So do I... I never meant to hurt you, Angel. The way things worked out—"

"How did things work out? I'm interested in your version of the events." The coolness of his tone shook her. "Your husband came home. Never told you where he was. You accepted him with open arms. You told me I wasn't wanted. You two were going to live happily ever after. Now he's been arrested and you need my help."

Leah buckled. Her body dropped to the chair beside her desk. The picture of her and Dell directly in front of her, smiling, happy, yes, happy ever after. They deserved that. Why shouldn't they?

"Is that the way it happened?" he asked again.

"That's not the way it happened. I told you from the very first day that I couldn't go through with it. That I felt a relationship with you was wrong, against everything I believed. I told you and I kept telling you. You can't think that I was out to hurt you, Angel. You don't believe that, do you?"

His presence undetectable. "Angel, are you there?"

"I don't want to have this conversation over the phone. Meet me at the Design Café on Lakeland. The one we held hands at."

"No. Absolutely not."

"Okay, but you're the one who wanted answers. I was just sitting here minding my own business. Watching the news. How long do you think Dell's going to get? Five years, ten, fifteen?"

Leah stood up, holding the phone like a walkie-talkie, yelling at it, understanding the implication. "I'll meet you!"

"See you in half an hour."

The line was quiet. They hung up at the same time. Leah didn't scare easily. Not since the time she'd gone home and performed the ritual. The kids in her fifth-grade class spent the entire lunch hour talking about Bloody Mary. "If you turn off the lights and close the door in the bathroom and spin in front of the mirror five times with your eyes closed, saying her name, Bloody Mary... Bloody Mary... she'll appear... Bloody Mary, dripping with blood, staring at you from the mirror and if you look at her, she'll steal your soul. If she doesn't appear, it means you're saved."

Leah didn't understand what "saved" meant. But couldn't wait to find out. She rushed home and stood in the center of the small white bathroom with the pink towels and pink toilet paper. Fearless, snapping the light switch off, standing in the dark. The fear didn't envelop her until she was on her last spin, until the last Bloody Mary spilled from her lips. When she stopped, dizzy, opening her eyes slowly to the darkness, waiting for the witch to appear looking back at her, there was nothing. Only the shadow of Leah's two Mickey Mouse curly pompoms on the sides of her head. Nothing. She'd held her breath for nothing. That was the day she stopped believing in the unknown. She stopped looking under her bed before she went to sleep at night, no longer checked the closets. Stopped looking behind her when she watched TV waiting for her mother to come home from work. If something was going to get her, jump out of the darkness and take her soul, it would have to do so when she wasn't looking. She wouldn't be waiting with open arms, which was the exact definition of fear. Sitting. Waiting. Paralyzed to act. That wouldn't be her. Angel Lopez wasn't going to scare her into doing nothing. For her husband, for her children, she had to do something.

Leah grabbed her purse and moved quickly, but not before leaving a note to anyone who might find it later.

chapter 39

IT WAS AMAZING HOW the advent of modems, cable, and satellite technology had transformed communication. As he sat on his couch, in the convenience of his own home, he watched his plan take shape and conclusion. Dell "Roadrunner" Fletcher, arrested for drug possession, with an added bonus, an unregistered gun. He must've been planning to shoot me, Lopez thought, a little impressed with the bravado. That could've worked, too bad he didn't think of it first. Leah would've condemned Dell Fletcher for putting a bullet through her lover. Her innocent sweet lover.

Lopez clicked the channels, one after the other—all eyes were on the crisis. Well, it's not like Dell Fletcher murdered anybody, he thought, but news was news. They'd take it any way they could get it.

Lopez had seen enough, time for the finale. His meeting with Leah was his first priority now. He imagined her eyes brimming with tears. Her slow blink, her head tilting to the side like a fragile tulip. *"Please help me, Angel. You have to help me."*

An ounce of the drug would have been sufficient, but he'd left a kilo. Nicely bundled. Dell Fletcher wasn't getting out of this one, the way money had the ability to buy freedom. Not even the best lawyer could talk him out of a twenty-year sentence.

He flicked off the remote. "Adios, my little friend," he mocked in his best Scarface voice.

The same little coffee shop they'd sat at before, this time it was the height of daylight. This time he wasn't wearing his uniform. The nameless face that poured him coffee countless times didn't seem to recognize him wearing a white knit shirt that hugged the bronze muscle of his biceps, his favorite thoroughly beaten jeans. *Leah's favorite jeans,* he could tell by the many times he'd caught her looking. She'd never admit that she had turned into a shallow visual creature. The trait of a man, completely absorbed by his physicalness. My, how the tables could turn. Lopez had stepped up the weights, a hundred pounds on each side of the barbell just for her. He wasn't Schwarzenegger big, not anywhere near, but he had the clean lines, the full cuts.

The minutes were ticking away. She was already ten minutes late. Lopez pulled the toothpick out of his mouth and broke it in two over his index finger. Idleness wreaked havoc on his stomach and his head. He took another sip of his coffee. It didn't taste so good today, missing that mud appeal. The ceramic white cup shook slightly in his hand. He was nervous.

She'd walk in any moment, her back straight, head held high, hips striding evenly. He thought of the way she concentrated before she spoke, lips barely touching, sensual. He wanted to kiss those lips deeply. Hold her by the back of her neck and plunge his tongue against hers. *Come on, Leah.* He checked his watch again. Sipped the bland coffee. Noticed two patrons had come and gone after being served full pancake-and-egg breakfasts in the time he'd been sitting.

Lopez kept his focal point on the open street outside the café. The blank asphalt, sandy black. Her burgundy Range Rover would pull up at any moment.

Only six days, but it felt like weeks, months since they'd last seen each other. Every day an eternity. By the time he'd put the bag in Dell Fletcher's car, he was already past the point of return. A crazy wreck. Now when he looks back on what he did, it seems a bit petty. Cowardice. He should have faced Dell Fletcher like a man. Fought for Leah. Showed her, without a doubt, her precious worth. Now he'd have to deal with her accusing eyes. The unmistakable dread of her disappointment. *What'd you do?* He had to ignore her question. Had to follow through.

The shiny burgundy SUV pulled up, rolling over a corner of the paved curb before stopping on even ground.

She was still polished after the stress of events, and he could see her spicy shaded lips from where he was sitting. Her sunglasses pushed close to her face. He stood up to get the door for her.

Light-headed. He still felt off-center when he was near her. Even though she'd broken his heart. Even though she'd pushed him down and kicked dirt in his eyes, he wanted to reach out and pull her in.

She brushed past him into the empty café. Her arm was pressed tight against her purse, clutching with both hands. She was afraid of him. That wasn't his goal. Not the purpose for which he set out. He simply wanted her to understand. Some things had to be done for a woman's own good.

"I can't stay long." She seemed to know exactly where he was seated, sliding into the booth where his coffee sat cold. "Tell me what you did? No, first tell me why, if you claim to care so much about me, how you could put my life in jeopardy. Those men had guns everywhere, point-blank in Dell's face. I walked into the entire thing. I could have been shot." She took off her sunglasses. The anger wasn't there, not like he thought it would be. Sadness. Always sadness.

"You're all I care about. Do you think I'd put you in harm's way? I wouldn't do anything like that. Leah, I love you." His hand moved to hers, still latched to the strap of her leather purse. She switched it to the other arm, then let him take hold of the now free hand. He fingered the pear-shaped diamond on her finger. Wishing it was he who'd put it here. He stroked the insides, the creases between her fingers. Her pulse was what he was looking for, the rhythm of her heart.

"Then tell me why you did it?" She tried to pull her hand away.

Lopez wrapped his other hand to her wrist. He leaned into her face, "I can ask you the same thing. Why? Why your actions said something completely different from your words? Words are meaningless, Leah. Communication comes from here." His finger ran down the length of her clavicle bone to the last closed button of her blouse. He felt the pulse quicken in the hand he still held. She tried to pull away, but he tightened his grip. "Why couldn't you follow your heart, Leah? Why couldn't you say what you meant... that you loved me, too... that you needed me? Why couldn't you admit that Dell coming home bailed you out of making a real decision? I know you were scared of letting go... afraid of what passion might mean. Loving someone without caution doesn't make you a bad person. Do you realize that I've never loved anyone... felt for anyone the way I feel for you? I know you felt it, too. You still do." He held up her hand in his, "I can feel it through your veins. You can't even sit here next to me without—"

"Shaking. That's what you feel, me not knowing what you're capable of next. You can't even admit to what you did. That makes me suspicious of you. How am I supposed to love someone who can't be honest with me? Okay, so you're right. I felt something for you that scared me. I admit it, now it's your turn to tell the truth."

Lopez let go of her hand and lifted the coffee cup sitting in front of him. He slid the napkin closer. "You have a pen?"

She reached in her purse and gave him her Mont Blanc.

He twisted the ballpoint to service and wrote the words, I DID IT NOW WHAT? He slid it in front of Leah, let her read it, then balled the napkin and dunked it into the black coffee. The horrified look on her face made him realize what he'd only guessed. She needed for him to say it out loud. He reached into her blouse, shifting his hand quickly side to side, then reached over her while she slapped at his hands. He grabbed her purse, pulling out the first thing he saw, a small tape recorder. At least he knew she hadn't gone to the police. If she had, the sting would've been a tad more sophisticated.

He held it up and pressed stop.

"He doesn't deserve your loyalty. Do you know that? Do you have any idea who it is you're trying to save?" He slid the recorder to the center of the table.

"He's my husband and whatever he's done in the past is in the past. He doesn't deserve what you're doing to him, Angel."

"Did he ever tell you the truth, about where he was while you were crying your eyes out?"

Leah shook her head, "It doesn't matter, now." She swallowed the lump she'd been holding. "All that matters is that you end this. Your superiors will understand, say you put the bag in the wrong car. Isn't that what you guys do, set people up who you know are already guilty. Say anything, just get him out of this."

"You figure it's safer if you don't know where he was, right?" he said, ignoring her pleas. "Then you won't have to pass judgment, make any kind of decisions."

"If you knew me at all, you'd know that's not true. I know exactly what I want and I stand by it."

Lopez leaned back in his seat. He folded his hands in front of him, shifting his thumbs from top to bottom, left to right. "Do you love him, or is this pure loyalty, guilt over what we had?"

She was silent, contemplating what would be the best answer.

He let his tired eyes wander to hers. "Tell me the truth... or do you even know what that is?" He wanted her answer first. He didn't want to destroy her. If she truly loved Dell Fletcher, there was no need for him to blow up her world, no need to make her stand on hollow ground, because it wouldn't be him that she reached for in need of solace.

"Dell and I have been through a lot. We've endured the pressure of his career, raising children, creating our own world where the rules may not apply somewhere else. It's not simple."

"Love is very simple, Leah. Very clear. That's how you know it's love. That's how I knew. There was no fog, no questions. When it came to you, boom, I just knew." He reached out and fingered her chin toward him. "Did you love me?"

She looked him straight in the eye, blinking only once, not contemplating or second-guessing what she knew was the right answer, "Yes."

"I didn't mean to hurt you, Leah. That wasn't what this was about. I put the bag there so you'd question what kind of person he was. Dishonest, sneaky. I guess I could have just told you the truth about where he was. The relationship he had with—"

The words were lost when three plain cars pulled up haphazardly to the curb of the café. Lopez looked to Leah, then back outside. Then back to Leah, who was now standing up, backing away, clutching her purse. She lifted her skirt, exposing her inner thigh where the wire was taped. He'd thought about touching her there, hadn't he? Dreamed about it, sliding his hands between the smoothness of her legs. She probably expected that he would, wearing the beige skirt that he loved to rake his hands over. In those brief moments when he looked back, he would always think that Leah wanted him to find the wire there. The look on her face told him so, *why didn't you check here?* She dropped the skirt back to its place, then continued to back away, out the door.

Lopez stood up, lifting his hands over his head, bending to his knees. He knew the rules. The handcuffs were put on one wrist at a time. The words were being spoken... his rights. Yes, he understood. As he watched Leah walk out the glass door, as she kept her back to him, never once turning around, he understood perfectly.

Leah ran to the long black sedan, tears in her eyes. Dell got out of the car and caught her in his awaiting arms.

"I was so scared, baby. I would rather die than see him hurt you."

She knew Dell heard everything that was said in the café. Listening with the officers as they sat with her as bait. In those crucial moments, she'd made her decision to follow through. She wanted Dell to be free so they could start again. Right past wrongs.

She turned her face up to his chin. "I only said that so he would—"

"Don't say a word. You don't have to explain. The only thing that matters is us, right here, right now. I made mistakes. If I have to spend the rest of my life making it up to you, I will. I will, Leah. I love you." He held her tight, Leah felt the rhythm of his heart, of his words.

"Let's go home."

* * *

Elicia was waiting in the lobby of the restaurant when Leah walked in. They hugged, cheek to cheek. It'd been a while since they last talked.

"You been waiting long?" Leah asked, eyeing the crowd in the restaurant.

"No. Our table is ready, though." Elicia signaled for the hostess with her manicured hand. She put an arm around Leah as they followed the bouncy blonde to their table. "So things are getting back to normal in the Fletcher household?"

"Absolutely not." Leah hugged her back around the waist. "We're doing things a lot differently around there. We actually have a family coach. You ever heard of such a thing? Sort of like a weight trainer, but he comes in and actually helps us strengthen our communication muscle."

The table was in the center of the restaurant. Elicia looked at Leah, "Is this okay?"

"Oh, it's fine."

"I know how you hate to be in the center of things... literally."

They sat down. The room was filled with natural light. There were no dark corners to hide in, Leah noticed, not even if she'd wanted to.

"So this person actually comes to your house... and does what? Like follow you guys around, monitoring how you react to each other?"

"Sort of... it's a therapist whose main purpose is to train athletes how to come back home, and fit in... you know like a normal husband, veg out on the sofa while watching sports and eating pretzels...." Leah laughed at herself. Seeing Dell without a care in the world, watching sports on television for the first time without feeling like he'd lost something—she welcomed it. "The therapist comes in once a week and makes us all sit down together and *share,* as he puts it."

Elicia threw up her hands, "Got a cure for everything."

"Not everything." Leah scrunched up her nose, trying to resist the need to cry. It didn't take much these days, the slightest breeze, the tune of a song. She was an oscillating fan, back and forth with her emotions. It was a struggle every day.

"You've been through so much. Has Angel tried to contact you at all?"

Leah felt the stab, the pierce between the lobes of her ears. She swallowed it down. "That was part of his sentence, part of his probation. He can't contact me or come anywhere near us."

"But doesn't it scare you that he's still out there? I mean a slap on the wrist, that's it and he's out there as if nothing ever happened."

"I think for him, losing his career and…"

"He never had you to begin with, Leah. You weren't his to lose."

"That's not what I was going to say. I meant, losing his face, the embarrassment of it all. I think that was punishment enough. He was the one who got away, made it out of his neighborhood, the upstanding one, and now he's no better than the criminals he's arrested in the past. People who looked up to him won't see him that way anymore." Leah used the napkin in front of her to pinch between her eyes. That was the reason for the tears, compassion, empathy, nothing more.

"Stop feeling guilty. I know what you're thinking. It's not your fault."

"I know." Leah moved the tissue to her nose and dabbed.

"Oh, I see someone. I've been hunting this guy down for an interview forever. He can't hide now. Do you mind if I go for a minute, sweetie"? Elicia reached out and touched Leah's shoulder. "I'll be right over there." Elicia rose up and clicked her heels in the direction of her victim.

Leah sat for a moment, feeling the pressure of a fish in a fishbowl. She could at least look good if someone recognized her. Tear-stained eyes, dry lips. She dug in her purse for her lipstick but remembered she'd changed purses to go with her shoes. She looked over at Elicia, gabbing with the hot new NBA player who had been on the cover of every newsstand magazine. Leah picked up Elicia's purse that sat on the table. It was big enough to carry every shade of lip color invented.

She felt around, then looked inside. Pushing aside a wallet, a daily planner, and an array of nail polish, Leah found a couple of tubes of lipstick. What she also saw stopped her from breathing. She stood up too quickly, knocking over the just-filled water glasses. The chair fell back with a snap. All eyes were on her. Elicia looked over too, realizing what was going on when she saw the silver-chained band in Leah's hand. Their eyes met.

Elicia rushed to her friend's side.

"No." Leah shook her arm loose of Elicia's grasp. She wasn't afraid. She didn't care who was looking. "What are you doing with this!" Her scream echoed in the silence of the still watchers. "You took this out of my house—why?"

"Leah, please, not here." Elicia tried to talk low, waiting for Leah to realize they were the main attraction. "Not here," she reiterated through gritted teeth.

"Tell me!"

Elicia picked up her purse and rushed out of the restaurant. Leah had no choice but to follow.

The wind whipped between them. Leah caught up. "Tell me!"

"I took the watch to show Dell... when he was sick, to test him to see if he'd really lost his memory. The watch, a picture of you and the kids. I just wanted to see if he was being honest about not knowing who he was."

"You knew where he was, the entire time?"

"Yes." Elicia pulled a thin stream of hair out of her face. The wind shifted, calming down just as quickly as it began.

"How did you know... how could you know and not tell me?"

"He needed to get well. He couldn't do that with everyone watching. The pressure you were putting him under, like he could just snap his fingers and make himself okay. I wanted to help. So I went in and took a few things that could jog his memory. I took what medicine I could find, too, just in case. I didn't know if he was going to have withdrawal."

"Why would he need you to take his medicine if he was already in a care facility? This isn't making any sense."

Elicia grabbed Leah's arms. "I helped him get better, Leah. He was beaten up, lost, he didn't even know who I was. When I found him, I wasn't sure if someone was still after him. I didn't know, so I hid him at my house."

Leah snapped her arms out of her grip. "What are you saying? He was there the entire time?"

The silence between them, growing wider, louder. Movement around Leah could be seen from her peripheral vision, but she could hear nothing. A numb buzzing in her ear, growing more intense. "You and Dell? Is that what you're telling me?" The hysterical laughter beat across her chest. Waves of tears and laughter intermingled. She took off her shoes and put them in her arms and started walking. A stagger that led her in no particular direction. Words were beating in her head. She could hear Squire, "And you're falling for it again." She could hear Angel, "Just a matter of time."

Elicia was screaming for her to stop. She caught up with her. "You didn't care. You kicked him out. You wanted him out. You told me over and over how you were sick and tired of him. How you didn't want to put up with him anymore. *Dell's sucking the life out of me, Elicia, poor me, what am I going to do?"* she mocked. "Why the hell didn't you just hand him over on a silver platter?"

Leah kept walking, she stopped long enough to find her car, pulling out her keys. Elicia was still in her ear. "He's better because of me. I helped him. You didn't. I sat by his side doing what you didn't want to do, wouldn't do. And now that he's healthy, he went running straight back to you!" She kept her hands on the door, keeping Leah from closing it.

"Did you ever love him? Did you really love him, because it's for better or worse, Leah, you don't give up when it's broke. You should be thanking me! Do you know how it feels to watch, to listen to your complaining? What the hell did you expect? You sit there telling me how miserable you are with this man, this man that I would give my right arm for, any woman would, but you, all you did was complain and bitch about how unhappy you were."

"Get away from the car." Leah stepped on the gas lightly, giving Elicia a chance to move back. She peeled her fingers away one last time, then rammed her foot on the pedal.

In the rearview mirror Leah saw Elicia fall backward but she didn't stop or slow down. Leah could still hear Elicia screaming in her ear even though she was miles behind. *All you did was bitch and complain! You should be thanking me!*

* * *

She pulled up to her house and tried to compose herself. *You were miserable!*

The house had a calm, tranquil effect as soon as she walked through the door. She heard voices, Dell and Josh, then Kayla. They were all three out back playing baseball, Kayla at bat, Josh playing catcher, and Dell pitching. The ecstatic scream from Kayla when she got a hit and ran to the makeshift base.

Josh saw her first and yelled for her to come out and join them. "It can be me and you against Dad and Kayla, Mom. Come on!"

She shook her head, no.

"Baby, come on." Dell waved his hands for her to come out. Leah stepped out to the patio where she stood, taking in each one of their faces. Her eyes landed back on Dell's. *Why didn't you just hand him over on a silver platter?* She swallowed the wave of emotion that traveled up her throat... *for better or worse, Leah, you don't quit when it's broke.*

Dell came to her where she stood. She felt his hand on the side of her face, "Baby? What's wrong?"

It all came flooding back, the way she felt when she believed Dell was out of her life for good. The torturous days and nights begging God for one more chance. It has been granted, her prayers answered.

She'd known what Angel had been trying to tell her in the café, of Dell's betrayal, but didn't want to hear it. Afraid of the decision she'd have to make.

She took in a long breath, holding it, then drawing his hand to her lips. "I just love you so much." He pulled her in his arms.

"I just love you," she mumbled into his chest, "you and the kids. I love you."

She touched his head, stroking the smoothness of his skin. In their world they would have to include forgiveness, patience, and all the other qualities that had been left out. Too busy existing, moving from one day to the other. They had left each other to their own survival. Neither one there for the other. It wouldn't happen again. She'd never let it happen again.

He lifted his dark wet eyes to hers, "I would die if I ever lost you."

They kissed, mingling both their tears, both their hearts.

Roadrunner Reader's Group Guide

Questions for discussion

1. The opening chapter of *Roadrunner* reveals Dell's state of despair. He relies on a cocktail of prescription drugs to take him to a zone where there are "no paparazzi, no reporters, no questions he couldn't answer." Do you get the impression that the bulk of these unanswerable questions comes from the press or from his family? From whom is he trying to escape? Is your first reaction to Dell pity or revulsion? Does that reaction change at any point in the story?

2. Just before their violent incident, Leah offers Dell a choice between his family and his misery. Do you think she is right to lay it all on the line at this point? How far should a spouse go to help his/her partner recover from an addiction or a debilitating depression? Does your answer change when you factor children into the equation? Why or why not?

3. Dell fantasizes about his pre-injury athletic prowess: "Crouched in stance, anticipating the speed and shape of the ball . . . the crack of the bat . . . the run!" But he also dwells on his golden reputation: "The high unmatched by any other, fans, superiority, and recognition."

Is he addicted to the game of baseball, or simply to fame? Do you think the cult of personality that the professional sports world engenders is necessarily corrupting? Or does it serve a useful purpose in providing kids recognizable heroes?

4. As the squad car pulls up to her house, Leah recognizes that a severe shift in balance has just occurred between "what her life really was and what she thought it ought to be." Weeks later, as she fends off one of Angel's stronger advances, she laments that "this wasn't supposed to be her life. . . . This wasn't supposed to be happening." Where else in the novel do we see the theme of shattered expectations and thwarted "supposed to"s? Which characters are able to adapt to the disappointments of reality, and which are destroyed by them?

5. What influence has Leah's mother had on her in terms of relationships? What influence has Angel's mother had on him? What do you think Josh learns from Leah through the course of the story?

6. Dell makes a show of thanking God for his successes in front of the media, but privately considers himself his own god, fully responsible for all of his own actions: "His days and nights had been filled with strategy, with maintaining control of his destination." In what ways is Angel similar? Do you think Angel truly feels for Leah all that he professes, or is his obsession with her all about him? Given Angel's background, what does the wife of a professional athlete symbolize to him?

7. Does Angel's tragic family situation cause you to sympathize with him? Why do you think he's unable to go through with the dire crimes he contemplates, Squire's murder and Dell's murder among them? Is he a coward?

8. In what ways does *Roadrunner* address the theme of addiction? What are Leah's addictions? Angel? Elicia? Does anyone make a full recovery by the end of the novel?

9. Angel's behavior with Kayla seems to confirm that he's a creep. Does he overstep his bounds earlier than this? At what point do you lose trust for Angel? Would Leah be justified in filing a sexual harassment charge against him? Why does she never consider doing so?

10. Dell often hides in his son's room because Leah "rarely came down the hall past the point where organization and structure became disheveled, where mess and clutter lurked behind every closed door... She simply asked that the children's doors be kept closed so what she didn't know wouldn't hurt her." Is this Leah's key problem—that she can't process life's messiness? If so, does Dell recognize it as a problem?

11. Right before Dell decides to piece together the puzzle of who and where he is, he awakens from an exhausting baseball dream to the realization that "he was merely a man, nothing more." Do you read this as a final defeat for Dell, or as a positive turning point?

12. Angel is profoundly affected by the discovery that his childhood idol has devolved into a drug-addled wife-beater. How much of his treatment of Dell is motivated by anger at having his illusion dispelled? Does he pursue Leah because he has a newly found sense of his own potential, or because he wants to prove a point about men like Dell wasting their precious gifts?

13. Since money is no object in the Fletcher household, are you surprised that Leah fails to hire detectives to hunt for Dell? Is her judgment impaired by her own ambivalent feelings about her marriage, and her growing weakness toward Angel's advances? Or is she simply so accustomed to Dell making the household decisions that she's paralyzed by his absence? What course of action would you take were you in her shoes?

14. As Leah contemplates the events that have led her and Dell into their predicament, she recalls him not as an equal partner, but as an "opponent," forging ahead rapidly toward his goals, while she is left "trailing behind like a quiet breeze." How much of her behavior toward him is motivated by jealousy and/or resentment that he was able to pursue his dream while she raised the kids? What could they have done to ensure more equality in the marriage?

Soon to be a major motion picture...

If you liked *Roadrunner*, you will love Trisha R. Thomas's critically acclaimed first novel, soon to be a major motion picture starring Halle Barry. *Nappily Ever After* is a fresh, funny, original debut novel about contemporary, independent black women, their lives, their loves, and their hair. Nominated for a NAACP Image Award and the 2001 Golden Pen Awards for Best New Author and Best Mainstream Fiction.

Nappily Ever After

0-609-80898-2

$12.00 paper (Canada: $18.00)

Available from Three Rivers Press wherever books are sold

www.randomhouse.com